AF606577

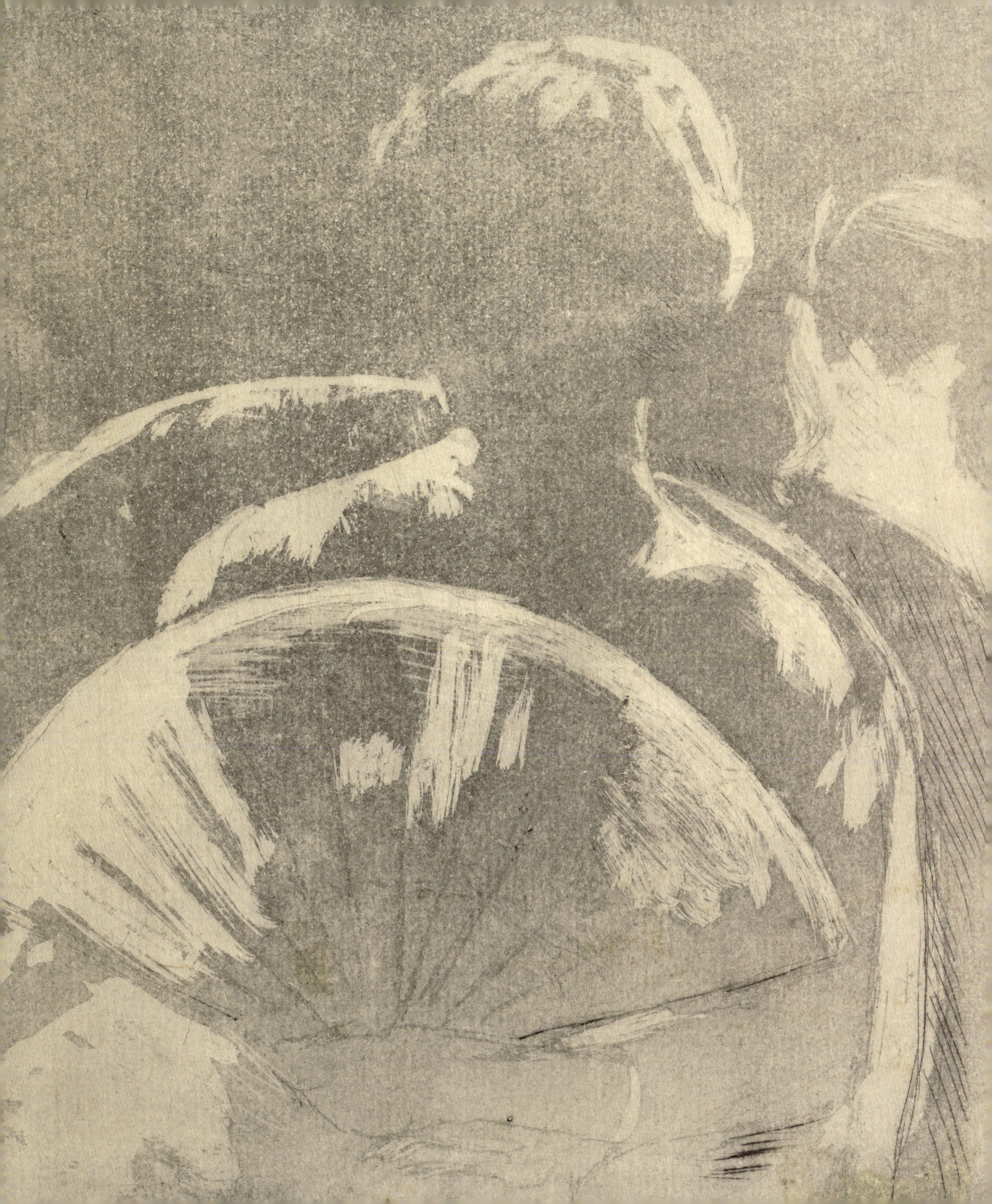

Inside Out
The Prints of Mary Cassatt

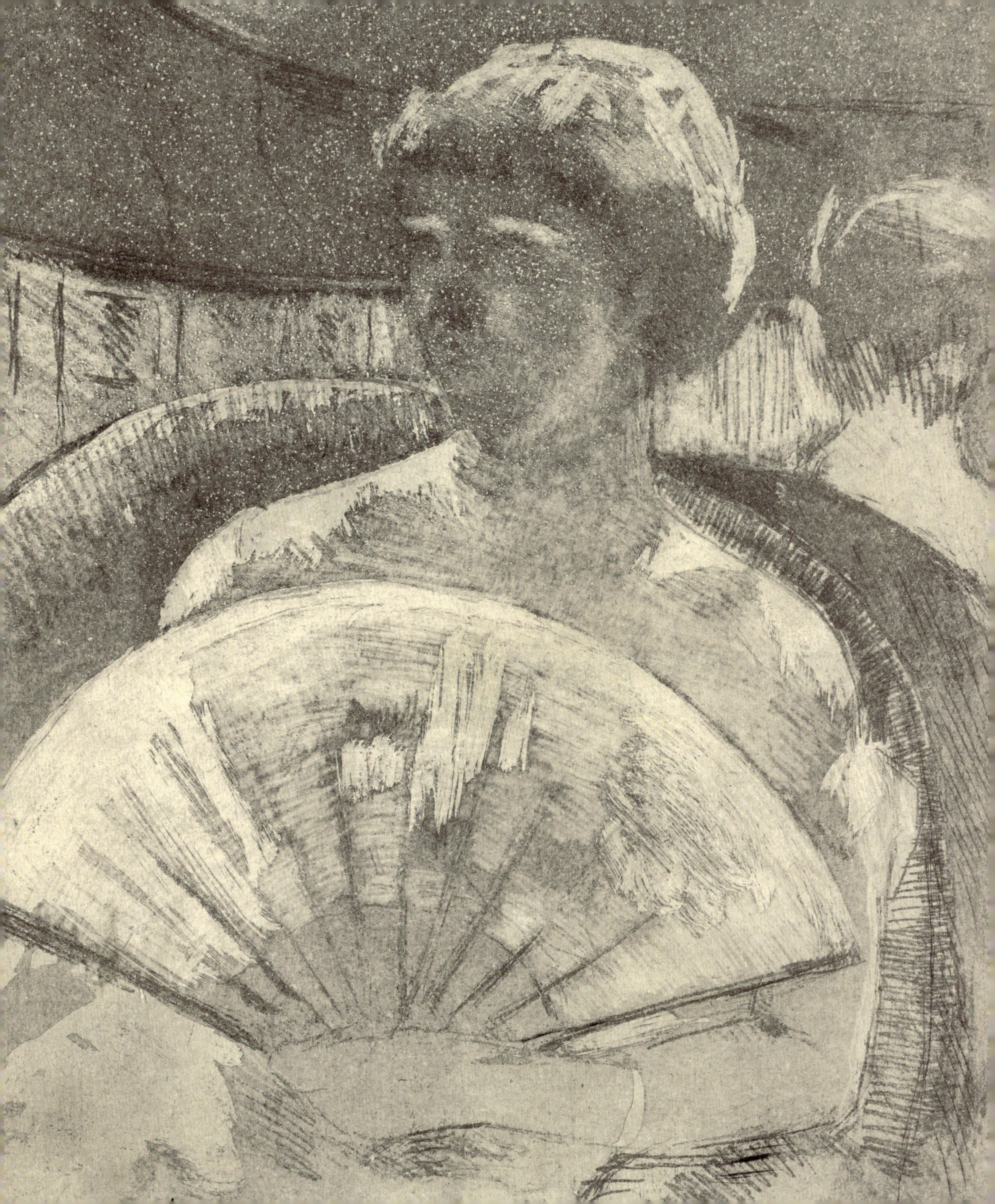

Edited by Shalini Le Gall
and Justin McCann

With contributions by
Justine De Young and
Daniel Harkett

Colby College Museum of Art
Waterville, Maine

DelMonico Books • D.A.P.
New York

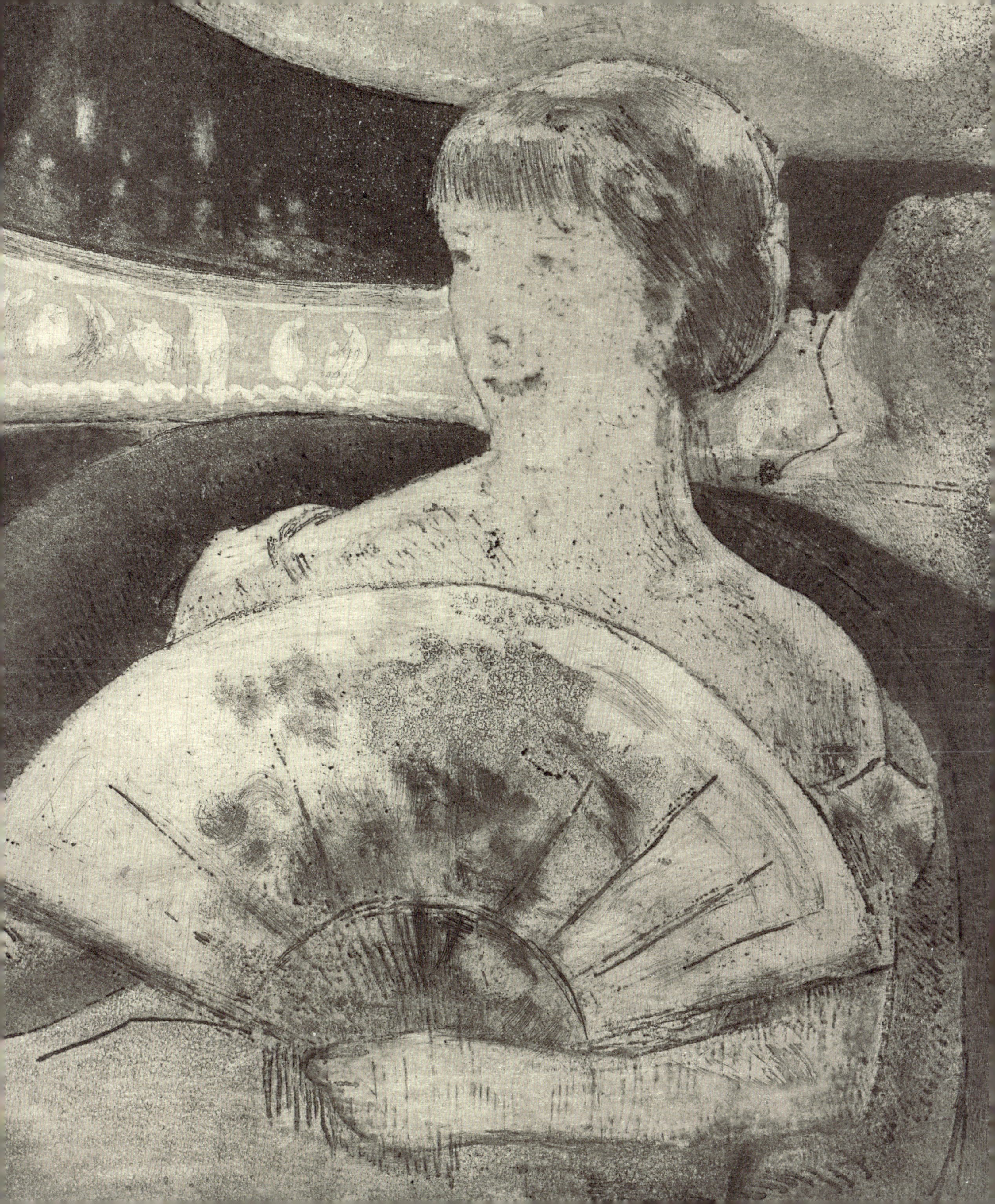

This book was published on the occasion of the exhibition *Inside Out: The Prints of Mary Cassatt* organized by Colby College Museum of Art and curated by Shalini Le Gall and Justin McCann.

June 3–November 1, 2021

Published in 2021 by Colby College Museum of Art and DelMonico Books • D.A.P.

Colby College Museum of Art
5600 Mayflower Hill
Waterville, Maine 04901
www.colby.edu/museum

DelMonico Books
available through ARTBOOK | D.A.P.
75 Broad Street, Suite 630
New York, NY 10004
www.artbook.com
www.delmonicobooks.com

Publication manager: Megan Carey
Publication coordinator: Olivia Fountain
Designer: Rita Jules, Miko McGinty Inc.
Typesetter: Tina Henderson
Pattern designer: Frances MacLeod
Editor: James Gibbons
Proofreader: Lindsey Westbrook
Printer: Trifolio S.r.l., Verona, Italy

This exhibition and publication are generously supported by the Lunder Collection Fund.

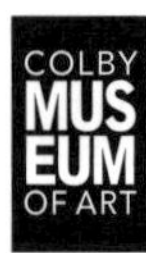

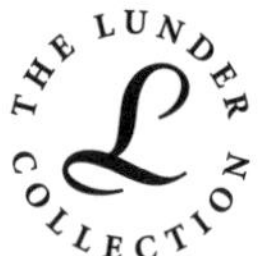

Image credits
Every reasonable attempt has been made to identify owners of copyright. Errors or omissions will be corrected in subsequent editions.

pp. 18 L, 33: Image © The Metropolitan Museum of Art / Art Resource, NY; p. 18 R: © National Gallery, London / Art Resource, NY; pp. 19, 21, 25, 49: Courtesy National Gallery of Art, Washington, DC; pp. 20, 64, 74–77, 82–84, 88–89, 92, 95, 97–105, 107–11, 113–19: Photos by Peter Siegel, Pillar Digital Imaging LLC; pp. 31, 35: Photograph © 2021 Museum of Fine Arts, Boston; p. 32: Image courtesy Melville McLean; p. 41: Credit Tokyo Fuji Art Museum, Tokyo, Japan / Bridgeman Images; p. 45: Images courtesy of Fashion Institute of Technology|SUNY FIT Library Special Collections and College Archives; p. 57: Photos courtesy Michael Urtado, Image © RMN-Grand Palais / Art Resource, NY; pp. 65–71, 79–81, 85, 91, 93–94: Photos by Pixel Acuity; p. 73: Photo by Jason Weller; pp. 87, 90: Photos by Luc Demers; p. 121: Photo by Peter Siegel, Pixel Acuity.

ISBN: 978-1-63681-006-5
Library of Congress Control Number: 2020924026

Cover: *Peasant Mother and Child* (detail), c. 1894. Drypoint and aquatint on paper. Tenth (final) state. 17¼ x 11¼ in. (43.8 x 28.6 cm). The Lunder Collection, 2017.468. Back cover: *Lydia Reading, Turned Toward Right* (detail), c. 1881. Softground etching and aquatint on paper. Second (final) state. 7 1/16 x 4⅜ in. (17.9 x 11.1 cm). The Lunder Collection, 2012.304. Page 1: *In The Opera Box (No. 2)* (detail), 1879–80. Softground etching on paper. First state (of three). 12 3/16 x 9 3/16 in. (31 x 23.3 cm). The Lunder Collection, 2012.292. Page 3: *In The Opera Box (No. 2)* (detail), 1879–80. Softground etching and aquatint on paper. Second state (of three). 12 3/16 x 9 5/16 in. (31 x 23.7 cm). The Lunder Collection, 003.2010. Page 5: *In The Opera Box (No. 3)* (detail), 1879–80. Softground etching and aquatint on laid paper. Fourth (final) state. 14 1/16 x 10⅝ in. (35.7 x 27 cm). The Lunder Collection, 2012.294

Contents

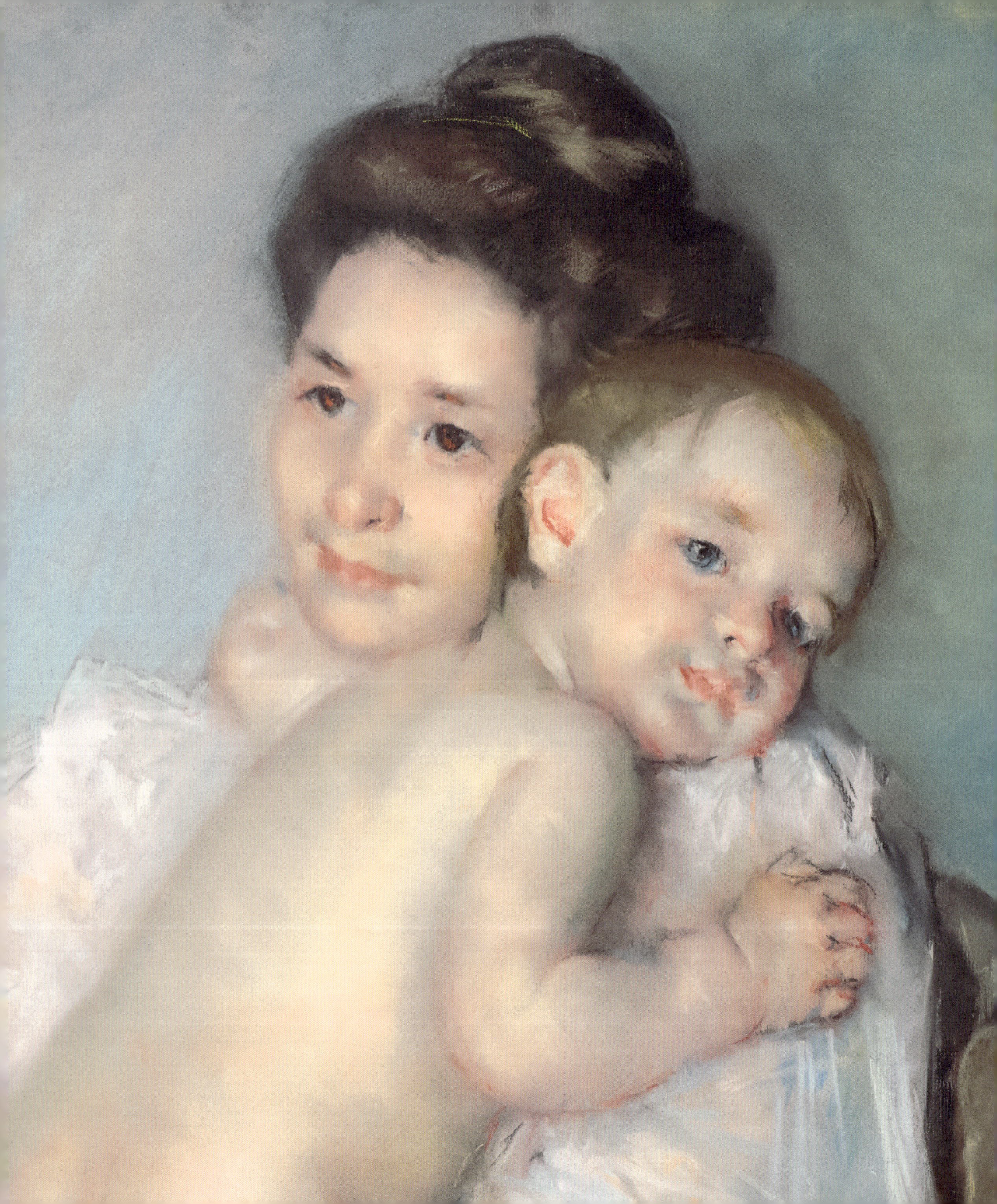

Director's Foreword

In 2013, Alan and Barbara Mirken donated to the Colby College Museum of Art the sumptuous pastel *Mother Berthe Holding Her Nude Baby* by Mary Cassatt. Set against a soft blue background, the child rests comfortably and securely in its mother's arms. The pair gaze in opposite directions, but they are united through their embrace and in Cassatt's sensitive use of flesh tones throughout the piece. It communicates an idyllic vision of the private domestic sphere of French bourgeois mothers. In style and subject matter, it is an exemplary work by Mary Cassatt.

The Mirken family gave the pastel to the Colby Museum in honor of Peter and Paula Lunder to celebrate their commitment to the collecting and study of American art at Colby. They also made the gift in recognition of the Lunders' appreciation of Mary Cassatt. In 1983, Peter and Paula purchased *Pensive Roman Girl* (p. 64), an early oil painting by the artist. In 2012, the Lunders made an exceptional gift to the Museum with the acquisition of forty-four prints by Cassatt. This extraordinary group of works included a selection of rare trial proofs that document her first forays into printmaking. Cassatt's experiments with softground etching found in the collection are complemented by her exquisite drypoints. Together, they make a profound statement about her ingenuity and accomplishments as a printmaker, and I am pleased that this collection has served as the basis for the exhibition and catalogue *Inside Out: The Prints of Mary Cassatt*.

Through this exhibition, co-curators Shalini Le Gall and Justin McCann reveal an artist trying to make sense of the meanings and expressions of interiority and selfhood at play in the modern world of nineteenth-century Paris. Cassatt made "the spaces of femininity," a term coined by the art historian Griselda Pollock, her primary subject. The essays in this catalogue by Le Gall, McCann, Justine De Young, and Daniel Harkett probe these spaces to explore notions of privacy and domesticity; art making and innovation; class, gender, and fashion; and solitude and interior states of mind.

As a child, I was mesmerized by the first work by Mary Cassatt I ever encountered—in the pages of a book. *The Child's Bath* (p. 37), in the collection of the Art Institute of Chicago, features a partially undressed young girl, perhaps age three or four, depicted from above and painted within a tightly composed pictorial space, one where half-tones and close chromatic relationships dominate. The child rests on the lap of a woman who gently washes the girl's feet. The image both drew me in and kept me at bay as an observer of a scene that wasn't mine to occupy. A similar dynamic is at play across the works in this exhibition, which show an artist engaging with subject matter, artistic process, a visual vocabulary, and social norms in ways that remain vital today.

It is thanks to the remarkable generosity of Peter and Paula Lunder and the Mirken family that Colby audiences have access, for years to come, not simply to images in a book but to tangible works of art—works that invite us to study them closely, over and over again.

Jacqueline Terrassa
Carolyn Muzzy Director

Mary Cassatt, *Mother Berthe Holding Her Nude Baby* (detail), 1898–99. Pastel on paper. 22½ x 17¼ in. (57.2 x 43.8 cm). Colby College Museum of Art, Waterville, Maine, gift of Alan B. Mirken '51 and Family in honor of Peter and Paula Lunder, 2013.549

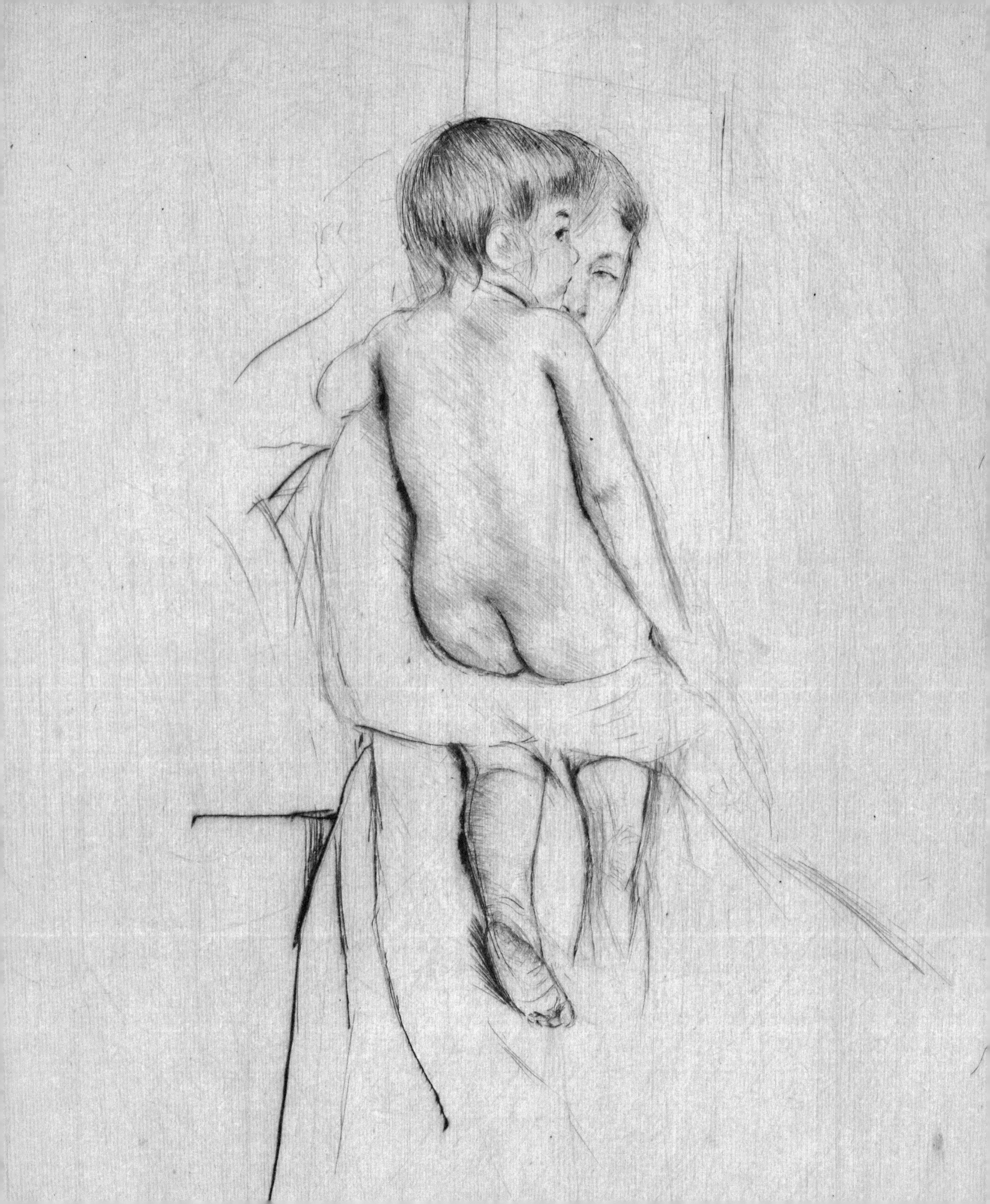

Introduction

In 1879, Mary Cassatt partnered with Edgar Degas and Camille Pissarro on a project to publish a journal, *Le Jour et la nuit* (Day and Night), that would be devoted to the fine art of printmaking. The publication never saw the light of day, but the prints Cassatt produced during this period reveal a different side of an artist at the center of the modern art world in France. Degas had invited her to exhibit with the Impressionists in 1877, and with this group Cassatt was free to pursue her own artistic agenda. Nowhere is that more evident than in her printmaking. Exploring themes of domesticity, fashion, solitude, and the creative process, *Inside Out: The Prints of Mary Cassatt* examines the artist's experimentation with the medium over a period of more than two decades and evaluates the range of public and private spaces visible across these works. In comparison to painting, black-and-white prints emphasize contrast and heighten the significance of light and shadow. With its evident careful study and laborious attention to detail, Cassatt's early print work unveils surprising reversals of meaning in images of modern life, where formality permeated domestic spaces and sharply etched lines conveyed unexpected intimacy in public settings.

A pivotal figure in a group of artists that included Degas, Claude Monet, and Pierre-Auguste Renoir, Cassatt has been the focus of numerous articles, books, and exhibitions. Her work defies simple categorization. Her many prints and paintings do not fit easily into established categories of nineteenth-century American or French art. While she worked alongside and exhibited with the Impressionist circle, she rarely engaged with the pure landscape subjects favored by Monet or Alfred Sisley or the scenes of popular entertainment or dandies depicted by Édouard Manet and Degas. Her best-known works are undoubtedly the images of women and children referred to as the "mother and child" scenes in numerous paintings and prints. While these scenes might resemble the sentimental domestic pictures then popular with collectors, the starkness and minimal ornamentation of Cassatt's compositions create a uniquely austere impression of these otherwise affective subjects.

For scholars, Cassatt's work exemplifies the challenges for women artists working in the nineteenth century. Given her privileged, wealthy background, there was little possibility that Cassatt could study nude male models or participate in the social activities enjoyed by her male colleagues in dance halls, cafés, and brothels without offending public expectations. Yet her interest in women's lives and domestic settings is not sufficiently explained by a lack of access to other subjects. Rather, Cassatt's prints reveal a deep understanding of the shifting boundaries between private and public spaces in modern Paris and the gendered dimensions of interiority.

Inside Out: The Prints of Mary Cassatt joins a dynamic curatorial and scholarly discussion reevaluating Cassatt's work, which has brought her printmaking front and center. In her own lifetime, Cassatt was the subject of extended critical attention, for instance in reviews penned by Félix Fénéon and Joris-Karl Huysmans and a book-length study by Achille Ségard.[1] Her friendship with the philanthropist and art collector Louisine Havemeyer spurred American interest in her

Mary Cassatt, *Baby's Back* (detail), 1890. Drypoint and softground etching on paper. Third (final) state. 9 3/16 x 6 7/16 in. (23.3 x 16.4 cm). Colby College Museum of Art, Waterville, Maine, The Lunder Collection, 2012.315

work and in French art more generally, and art historian Adelyn Breeskin conducted research over several decades and published catalogues raisonnés of Cassatt's known paintings and prints. In the 1970s and 1980s, art historians directed their critical acumen to Cassatt's identity as a woman artist in France and to her overwhelmingly domestic subject matter. As Griselda Pollock wrote, Cassatt's work navigated "the intellectual or rather inner world of thoughtful reflection and subjective identity, traditionally reserved for representations of men."[2]

Alongside art historians who have brought a keen critical eye to Cassatt's position as an artist and her complex renderings of her female subjects, museum curators have mounted exhibitions that challenged assumptions about her work and reconsidered the modernity of her practice. *Mary Cassatt: Modern Woman* (1999), *Degas/Cassatt* (2014), and, more recently, *Mary Cassatt: An American Impressionist in Paris* (2018) and *Innovative Impressions: Prints by Cassatt, Degas, and Pissarro* (2018) are only a few of the exhibitions to have importantly shed light on the many aspects of Cassatt's artistic practice, particularly her printmaking. As Amanda Zehnder writes in the catalogue for *Degas/Cassatt*, Cassatt was "a single female artist in late nineteenth-century France engaged in a messy, labor-intensive, technical process with older male artists connected to a then-radical art movement."[3] As Zehnder notes, one cannot overstate how unusual it was for Cassatt, a respectable woman from an established American family, to join a renegade group of artists and experiment with printmaking, especially in light of the traditional academic training she had received as a young woman.

Although her academic training in the United States and Europe initially made Cassatt skeptical of printmaking, she embraced the medium shortly after joining the Impressionists. Born in Allegheny City (today part of Pittsburgh) in 1844, Cassatt took classes at the Pennsylvania Academy of Fine Arts in Philadelphia, and then lived most of her life as an expatriate in France from 1866 until her death in 1926. She continued her academic study of art first in the atelier of Jean-Léon Gérôme and then with Charles Chaplin, Paul Soyer, and Thomas Couture. Art academies privileged painting and sculpture over printmaking, which they viewed as a reproductive medium and not as a fine art. Nevertheless, just as Cassatt arrived in Europe, the Etching Revival was well under way in Britain and France. This revival reconsidered the artistic merit and expressive capabilities of etchings, aquatints, and lithographs.

In 1879, Cassatt joined forces with Degas and Pissarro on the print publication *Le Jour et la nuit*. As Sarah Lees illuminates in *Innovative Impressions*, this collaborative artistic initiative aimed to highlight creative and technical advancements in printmaking. From the beginning, Cassatt embraced the venture with an eye toward experimentation and improvisation, and her earliest graphic works demonstrate her bold, radical steps in exploring various printmaking techniques. The forty-nine prints by Cassatt in the Lunder Collection at the Colby College Museum of Art span most of her printmaking career.[4] These include trial proofs for *At the Dressing Table* (p. 68) and *In the Opera Box (No. 3)* (p. 76) in addition to rare impressions of *The Corner of the Sofa (No. 2)* (p. 65), *Lydia Reading, Turned Toward Right* (p. 87), and *Before the Fireplace (No. 2)* (p. 83), a portrait of Cassatt's ailing sister Lydia, impressions of which were only given to family members. In addition to Cassatt's exemplary work in softground etching and aquatint, the Lunder Collection also includes a number of exquisite drypoints by Cassatt, including

Baby's Back (pp. 104–5), *The Mirror* (pp. 114–15), and *Tea* (p. 113). In 2017, *Peasant Mother and Child* (p. 120) entered the Lunder Collection, a superb color lithograph that was first given by Cassatt to Violet Paget, the British author and aesthete better known by her pseudonym, Vernon Lee.

The prints by Cassatt at the Colby Museum illustrate the artist's ingenuity and creativity. Her technical skill with the medium expands the interpretive range we can now bring to these works almost 150 years after they were first made. For example, the etchings from the series *In the Opera Box* (pp. 74–77) are among the best known of Cassatt's prints. They exemplify her study of the uncertainty around private and public spaces. A young woman in the opera box is the focus of many gazes, yet Cassatt employs the fan in the foreground as a marker of psychological and spatial distance. In other works, such as *The Visitor* (p. 81) or *Knitting in the Library* (p. 85), she backlights the sitters, enveloping the women in shadows. In these trial states, the boundaries between the visible and the invisible are indeed muddled, and her representations of these modern social spaces contrast sharply with those by her male Impressionist colleagues. Her studies of more traditionally private domestic spaces are equally complex. *Before the Fireplace (No. 2)* depicts Cassatt's sister Lydia in the drawing room of the family residence in Paris. The decorative armchair, detailed fireplace, and collection of objects conjure an image of an established family's interior. Yet Lydia's gaze, off to the side, is distant, and the negative space surrounding her isolates the human presence in the scene. Her physical form is visible, but her thoughts, the object of her attention, remain unknown to us.

Rather than provide a comprehensive overview of Cassatt's printmaking, the essays in *Inside Out: The Prints of Mary Cassatt* explore specific themes and techniques found in works from the Lunder Collection. They are unified in their examination of identity and interiority, privacy and intimacy. In his essay, "Mary Cassatt at Work, 1879–80," Justin McCann examines Cassatt's embrace of etching and her experimental approach to the medium. The link between Cassatt's maternal scenes and the serial process of printmaking is the focus of Shalini Le Gall's essay, "Serial Motherhood in Cassatt's Early Prints." Justine De Young in her essay, "Dressing the Modern Woman: Mary Cassatt and 1890s Fashion," examines Cassatt's fashion choices in her prints, claiming that she was far more attentive to trends than has been previously remarked, with some surprising revelations about familiar works. Finally, in "Intimacy and Privacy in Cassatt's Prints," Daniel Harkett offers a poignant reflection on the artist that explores her images of public and private life, arguing that she holds open a space for the self even when her figures are deeply embedded in social relations.

Peter and Paula Lunder acquired Cassatt's painting *Pensive Roman Girl* (p. 64) in 1983. Since then they have assembled one of the finest and most distinctive collections of prints by the artist, and we are so pleased to be able to present them to a wider audience with the support of so many individuals who have been central to this project. Sharon Corwin, former Carolyn Muzzy Director of the Colby Museum, championed this project at its inception and supported it through its many stages of development. Jacqueline Terrassa warmly embraced the exhibition upon her arrival at Colby as the Carolyn Muzzy Director, and we are thankful for her thoughtful and timely insights into our work. Susan Schulman's scholarly and technical expertise has been indispensable in the development of the print collection at

Colby. In addition to contributing insightful essays and original scholarship to this catalogue, both Daniel Harkett and Justine De Young were key interlocutors in the early stages of the project, as was Hollis Clayson. We are indebted to an entire team of colleagues who have brought *Inside Out: The Prints of Mary Cassatt* to life in the gallery and in the pages that follow. Megan Carey and Olivia Fountain have expertly and patiently managed the book project from beginning to end. They assembled a talented and creative group of designers and editors to whom we are most grateful: Miko McGinty and Rita Jules, Frances MacLeod, James Gibbons, and Lindsey Westbrook. Additionally, the project could not have come to fruition without the efforts of our deputy director, Julianne Gilland, and our registration and installation team, Elizabeth Carpenter, Lorraine DeLaney, Paige Doore, Chris Patch, and Jason Weller. The suite of exhibition-related public and academic programs was developed by our colleagues in education and public programming, Jordia Benjamin-Sands, Kristin Bergquist, Sheri LaVerdiere, Abigail Newkirk, and Miriam Valle-Mancilla, and we are thankful for their commitment to this project. We are additionally grateful to the Portland Museum of Art for lending *Anne and Her Nurse*, an oil painting by Cassatt, to the exhibition.

Inside Out: The Prints of Mary Cassatt was originally scheduled to open in 2020. The COVID-19 global pandemic prevented that from happening. We were entering the final stages of work on the exhibition and catalogue when the world came to a halt. The experience of quarantine, masks, and social distancing undoubtedly impacts our view of Cassatt's scenes of seclusion and solitude. This tragic pandemic has dramatically altered how we behave, live, and relate to one another. We invite visitors to this exhibition and readers of this catalogue to bring their own reevaluated notions of intimacy, privacy, and socializing to this study of Cassatt's work.

Shalini Le Gall
Chief Curator, Susan Donnell and Harry W. Konkel Curator of European Art, and Director of Academic Engagement, Portland Museum of Art

Justin McCann
Lunder Curator for Whistler Studies, Colby College Museum of Art

Notes

1. Félix Fénéon, "Cassatt, Pissarro," *Chat Noir* (April 11, 1891): 1728; Joris-Karl Huysmans, L'Art moderne (Paris: Charpentier, 1883), 232; Achille Ségard, *Un Peintre des Enfants et des Mères, Mary Cassatt*, 3rd ed. (Paris: P. Ollendorff, 1913).

2. Griselda Pollock, *Mary Cassatt* (London: Chaucer, 2005), 22.

3. Amanda T. Zehnder, "Forty Years of Artistic Exchange" (2014) in *Degas/Cassatt*, ed. Kimberly A. Jones (Washington, DC: National Gallery of Art, 2014), 7.

4. The Lunders acquired a collection of forty-four prints by Cassatt in 2012. Details about the prints can be found in R. Stanley Johnson, *Mary Cassatt: Early Graphic Works 1878–1891* (Chicago: R. S. Johnson Fine Art, 2011).

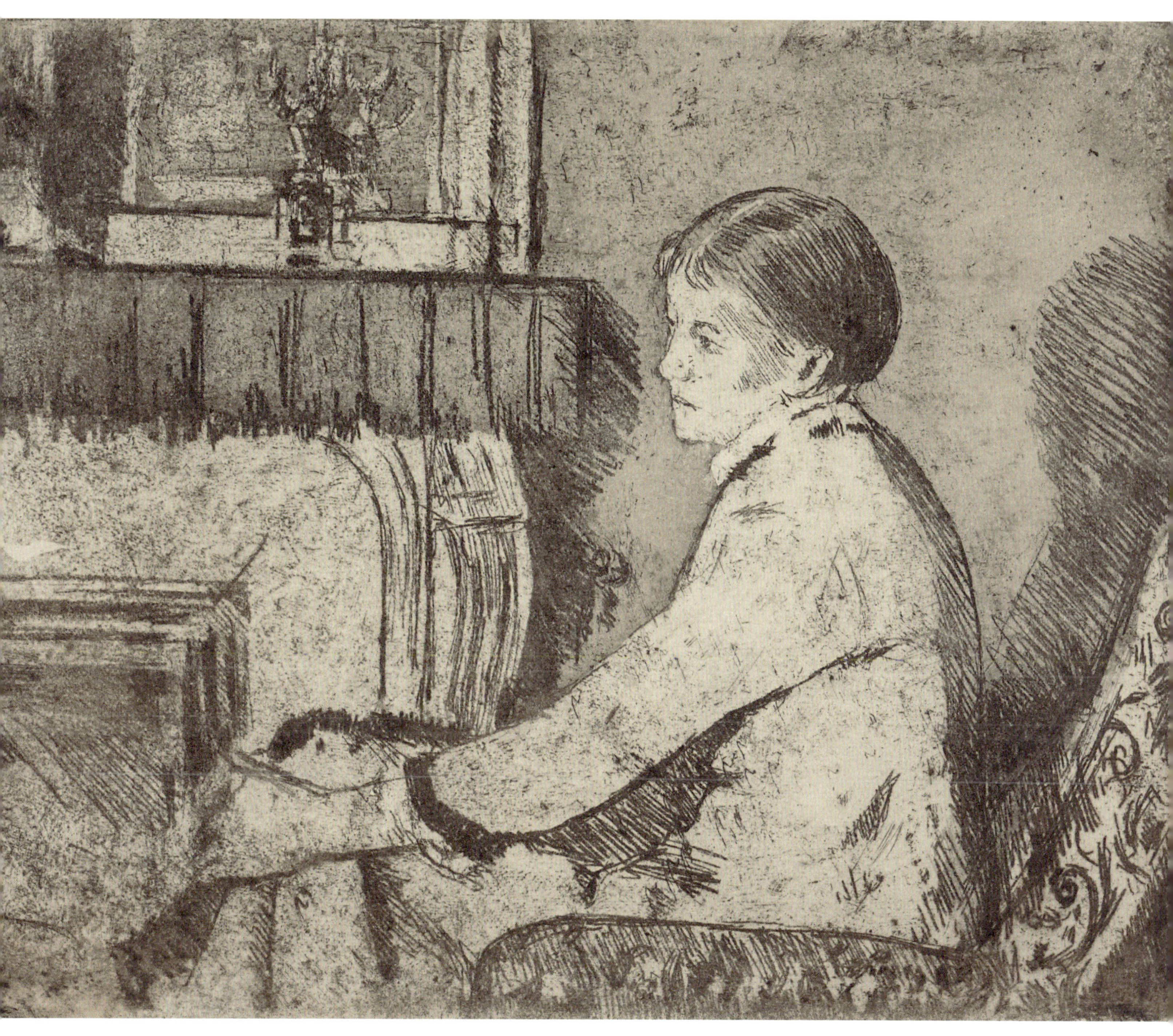

Mary Cassatt, *Before the Fireplace (No. 2)* (detail), c. 1882. Softground etching and aquatint on paper. Only known state. 6 5/16 x 8 5/8 in. (16 x 21.9 cm). Colby College Museum of Art, Waterville, Maine, The Lunder Collection, 2012.305

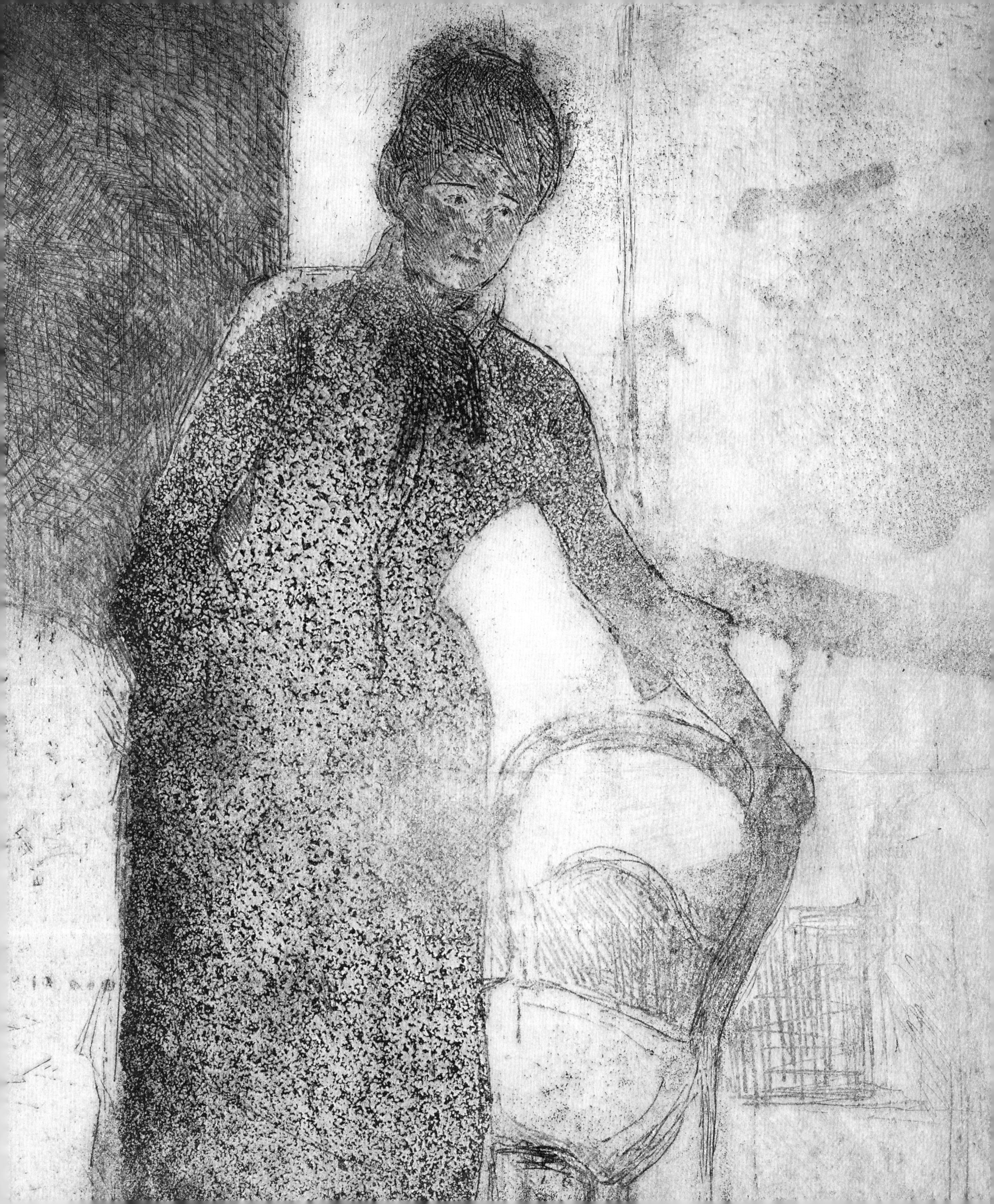

Mary Cassatt at Work, 1879–80

Justin McCann

Mary Cassatt's life was at a turning point in 1878. A year earlier, Edgar Degas had invited her to exhibit with the Impressionists. Cassatt was overjoyed. "At last," she remarked years later, "I could work with absolute independence, without considering the opinion of a jury. I had already recognized who were my true masters. I admired Manet, Courbet, and Degas. I hated conventional art. I began to live."[1] Cassatt had spent the better part of a decade making "conventional art," paintings that would be promising candidates for exhibition in the annual Salon in Paris. Many of these works, like *Pensive Roman Girl* (p. 64), satisfied a popular taste for costume genre scenes that reflected Old Master traditions from the seventeenth century. Cassatt seemed on her way to the success she had imagined for herself when the Salon accepted her painting of a peasant playing the mandolin—*The Mandolin Player*—in 1868. Other successes followed in the early 1870s, but by the middle of the decade Cassatt feared her career might be stalling. Increasingly frustrated with the politics of the Salon, she began to rebel against the art establishment, abandoning her academic style in favor of society portraits and scenes of everyday life.[2] Degas's perfectly timed invitation to join him and other "indépendants" promised a stimulating, sympathetic venue for Cassatt's art.

As she prepared for her first exhibition with the Impressionists, Cassatt executed a self-portrait that captures her state of mind at this time (fig. 1). Her floral bonnet and white dress with gloves show her to be appropriately attired for a young woman in Paris. Her pose, though, is anything but ladylike according to the standards of the period, and calls to mind Titian's *Portrait of Gerolamo (?) Barbarigo* (fig. 2). Artists such as Rembrandt van Rijn and Joshua Reynolds had used this pose in their

Mary Cassatt, *The Visitor* (detail), c. 1880. Softground etching, aquatint, etching, drypoint, burnishing, and fabric texture on paper. Second state (of six). 15½ x 12³⁄₁₆ in. (39.4 x 31 cm). Colby College Museum of Art, Waterville, Maine, The Lunder Collection, 2012.297

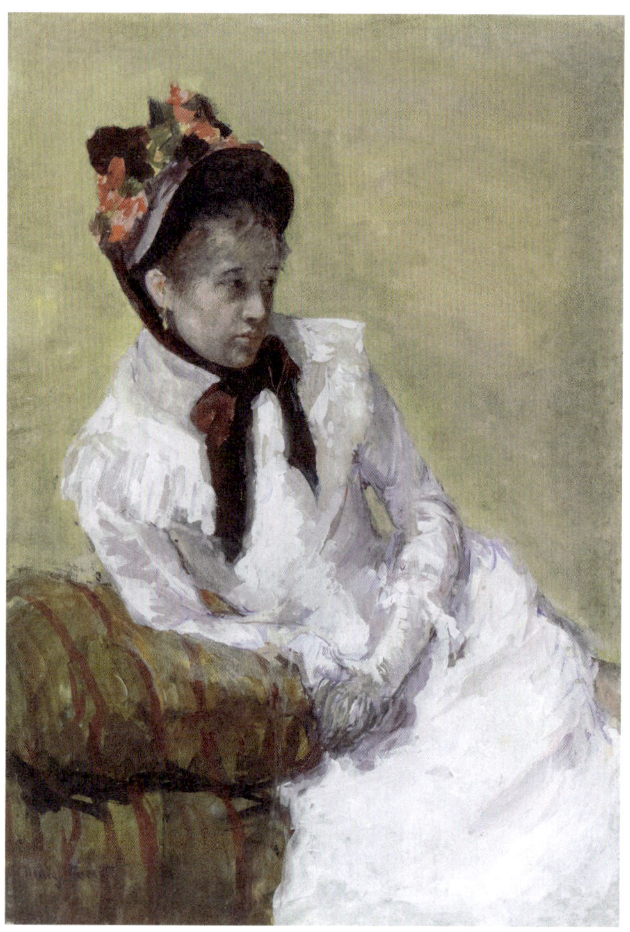

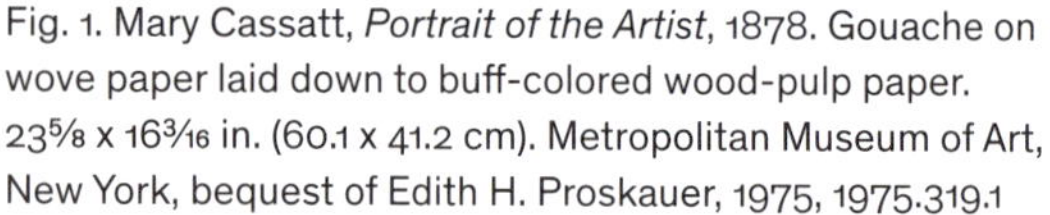

Fig. 1. Mary Cassatt, *Portrait of the Artist*, 1878. Gouache on wove paper laid down to buff-colored wood-pulp paper. 23⅝ x 16 3/16 in. (60.1 x 41.2 cm). Metropolitan Museum of Art, New York, bequest of Edith H. Proskauer, 1975, 1975.319.1

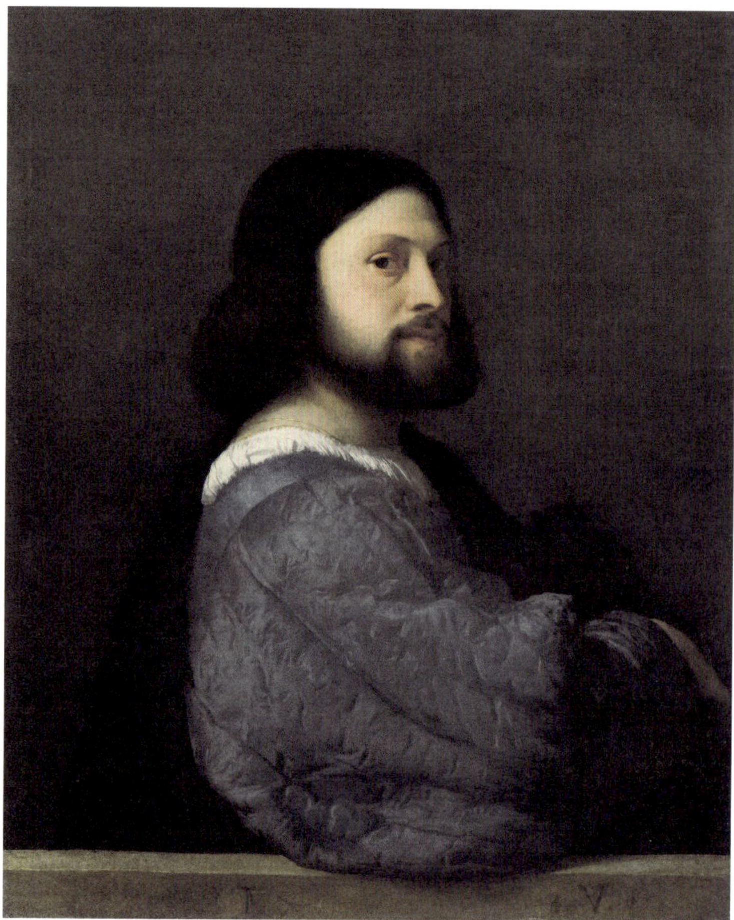

Fig. 2. Titian, *Portrait of Gerolamo (?) Barbarigo*, c. 1510. Oil on canvas. 32 x 26 in. (81.2 x 66.3 cm). National Gallery, London, NG1944

own self-portraits to communicate authority and self-possession. Cassatt, for her part, offers her own variation on the pose. She leans across a plush cushion and, although her body faces us, she has turned her head to the left and gazes confidently into the distance, flouting the traditional image of a female artist. Cassatt's self-portrait is like a calling card announcing her newfound creative freedom and her intention to follow her own vision in her art. But what she did not know when she painted this self-portrait was that some of her most innovative and experimental achievements over the next two years would be works in a medium altogether new to her: printmaking.

Up to this point, Cassatt had thought of herself as a painter. She had had no formal training in printmaking when Degas introduced her to etching in 1879.

The two artists had first met two years earlier in Cassatt's studio, brought together by their mutual friend Léon Tourny.[3] Degas may have been aware of Cassatt's work as early as the 1874 Salon, supposedly remarking upon seeing her painting *Ida*, "It's true. Here is someone who feels as I do." Cassatt encountered Degas's work in a Parisian gallery around the same time—she was not in Paris to attend the first Impressionist exhibition—and in 1877 she encouraged her friend Louisine Elder, later Louisine Havemeyer, to purchase his work.[4] Although we do not know the details of their first conversation, we might imagine that they spoke of their mutual admiration for each other and their shared disdain for the Salon, with Degas inviting Cassatt to join the Impressionists.

For the next several years, the two artists collaborated closely.[5] Cassatt began work on the painting *Little Girl in a Blue Armchair* (fig. 3) for the next Impressionist exhibition, moved to 1879 from its originally scheduled 1878 opening. As the work was being made, Degas advised Cassatt on how to complete it and even had a hand in painting the background.[6] Its bright palette and modern subject matter, as well as its cropped, asymmetrical composition, heralded Cassatt's new artistic direction and partnership with Degas. Although the painting marked a radical departure from her prior work, one important interest of Cassatt's carried over: a focus on the sitter's interior state. We see this in *Meditation* (fig. 4) from 1906 and the painting *Pensive Roman*

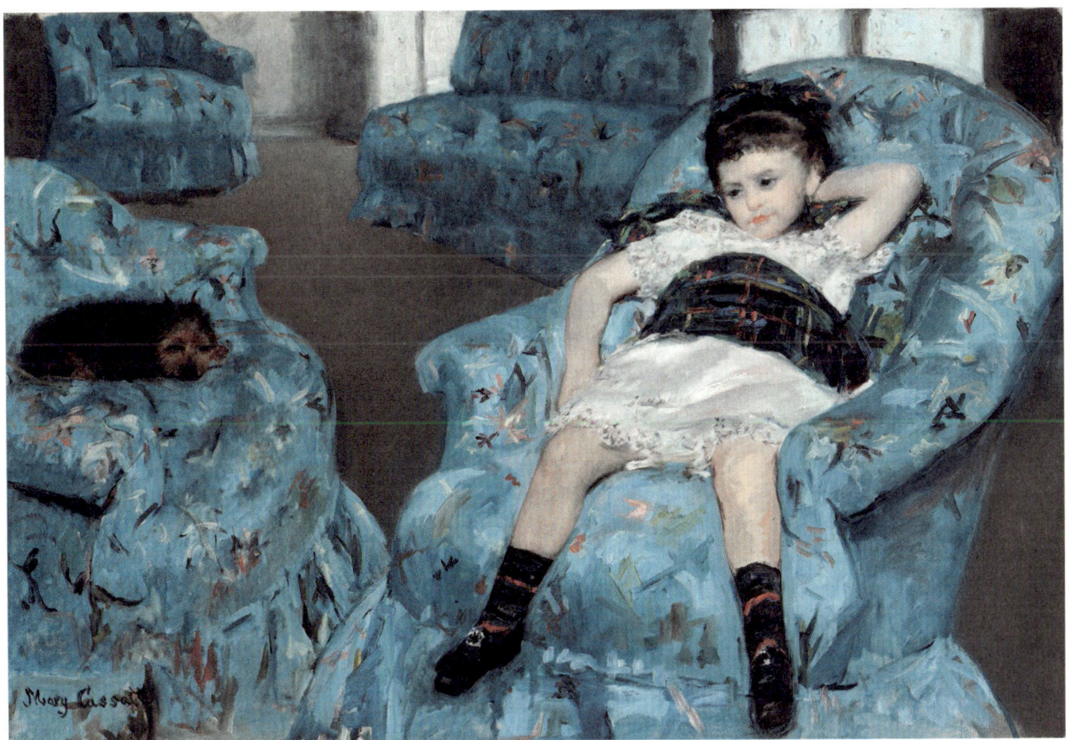

Fig. 3. Mary Cassatt, *Little Girl in a Blue Armchair*, 1878. Oil on canvas. 35¼ x 51⅛ in. (89.5 x 131.8 cm). National Gallery of Art, Washington, DC, Collection of Mr. and Mrs. Paul Mellon, 1983.1.18

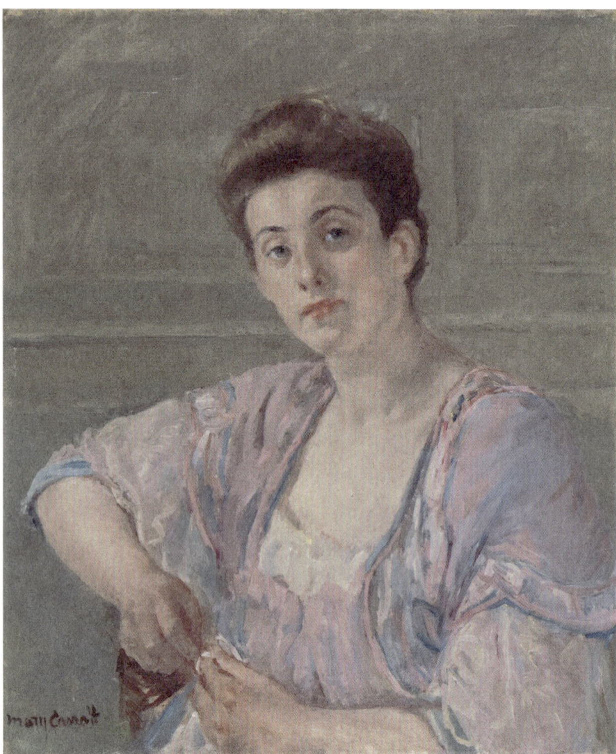

Fig. 4. Mary Cassatt, *Meditation*, 1906. Oil on canvas. 26½ x 22½ in. (67.3 x 57.2 cm). Colby College Museum of Art, Waterville, Maine, gift of Thomas J. Watson, Jr., 1972.002

Girl from circa 1872, where the child looks longingly upward. In *Little Girl in a Blue Armchair* the girl, now a child of a bourgeois family, stretches out over the armchair and looks downward, either bored or exhausted. Cassatt's exploration of interiority and solitude remained consistent throughout her career, and when she started to etch the following year, she would find the medium suited her purposes well.

Featuring eleven works, Cassatt's Impressionist debut on April 10, 1879, was a success with critics and buyers alike.[7] Cassatt reveled in the acclaim but quickly turned her attention to a new project. The writer Ludovic Halévy visited Degas's studio in May shortly after the close of the exhibition. He recorded: "Visit to Degas: Met him with the independent Miss Cassatt. . . . They are in a state of high excitement. They each received 440 francs from their exhibition and are thinking of starting a review."[8] The "review" was a journal, *Le Jour et la nuit* (Day and Night), which was to be devoted to prints. The first issue, according to an announcement in the periodical *Le Gaulois* in January 1880, would include work by Cassatt and Degas, among other artists, including fellow Impressionist Camille Pissarro.[9] In the end, the journal was not realized, but before the project fell apart Cassatt produced a series of technically daring, innovative etchings during the fall and winter of 1879–80.[10]

Printmaking had become a vehicle for a radically modern art by the 1870s. Just a few decades earlier, the medium (itself encompassing several distinct mediums) was primarily associated with the reproduction of images for wider circulation and therefore was not necessarily regarded as a means to make original works of art. However, artists at midcentury began to reassess the potential of etching in particular, and by the 1860s a shift in the status of prints more generally was underway. The Société des Aquafortistes (Society of Etchers) was formed in Paris in 1862, led by the publisher Alfred Cadart and the printmaker Félix Bracquemond. Artists associated with the Etching Revival, as it has since been called, prized originality, drama, experimentation, spontaneity, and expressiveness above all else in their work.[11] As Charles Blanc, an art critic and editor, put it, "Etching represents improvisation, liberty, and color."[12] The Society published three hundred etchings in five albums between 1862 and 1867. Artists also published prints in periodicals and issued portfolios of their own. The innovative work of Bracquemond in

France and James McNeill Whistler in England, among many others, demonstrated etching's effectiveness as a medium for vanguard artists and set the stage for further developments. Cassatt would have been aware of this surge in interest, but it may have been her personal encounter with Degas's prints from the mid-1870s that inspired her to consider printmaking in a fresh light. In these works, Degas blended various techniques that produced dramatic effects of lighting and shadow, aesthetic qualities that spoke to Cassatt's painterly imagination.[13] She also visited the *Exhibition of Works in Black and White*, which showcased many leading contemporary printmakers, in Paris during the summer of 1876.[14] Cassatt reevaluated printmaking during the exact period when she was rethinking her painting practice and her relationship to the Salon. Her success at the Impressionist exhibition doubtless emboldened her to embrace a new medium and to take a headline role in *Le Jour et la nuit*.

Cassatt worked feverishly throughout the fall and winter of 1879–80 on *In the Opera Box (No. 3)*, her planned contribution to the journal, seeing it through several different plates, states, and trial proofs (pp. 74–77).[15] She worked in Degas's studio while he worked on his contribution, *Mary Cassatt at the Louvre: The Etruscan Gallery* (fig. 5).[16] In addition to *In the Opera Box*, several other etchings by Cassatt from this period reveal an inquisitive and experimental artist reveling in the medium's creative possibilities. From the beginning she was interested in exploring different techniques, not only to learn about etching but also to arrive at her desired aesthetic effects. This was her "cookery," and her inventive and exploratory mind is clearly in evidence in the Colby Museum's collection.[17]

Cassatt chose to work primarily with softground etching and aquatint during this initial period. The combination of the two techniques can create a range of tones and textures that she could use to depict various effects of light. Softground etching—as opposed to hardground—produces soft, graveled lines similar to those of a graphite sketch. The Lunder Collection's *Standing Nude with a Towel* (p. 67), one of her earliest etchings, reveals Cassatt's investigation of these two techniques.[18] The subject is certainly unexpected and was indeed unprecedented for Cassatt at this point in her career. Since she was working in Degas's studio at the time, she may have selected the subject so as to be in dialogue with him. Her

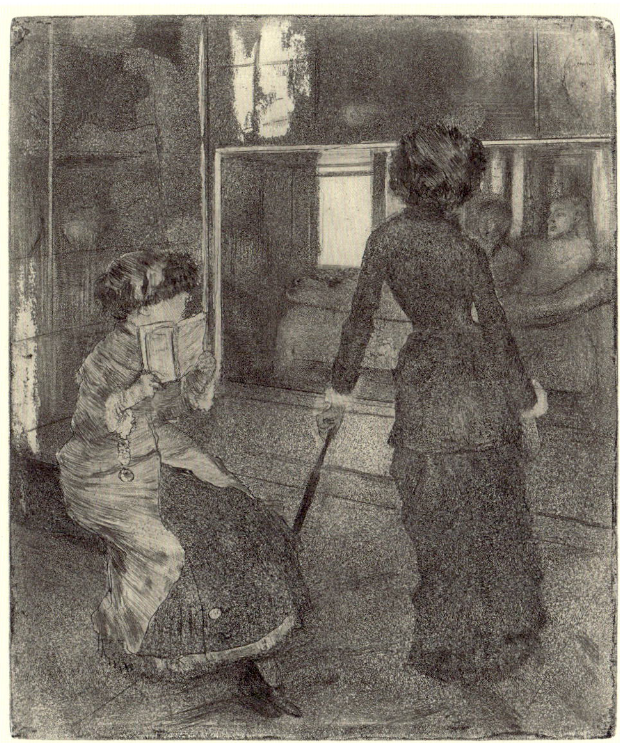

Fig. 5. Edgar Degas, *Mary Cassatt at the Louvre: The Etruscan Gallery*, c. 1879–80. Etching, aquatint, and electric crayon on paper. Fourth (final) state. 10⁹⁄₁₆ x 9³⁄₁₆ in. (26.8 x 23.4 cm). National Gallery of Art, Washington, DC, Rosenwald Collection, 1943.3.3366

figure, as many art historians have noted, bears striking similarities to Degas's nudes from the same moment. In this impression, the contour of the body is delineated with thick, darkly inked lines, indicating that perhaps Cassatt was getting a feel for the pressure she needed to apply with the pencil as she transferred her drawing from paper to the copperplate. The print also shows Cassatt experimenting with aquatint to produce various tonal effects. Here the aquatint is applied in a general and imprecise way, forming an uneven layer from which Cassatt could judge its initial effect. In later states, she applied the aquatint more aggressively and used foul biting and wire brushes to create pools to hold large amounts of ink. *Standing Nude with a Towel*, never intended to be a finished or exhibited work, represents one step in a series of trial runs that demonstrates Cassatt's curious and creative mind at work as she mixed and matched techniques.

Cassatt's other etchings from this early period relate mainly to the theater—which she attended regularly—and to scenes of domesticity. The Lunder Collection contains a rare, perhaps unique trial proof of *In the Opera Box (No. 3)* (p. 76).[19] In this impression Cassatt has printed just the lower portion of the composition that includes only the arms and the fan. Planning to contribute *In the Opera Box (No. 3)* to *Le Jour et la nuit*, Cassatt wanted to ensure that every part of the plate was just as she wanted it to be. Printing a trial proof of this specific section allowed her to examine each detail as an isolated unit. This type of select proofing of the print, not uncommon for Cassatt, can also be seen in *At the Dressing Table* (p. 68).[20] This is a trial proof of the upper half of an etching that depicts a woman dressing, perhaps getting ready to go to the theater. *The Bouquet* (p. 79) might be the ghostliest of all of Cassatt's early prints in the Lunder Collection.[21] A well-dressed but faceless woman sits alone, set against a dark background. Cassatt has used aquatint to cast a shadow across the figure, applying stopping-out varnish for the highlights on her dress, shoulders, and the top of her head. The bouquet that is supposed to sit in her lap has not yet been added. This print is one of the most startling and difficult etchings to make sense of. The subject relates to the other theater scenes she was working on at the time. *The Bouquet* may have been an attempt to transform her painting *The Loge*, now at the National Gallery of Art in Washington, DC, into a print. She was working on the painting during the same period. She abandoned *The Bouquet* after three states in favor of another composition that references *The Loge* more directly: *Two Young Ladies Seated in a Loge, Facing Right* (fig. 6).[22] Perhaps *The Bouquet*, then, was a test run to flesh out the use of materials, as there was no room in the composition for a second figure. Or perhaps she was attempting to do something she could not achieve in painting but that might work in softground etching and aquatint. Whatever the case, Cassatt's series of theater paintings and prints from the period show her thinking innovatively across media.

The Visitor (p. 81) is a prime example of Cassatt's evolving aims as a printmaker during this creatively fecund phase.[23] In perhaps her most ambitious work to date, a woman, taking hold of a chair to sit down and visit with a friend—not yet pictured—is dramatically backlit against a large window that casts her in shadow. The Lunder Collection's rare second-state impression illustrates Cassatt's inventive and exploratory use of different tools and techniques—six techniques in total—that enabled her to achieve her desired textures and lighting effects. The first step in her working process for this composition—and

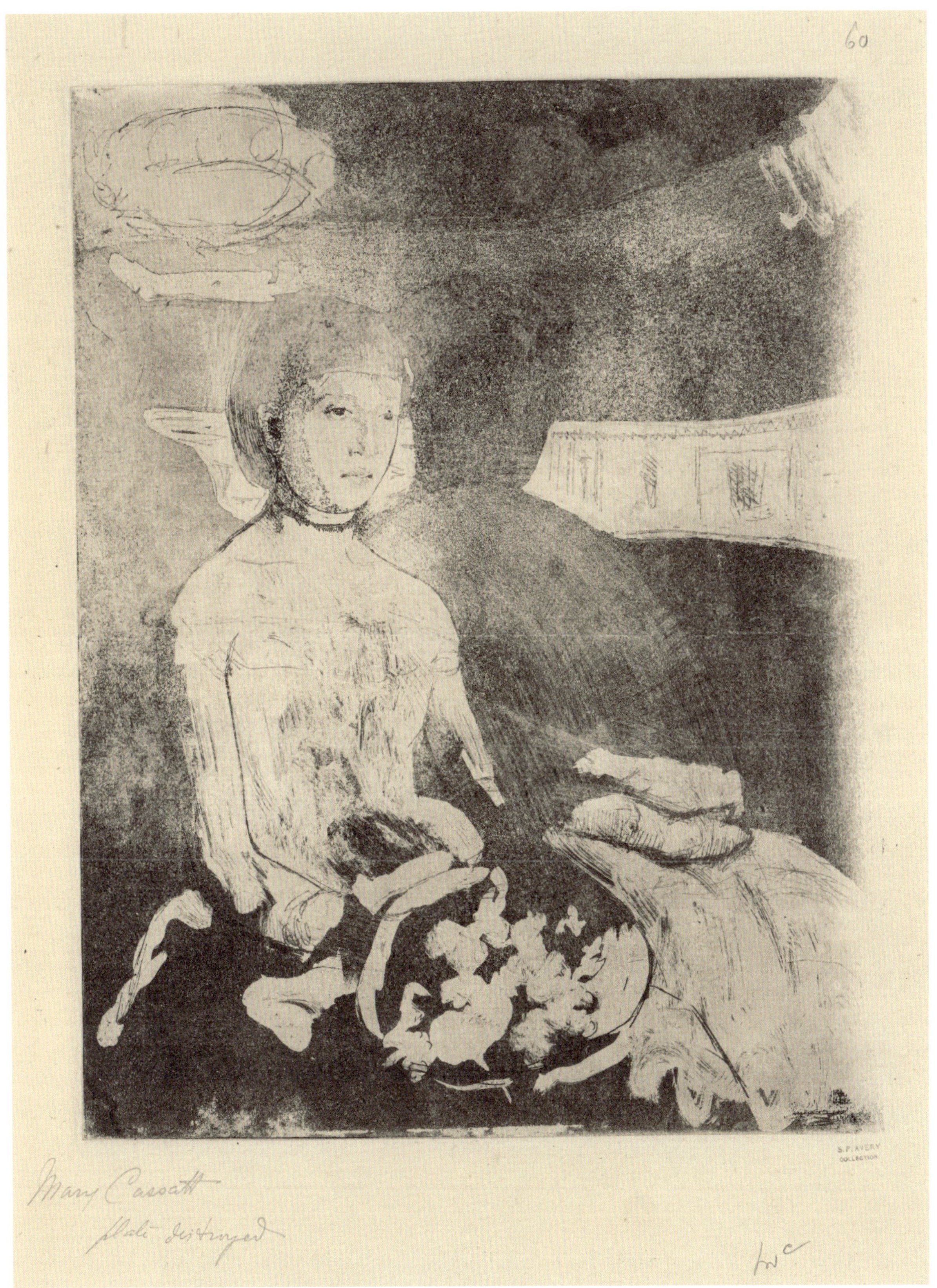

Fig. 6. Mary Cassatt, *Two Young Ladies Seated in a Loge, Facing Right*, 1882. Softground etching, aquatint, and drypoint on paper. First state (of two). 10⅞ x 8⁹⁄₁₆ in. (27.6 x 21.7 cm). The New York Public Library, The Miriam and Ira D. Wallach Division of Art, Prints and Photographs: Print Collection, 108212

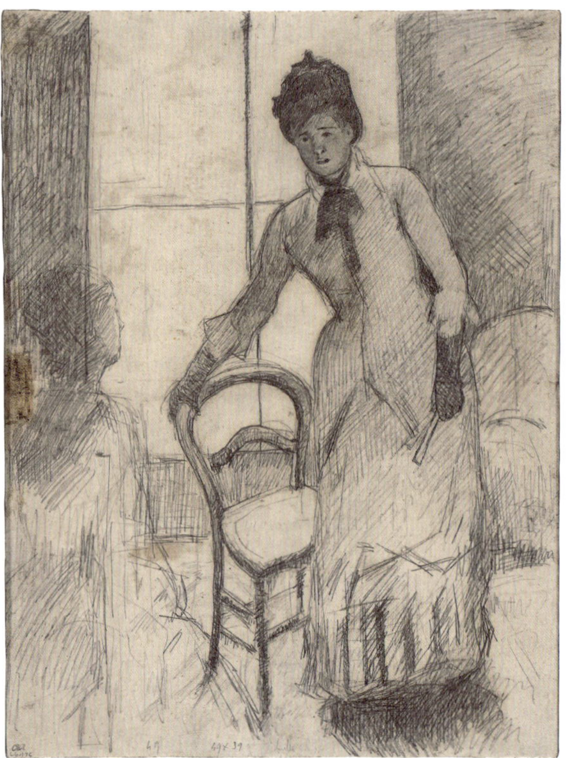
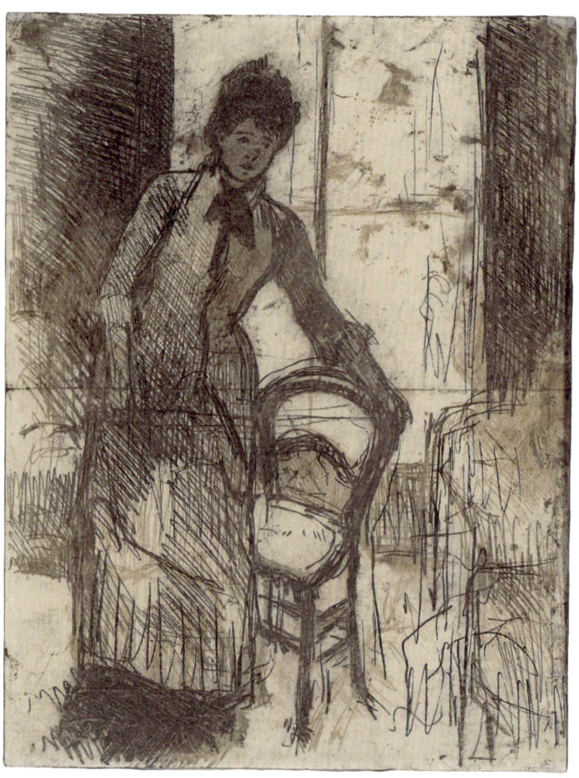

Fig. 7. Mary Cassatt, *The Visitor* (recto); *The Visitor* (verso), c. 1881. Black and tan pencil on paper. 5¾ x 12³⁄₁₆ in. (40 x 30.9 cm). Cleveland Museum of Art, gift of Fifty Members of The Print Club of Cleveland on the Occasion of the Fiftieth Anniversary, 1966.176

perhaps many others during this period—was to sketch the scene on paper, and then transfer the drawing to a copperplate. Figure 7 illustrates Cassatt's working drawing for *The Visitor* and the reverse tracing in softground.[24] The transfer was made by laying the paper over a plate coated in acid-resistant wax. Cassatt would then take a pencil and trace the drawing. The drawn lines push into the wax, and when the drawing is peeled off the waxed lines also come up, stuck to the backside of the paper. The image appears as lines of exposed metal on the plate, which was then placed in an acid bath. Cassatt could make trial proofs of the print to check on its progress, then reground the plate and add additional lines. In the case of *The Visitor*, she repeated this process several times, producing at least six unique states in addition to perhaps other intermediary states. The Lunder Collection's impression shows the composition in an early stage, featuring the central figure. The interior of the room is just sketched in. In later states, Cassatt would add the figure of the seated woman, along with pattern to the armchair and an additional gauzy texture to the curtain behind her (fig. 8).

The Colby Museum's *The Visitor* is a peek into Cassatt's working methodology early in a composition's

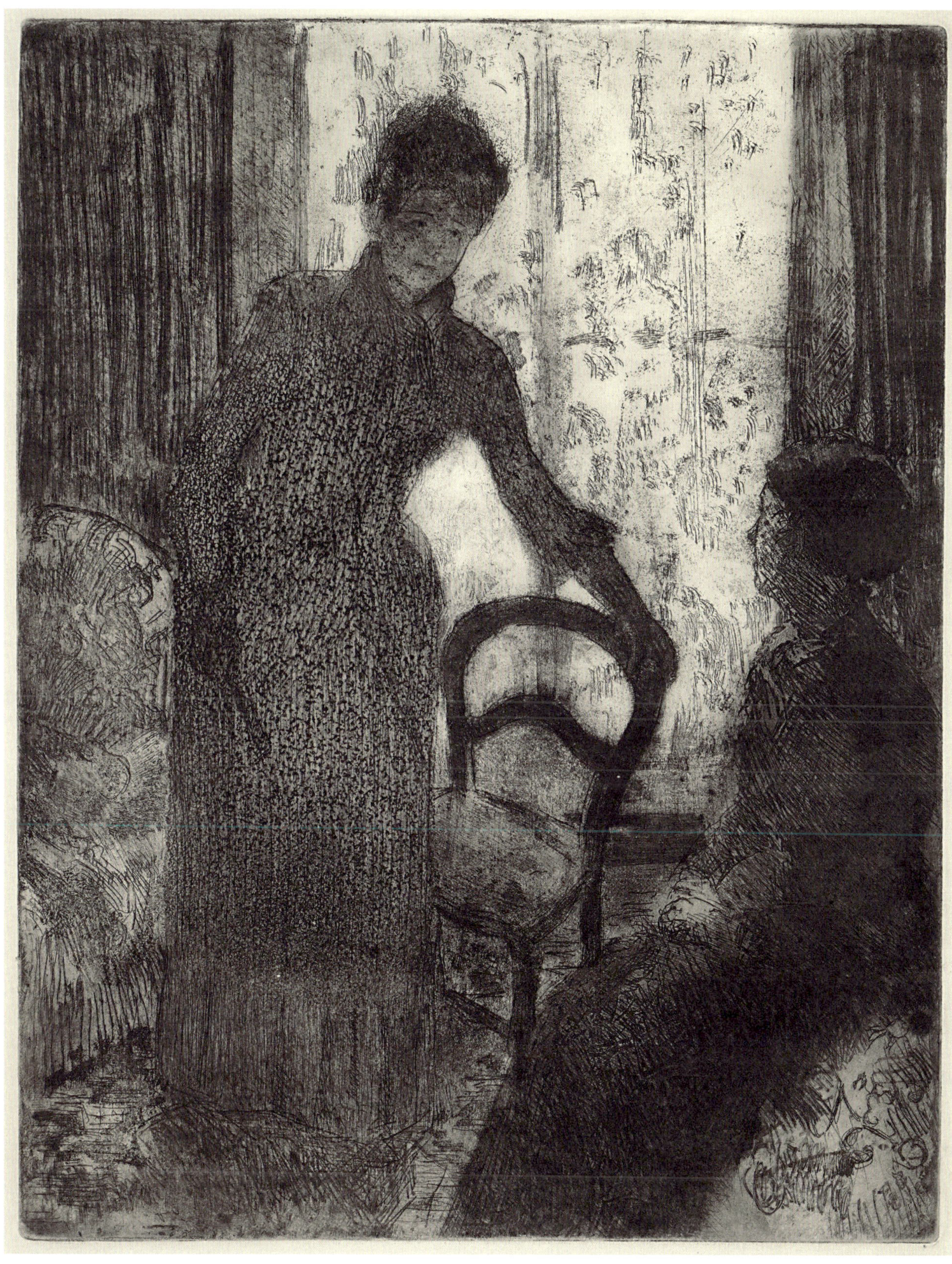

Fig. 8. Mary Cassatt, *The Visitor*, c. 1880. Softground etching, aquatint, and drypoint on paper. Sixth (final) state. 15⅝ x 12¼ in. (39.7 x 31.1 cm). National Gallery of Art, Washington, DC, Rosenwald Collection, 1946.21.94

development, one step in an experimental but meticulous process. For this early period of printmaking, though, it is difficult to assess which works Cassatt considered "finished." *The Visitor* and *In the Opera Box (No. 3)* are most certainly finished works. However, Cassatt was satisfied to leave other works, even after multiple state changes, unfinished. Perhaps, having learned what she wanted from the plate, she was content to move on. Perhaps she was juggling work on several plates at once and simply went where her creative momentum took her. Regardless, it might be this unfinished quality that inspired Martha Tedeschi to refer to the crop of trial proofs and early-state impressions in the Lunder Collection as "ghostly experiments."[25] These prints are artifacts of works in process, and they are difficult to decipher and understand. We naturally want to see the "finished" product. We want to arrive at a satisfactory meaning that we hope might come from more resolved details. We search for clues within *The Bouquet* or *Waiting* (p. 69) for narrative, for sentiment, for a message, but the work does not yield that type of meaning. Instead, in these unfinished works we see Cassatt in mid-thought. We see her starting and stopping, then changing course. We can feel her creativity and physical effort mingling together, so to speak, on the plate. We are left with the traces of Cassatt's manual work at every step of the etching process. Defying gender conventions, she installed herself in Degas's studio and pulled her own prints, turning the heavy rollers that slid the plate through the press. She handled acid, inks, wire brushes, and other sharp implements. Making prints was a messy, dirty, even dangerous practice. After pulling impressions, Cassatt most likely examined them with Degas, critiquing them and noting the changes she wanted to make. Now, more than a century later, we can examine and exhibit her working practice. Cassatt's trial proofs and early-state impressions reveal her step-by-step process, and as we look at them we see her learning and taking risks, fearlessly innovating and experimenting. They are some of the most intimate and captivating works of art she ever created.

Notes

1. Quoted in Adelyn Dohme Breeskin, *Mary Cassatt: A Catalogue Raisonné of the Graphic Work* (Washington, DC: Smithsonian Institution Press, 1979), 15.

2. Nancy Mowll Mathews, *Mary Cassatt: A Life* (New Haven, CT: Yale University Press, 1994), 96–108.

3. Amanda T. Zehnder, "Forty Years of Artistic Exchange," in *Degas/Cassatt*, ed. Kimberly A. Jones (Washington, DC: National Gallery of Art, 2014), 6–7.

4. George T. M. Shackelford, "*Pas de deux*: Mary Cassatt and Edgar Degas," in *Mary Cassatt: Modern Woman*, ed. Judith A. Barter (Chicago: The Art Institute of Chicago, 1998), 109–10.

5. For the collaboration between Cassatt and Degas during this period, see Zehnder and Shackelford's respective essays cited above and, more recently, Sarah Lees, "Innovative Impressions: Cassatt, Degas, and Pissarro as Painter-Printmakers," in *Innovative Impressions: Prints by Cassatt, Degas, and Pissarro*, ed. Sarah Lees (Tulsa: Philbrook Museum of Art, 2018), 11–91.

6. Ann Hoenigswald and Kimberly A. Jones, "'All the Vocabularies of Painting': Adaptation and Experimentation, 1878–1879," in *Degas/Cassatt*, 114.

7. Mathews, *Mary Cassatt: A Life*, 133–37.

8. Quoted in Zehnder, "Forty Years of Artistic Exchange," 7.

9. Ibid., 6–9; Shackelford, "*Pas de deux*: Mary Cassatt and Edgar Degas," 118–20; Lees, "Innovative Impressions," 31–40.

10. This essay focuses on a collection of trial proofs and early prints by Cassatt, which the Lunders acquired in 2012. The collection is well documented in R. Stanley Johnson, *Mary Cassatt: Early Graphic Works 1878–1891* (Chicago: R. S. Johnson Fine Art, 2011).

11. On the Etching Revival see Elizabeth Heisinger and Martha Tedeschi, eds., *The Writing of Modern Life: The Etching Revival in France, Britain and the U.S. 1850–1940* (Chicago: The Smart Museum of Art, The University of Chicago, 2009); Michel Melot, *The Impressionist Print*, trans. Caroline Beamish (New Haven, CT: Yale University Press, 1996); Lees, "Innovative Impressions," 11–27.

12. Quoted in Lees, "Innovative Impressions," 13.

13. Marc Rosen and Susan Pinsky, "The Medium as Muse: Innovations and Intersections in Printmaking," in *Degas/Cassatt*, 100–101.

14. Mathews, *Mary Cassatt: A Life*, 140.

15. Martha Tedeschi, "Mirror Images: A Reflection on Mary Cassatt's Opera Box Prints," in *The Lunder Collection: A Gift of Art* (Waterville, ME: Colby College Museum of Art, 2013), 219–22; Breeskin, *Mary Cassatt: A Catalogue Raisonné of the Graphic Work*, no. 21 and no. 22.

16. Rosen and Pinsky, "The Medium as Muse," 101.

17. Tedeschi uses the word "cookery" to describe Cassatt's combination of various printmaking methods. Also see Shackelford, "*Pas de deux*: Mary Cassatt and Edgar Degas," 120.

18. Breeskin, *Mary Cassatt: A Catalogue Raisonné of the Graphic Work*, no. 9.

19. Johnson, *Mary Cassatt: Early Graphic Works*, 44–45.

20. Breeskin, *Mary Cassatt: A Catalogue Raisonné of the Graphic Work*, no. 10.

21. Ibid., no. 19.

22. Ibid., no. 18.

23. Ibid., no. 34.

24. For an overview of Cassatt's softground etching process here and on other prints from the same period see Louise S. Richards, "Mary Cassatt's Drawing of the Visitor," *Bulletin of the Cleveland Museum of Art* 65, no. 8 (October 1978): 268–76; Tedeschi, "Mirror Images," 220; Breeskin, *Mary Cassatt: A Catalogue Raisonné of the Graphic Work*, 36.

25. Tedeschi, "Mirror Images," 219.

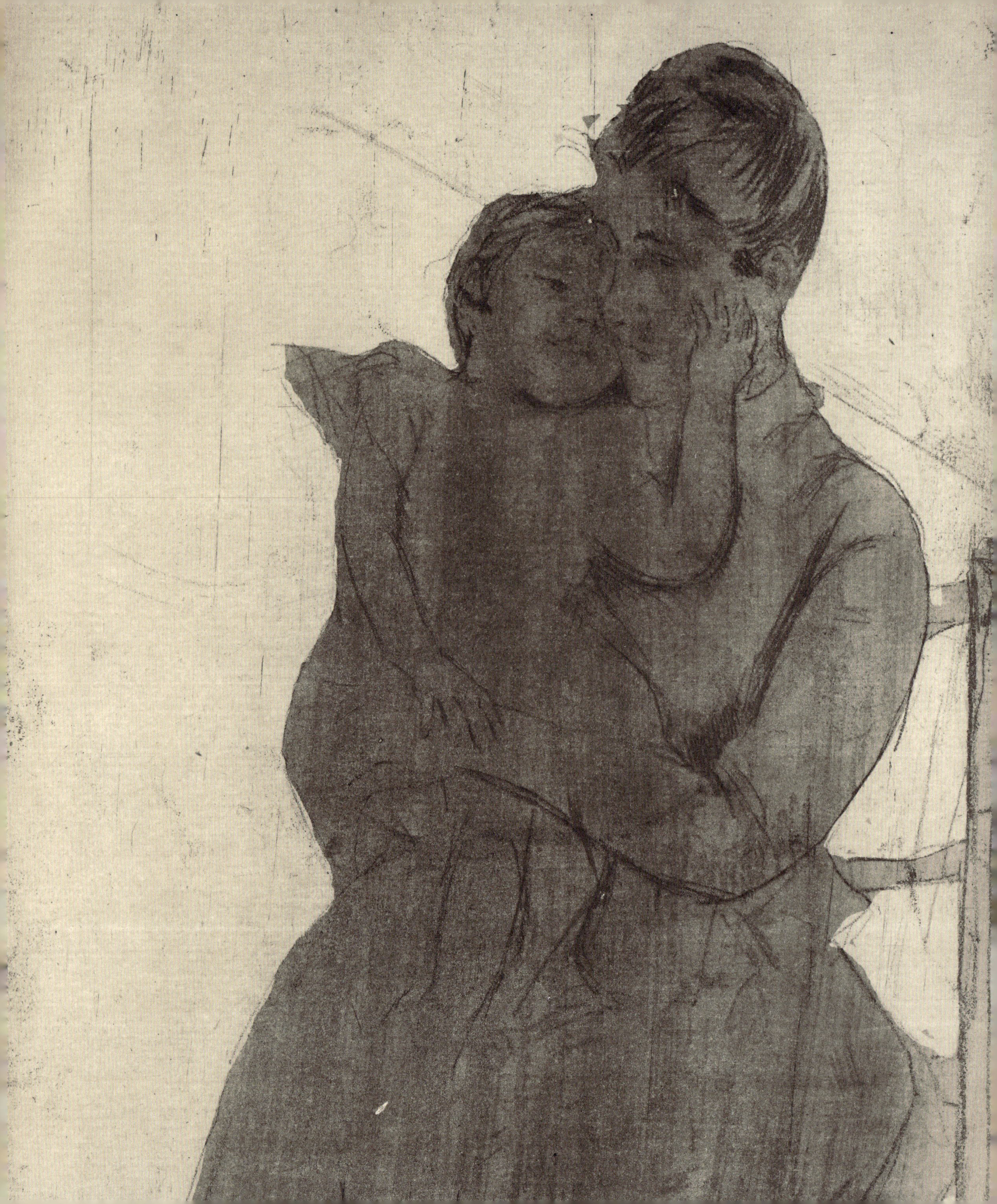

Serial Motherhood in Cassatt's Early Prints

Shalini Le Gall

In his 1913 survey of Mary Cassatt's work, *Un peintre des enfants et des mères, Mary Cassatt* (A Painter of Children and Mothers, Mary Cassatt), the French art critic Achille Ségard praised Cassatt's focus on *l'amour maternel* (maternal love) as a singular achievement in the representation of motherhood.[1] The subject's importance to Cassatt has been highlighted by numerous exhibitions and scholarly analyses that have explored her depictions of women and children, along with her representations of domesticity and motherhood, in prints, paintings, and pastels.[2] Yet Cassatt did not always specialize in such scenes; her early works included more varied images of private and public spaces alike, and made reference to broader European artistic traditions. Cassatt began to depict women and children in serial fashion in 1888–89, while experimenting with etching techniques alongside her Impressionist colleagues. Almost a decade earlier, shortly after the Fourth Impressionist Exhibition in 1879, Edgar Degas had invited Cassatt to join a group of artists, including Félix Bracquemond and Camille Pissarro, who were working to launch a journal entitled *Le Jour et la nuit* (Day and Night). The title alluded to artistic explorations in black-and-white imagery achieved through printmaking. Although the journal was never realized, the project offered Cassatt an opportunity to closely study contrasts between illumination and darkness, as well as positive and negative space, and to develop serial figurative studies that explored the formal flatness and social ambiguity of nineteenth-century domestic life.

Although Cassatt was not a mother herself, nineteenth-century critics credited her aptitude for depicting scenes of motherhood, and of women and children, to the fact that she was a woman. Joris Karl-Huysmans famously wrote, after seeing

Mary Cassatt, *Emmie and Her Child* (detail), c. 1889. Softground etching, aquatint, and drypoint on paper. Only known state. 8⅜ x 6⅛ in. (21.3 x 15.6 cm). Colby College Museum of Art, Waterville, Maine, The Lunder Collection, 2012.309

Cassatt's paintings, "seule, la femme est apte à peindre l'enfance" (only a woman is able to paint childhood), and later critics similarly focused their praise on her skill in painting maternal subjects.[3] In response to this line of criticism, Griselda Pollock has persuasively written about Cassatt's unique role as a woman artist, her insight into maternal subjectivity, and her reconceptualization of the "space of femininity."[4] Rather than focus on Cassatt's gendered experiences in nineteenth-century artistic and domestic spheres, I will instead concentrate here on her serial treatment of motherhood as a subject in 1889–90. The printmaking process informed her intensive study of women and children during this period, and small alterations in lighting, position, and background detail significantly impacted the interpretive scope that could be brought to these works.

The prints *Nurse and Baby Bill (No. 1)* (p. 101), *Nurse and Baby Bill (No. 2)* (pp. 102–3), *Solicitude* (p. 99), *On the Bench* (p. 100), and *Repose* (pp. 108–9) all date to the 1889–90 period, when Cassatt was treating the subject in multiple media. One of her earliest depictions of the mother and child theme, *Solicitude* is a drypoint that reflects Cassatt's extensive interest in interior light and shadow. As she made changes to the plate across multiple states and added drypoint lines in close proximity to one another, Cassatt significantly darkened the right half of the background and areas around the larger figure's neck and shoulder. In various states of *Nurse and Baby Bill (No. 1)*, Cassatt altered the features of the baby's face and hand, as well as the folds in the woman's dress, and even experimented with color. Comparison of the second and third states of *Baby's Back* (pp. 104–5) reveals changes to the child's foot and the background, along with significant lightening of the child's back. Examples of such increased detail appear across the various states of similar prints, including *The Stocking* (pp. 110–11), *Repose,* and *The Mirror* (pp. 114–15).

Like her Impressionist colleagues, Cassatt explored different iterations of a single subject.[5] Her extended study of the compositional variations of these coupled figures is similar to Monet's studies of haystacks or of the cathedral at Rouen, in each instance paintings in series made in the 1890s and later widely hailed for their modernist qualities.[6] Perhaps because of the domestic subject matter, critics have rarely treated Cassatt's serial studies of women and children as modernist formal experiments. The circumscribed interpretive scope afforded these works has been complemented by the overall disciplinary neglect of prints in general, in favor of paintings and other works of art more clearly intended for public display. Of course, Cassatt and other artists associated with the nineteenth-century Etching Revival included prints in public exhibitions of their work, but art historians have privileged painting in their examinations of this period.[7] Consequently, studies discussing Cassatt's women and children have often focused on the significance of this subject exclusively in her painting, with the unfortunate effect of neglecting how printmaking shaped her approach to the theme.

Considered through the lens of seriality, as an idea explored simultaneously in painting and printmaking, we find that the representation of women and children opened up new ways for Cassatt to activate seemingly static interiors, to shape contours of juxtaposed bodies, and to probe the psychological dynamics at work when a woman performs endlessly repetitive tasks of domestic labor. Perhaps surprisingly, in the variations Cassatt made across multiple states, she rarely added significant background detail or ornament to a composition. The backgrounds remain consistently stark; a few lines suggest benches, chairs, walls, or doorways, but otherwise these backgrounds express the Impressionist preference for flat pictorial space. This is especially apparent in the final state of *Repose*, where polka dots have been added to the adult figure's dress (undecorated in earlier states), while in the background a disorienting series of lines now designate walls, floors, and an open door or window. Rather than introduce new elements or details, most of the variations across the multiple states serve to refine limbs and facial features, alter shading, or further define compositional space in the background. Like her Impressionist peers working in series, Cassatt produced these multiple iterations to experiment with formal elements of her chosen medium, rather than to introduce narrative detail or enhance the setting. However, exploring this particular subject in serial form not only provided an opportunity to rework elements of positive and negative space. The succession of variations also offered insights into the routine, predictable nature of childcare.

The multiple iterations of *Nurse and Baby Bill (No. 1)*, for example, point to specific questions regarding seriality and the representations of motherhood and domestic labor. Unlike the ambiguous relationship between an adult female figure and a young child perceptible in other prints, the title of this series clearly identifies the woman as a caretaker. In her essay for this volume, Justine De Young addresses the challenges of recovering Cassatt's original titles, and in this case the difficulty in differentiating between mothers and paid caretakers merits further exploration. In an early state of this print, the adult and the child are modeled via the barest of lines, and the juxtaposed faces and the physical contact between limbs and bodies receive greater attention. In the only known final version of this print, now in the collection of the Museum of Fine Arts, Boston (fig. 1), the addition of green and brown ink has created a striking contrast between the two figures. Cassatt has guided the viewer to observe the scene as an image of domestic labor and to expect that the woman and child will be separated by psychological distance.

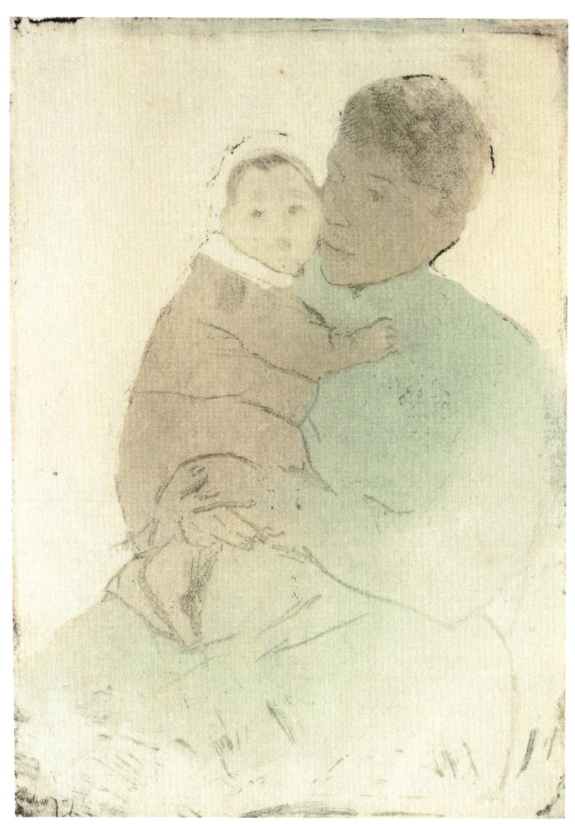

Fig. 1. Mary Cassatt, *Nurse and Baby Bill (No. 1)*, c. 1889. Softground etching and aquatint printed in green and brown ink on paper. Fourth (final) state. 7⁵⁄₁₆ x 5³⁄₈ in. (18.6 x 13.6 cm). Museum of Fine Arts, Boston, gift of Mr. and Mrs. Peter A. Wick, 58.1370

Cassatt's focus on the household workers in wealthy French homes is central to understanding many of her domestic scenes, including the striking drypoint *Susan Looking Down at Her Hands* (p. 95).[8]

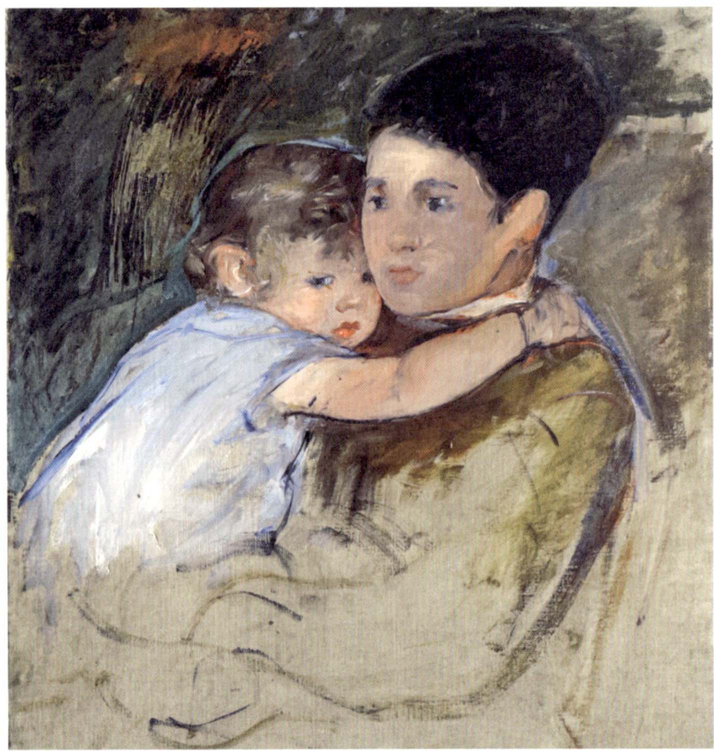

Fig. 2. Mary Cassatt, *Anne and Her Nurse*, c. 1897. Oil on canvas. 27½ x 23½ in. (69.9 x 59.7 cm). Portland Museum of Art, Maine, gift of Elizabeth B. Noyce in honor of Roger and Katherine Woodman, 1996.12

Susan was the cousin of Cassatt's housekeeper, Mathilde Valet, and here she poses as a housekeeper, an apron splayed across her dress. Perched on a bench or ledge, she scrutinizes her hands. The moment of rest represented in this print actually masks Susan's labor as Cassatt's model. Similarly, the caretaker holding baby Bill works doubly, at once caring for the child and modeling for the artist. Whereas affluent women employed household staff to care for their children's daily needs, laboring working-class women were compelled to place their children in home care settings, or emerging public care facilities known as crèches.[9]

Art historians, sociologists, and others have studied the system of domestic labor that fueled affluent lifestyles in general and Cassatt's artistic practice in particular.[10] The presence of paid workers in domestic settings doubtless endowed these spaces with an aura of formality and may have contributed to the stiffness and reserve some observe in Cassatt's images, such as the *Nurse and Baby Bill* prints or the painting *Anne and Her Nurse* (fig. 2). Yet this sense of psychological distance, imparted by the disparate gazes of the central figures and the relative absence of facial expressions, is also conveyed in prints portraying a mother and her child.

Writing during Cassatt's lifetime, both Ségard and Frank Weitenkampf praised the relative absence of sentimentality in her images of mothers and children, pointing to the simplicity and subtlety of the depictions.[11] In the various states of these prints, Cassatt experimented with background lines, clothing patterns, and limb articulation, but rarely did she depart from her original conception of the figures' gazes or facial expressions. In print after print, and indeed state after state, the subjects' psychological dimension is consistent, mimicking the repetitive nature of childcare. The details may vary, but the essential routine that structures childcare, particularly infant care, remains stable. Feeding, bathing, dressing, sleeping, playing: Cassatt shows us these moments in a young child's day, along with the individual responsible for ensuring the safety of such moments. Seriality here points not only to the process of printmaking but to the lived experience of childcare, ordered through routines.

Some of the prints that more explicitly represent motherhood introduce affective elements and thus appear to contrast with works such as the *Nurse and Baby Bill* prints. *Emmie and Her Child* (p. 97) is backlit, and the dramatic reversal of positive and negative space strongly ties the bodies together in a single, unified figure. As Hollis Clayson has argued, Cassatt's study of illuminated interiors added compositional and psychological dimensions to her prints, allowing her to link forms and figures in unexpected ways.[12] Physically linked bodies also appear in two other works in Colby's collection, the color print *Peasant Mother and Child* (p. 120) and the later pastel *Mother Berthe Holding Her Nude Baby* (p. 123).

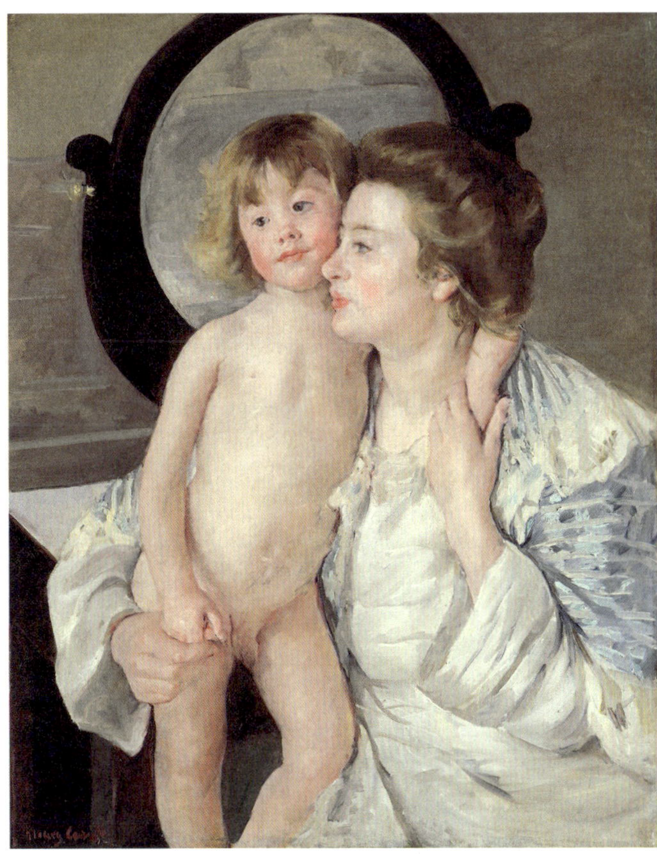

Fig. 3. Mary Cassatt, *Mother and Child (The Oval Mirror)*, c. 1899. Oil on canvas. 32⅛ x 25⅞ in. (81.6 x 65.7 cm). Metropolitan Museum of Art, New York, H. O. Havemeyer Collection, bequest of Mrs. H. O. Havemeyer, 1929, 29.100.47

Cassatt's depictions may have been based on scenes she observed and composed in affluent Parisian households, but viewers at the time would have immediately associated images of seated mothers holding infant children with representations of the Virgin Mary and the infant Christ. Whether or not Cassatt intentionally alluded to this tradition of religious painting, her contemporaries often made the connection. In reaction to the painting *Mother and Child (The Oval Mirror)* (fig. 3), Edgar Degas told Cassatt, "It's the infant Jesus and his English nurse," and the painting was later referred to as "the Florentine Madonna."[13] The contrapposto position of

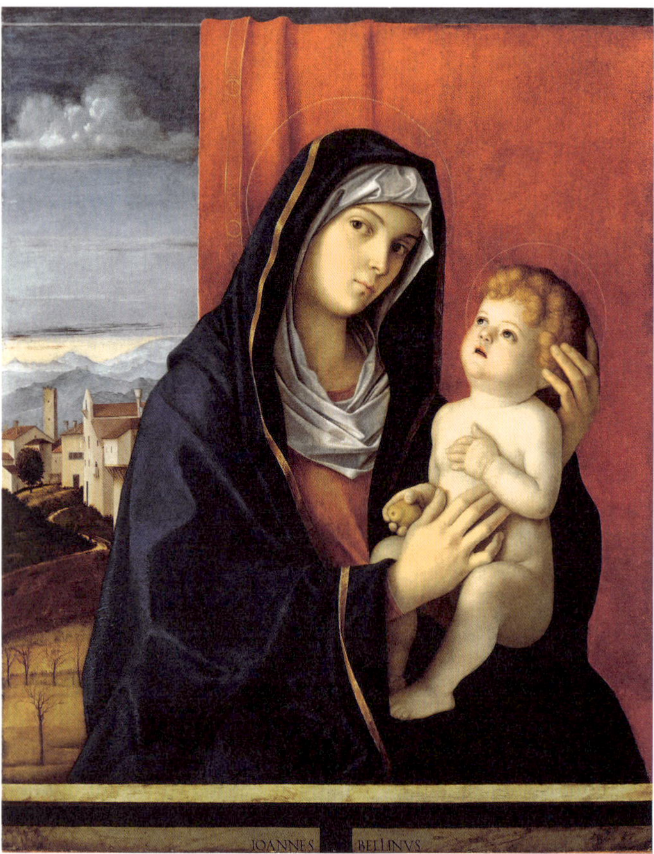

Fig. 4. Giovanni Bellini, *Madonna and Child*, late 1480s. Oil on wood. 35 x 28 in. (88.9 x 71.1 cm). The Metropolitan Museum of Art, New York, Rovers Fund, 1908, 08.183.1

the child's body, the halo effect created by the oval mirror in the background, and the blue of the woman's clothing all make reference to artistic conventions found in Italian paintings of the Virgin and Child. In a review of Cassatt's 1891 exhibition at Paul Durand-Ruel's gallery, Georges Lecomte coined the phrase "sainte famille moderne" (modern holy family) to describe her innovative approach to this traditional subject.[14] Although Cassatt did not seem especially interested in religious subjects, she would have seen Virgin and Child paintings during her travels in Italy and when studying works at the Louvre. Her images of seated women embracing children echo this Catholic tradition even as they add a secular dimension to an otherwise sacred subject.

In the stiff formality sometimes observed in the awkward contact between Cassatt's bodies, especially the limbs, the artist may have drawn from conventions found in images such as Giovanni Bellini's *Madonna and Child* (fig. 4). In this painting, Mary and Jesus are presented not as individuals in a familial relationship, but rather as religious icons intended to inspire reverence. The serial unfolding of various, though closely related, representations of the Virgin and Child subject across centuries and vast geographic expanses relies on the relative stability of artistic conventions, including the presence of red and blue garments, seated frontal postures, halos, and gestures of benediction. While Cassatt was more naturalistic in her approach than her Italian counterparts, her seriality is also fixed by certain formal guideposts: seated female figures occupying three-quarters of the picture plane; proportionally larger children being supported by adult arms grasping their legs; faces shown in close proximity but from different angles; a flatness of pictorial space conveyed by sparse background detail; and the use of angled perspectives.

Cassatt's interest as a printmaker in serial depictions of motherhood hinged on the formal experimentation that accompanied these explorations. The relative stability of her subjects in 1889–90 soon yielded to a new approach toward scenes of motherhood and childcare, a fresh orientation informed by her close study of Japanese woodblock prints in the wake of a groundbreaking exhibition at the École des

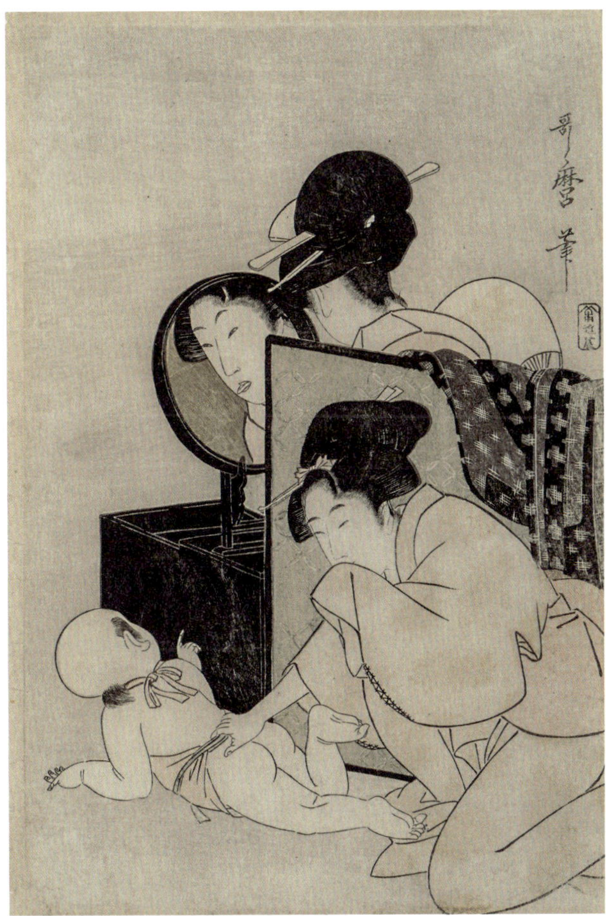

Fig. 5. Kitagawa Utamaro I, *Peeping*, c. 1799–1800. Woodblock print (nishiki-e); ink and color on paper. 15¼ x 10¼ in. (38.8 × 26.1 cm). Museum of Fine Arts, Boston, anonymous gift, 1999.229

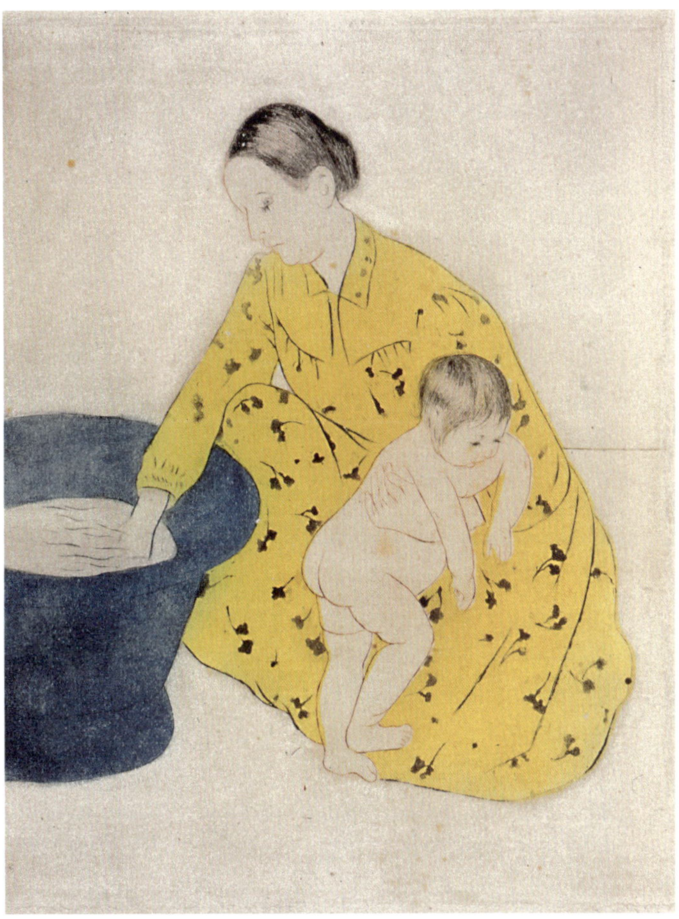

Fig. 6. Mary Cassatt, *The Bath*, c. 1891. Drypoint, softground etching, and aquatint in color on paper. 12¾ x 10 in. (32.4 x 25.4 cm). Museum of Fine Arts, Boston, bequest of W. G. Russell Allen, 63.310

Beaux-Arts in 1890. After Japanese ports opened to trade in 1853, following the military and economic pressure applied by Commodore Matthew Perry's US Navy squadron, Japanese goods inundated European markets. Like other Impressionist artists, Cassatt assembled a personal collection of Japanese prints, including several works by Kitagawa Utamaro, a Japanese artist active in the late eighteenth and early nineteenth centuries who specialized in scenes of women and children in domestic settings. The Utamaro print *Peeping* (fig. 5), formerly in Cassatt's collection and now at the Museum of Fine Arts, Boston, depicts the extended body of a young child edging forward from behind a screen in order to glimpse a woman reflected in an oval mirror; another woman holding the child steady attempts to restrain her laughter at such mischievous behavior. Such playful attitudes and voyeuristic insinuations are absent from Cassatt's domestic scenes. Nevertheless, Utamaro's work introduced new elements into the artist's formal experiments.

Cassatt's print *The Bath* (fig. 6) and the painting *The Child's Bath* (fig. 7) offer examples of her use and understanding of Japanese design principles. The print's compositional structure, the decorative motif of the woman's dress, and the lines of the child's fleshy body draw from artistic elements in Utamaro's work. In the painting, the child's large extended body serves as a meeting point for the work's various decorative motifs, including the diamond-patterned rug, the striped dress, and the floral wall and dresser. Central to the work of many Impressionist painters, Japanese prints held special significance for Cassatt at this historical moment. In Utamaro's prints, women and children are simultaneously quotidian subjects and vehicles for formal experiments with line, color, and flatness. It is little wonder that Cassatt found in them both validation for her own experiments and a means to reinvigorate a centuries-old European subject. Connected to both Japanese woodblock and European etching traditions, Cassatt's serial approach to printmaking probed the pictorial aspects of domestic spaces and gave form to the layered experiences that structured motherhood and childcare in nineteenth-century France.

Notes

1. Achille Ségard, *Un Peintre des Enfants et des Mères, Mary Cassatt*, 3rd ed. (Paris: P. Ollendorff, 1913), 142. All translations are my own.

2. Judith A. Barter, ed., *Mary Cassatt: Modern Woman* (Chicago: The Art Institute of Chicago, 1998); Mallory Farrugia, ed., *Cassatt: Mothers and Children* (San Francisco: Chronicle Books, 2019); Nancy Mowll Mathews and Pierre Curie, eds., *Mary Cassatt: An American Impressionist in Paris* (New Haven, CT: Yale University Press, 2018).

3. Joris-Karl Huysmans, *L'Art moderne* (Paris: Charpentier, 1883), 232. See also Camille Mauclair, "Un peintre de l'enfance: Miss Mary Cassatt," *L'Art decoratif*, August 1902, 177.

4. Griselda Pollock, *Mary Cassatt: Painter of Modern Women* (London: Thames & Hudson, 1998), 30, 33, 126.

5. Ibid., 163.

6. Paul Hayes Tucker, *Monet in the 90s: The Series Paintings* (New Haven, CT: Yale University Press, 1990); John House, *Nature into Art* (New Haven, CT: Yale University Press, 1988).

7. Hollis Clayson, "Mary Cassatt's Lamp," in *Is Paris Still the Capital of the Nineteenth Century? Essays on Art and Modernity, 1850–1900*, ed. Hollis Clayson and André Dombrowski (London: Routledge, 2016), 273.

8. Pollock, *Mary Cassatt: Painter of Modern Women*, 187.

9. Debra N. Mancoff, *Mary Cassatt: Reflections of Women's Lives* (New York: Steward, Tabori & Chang, 1998), 79. For information on childcare options for working-class women, and especially the history of the crèche, see Ann F. La Berge, "Medicalization and Moralization: The Crèches of Nineteenth-Century Paris," *Journal of Social History* 25, no. 1 (Autumn 1991): 65–87.

10. For an introductory overview, see Raffaella Sarti, "Historians, Social Scientists, Servants, and Domestic Workers: Fifty Years of Research on Domestic and Care Work," *International Review of Social History* 59, no. 2 (August 2014): 279–314.

11. Weitenkampf, writing in 1916, cited in Pollock, *Mary Cassatt: Painter of Modern Women*, 166–67. For full discussion see Ségard, *Un Peintre des Enfants et des Mères*, 36–44.

12. Clayson, "Mary Cassatt's Lamp," see 259 for discussion of "illumination discourse."

13. Natalie Spassky et al., *American Paintings in the Metropolitan Museum of Art*, vol. 2 (New York: Metropolitan Museum of Art, 1985), 646.

14. Georges Lecomte, "A coté des peintres-graveurs," *L'Arts dans les deux mondes*, April 18, 1891, 261, cited in Mathews and Curie, *Mary Cassatt: An American Impressionist in Paris*, 88.

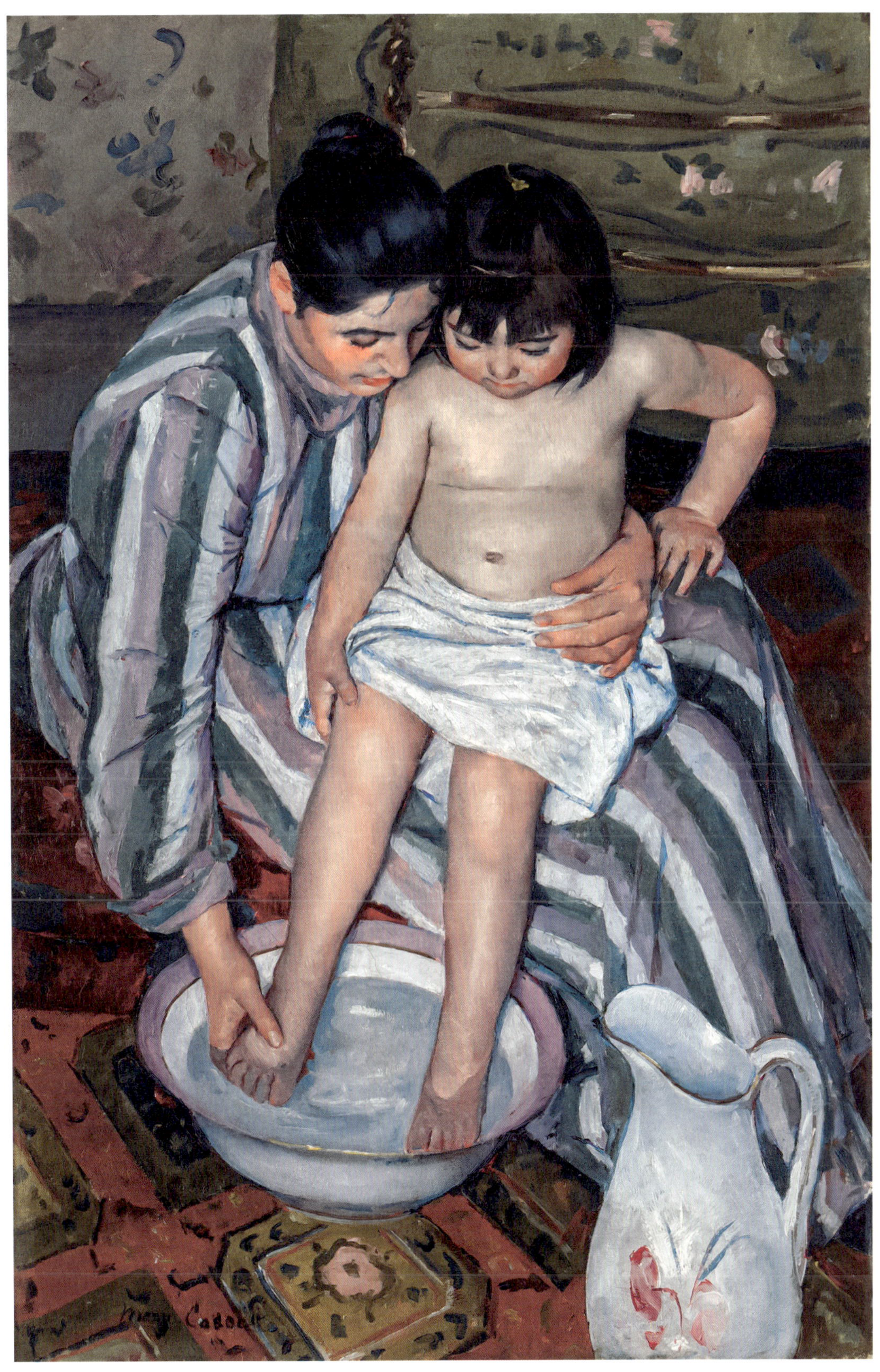

Fig. 7. Mary Cassatt, *The Child's Bath*, 1893. Oil on canvas. 39½ x 26 in. (100.3 x 66.1 cm). Art Institute of Chicago, Robert A. Waller Fund, 1910.2

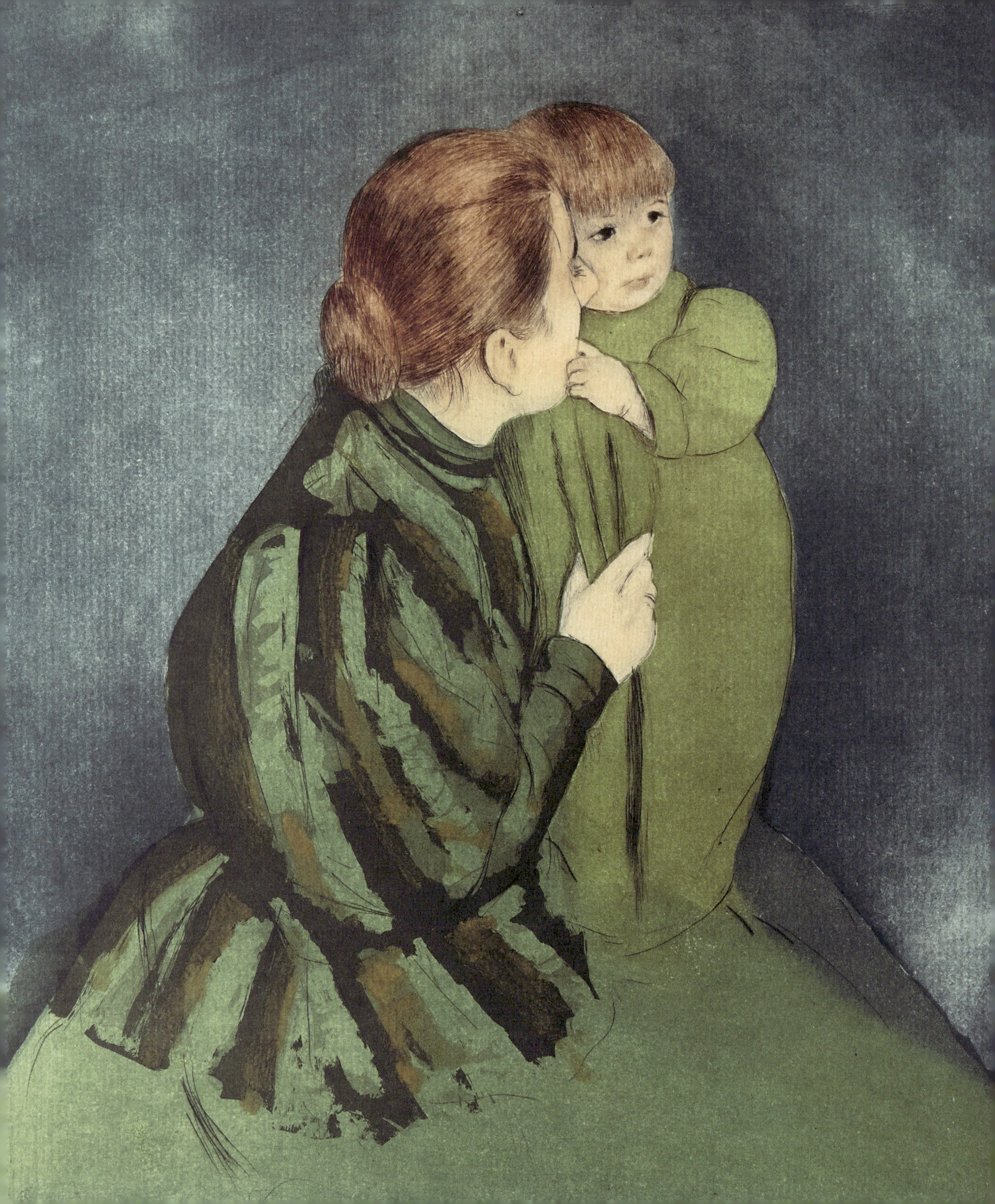

Dressing the Modern Woman: Mary Cassatt and 1890s Fashion

Justine De Young

Mary Cassatt came from a wealthy Philadelphia family and, like any woman of her class, she was expected to dress well. Dressing well meant dressing not only appropriately for the occasion, the season, and the time of day, but also with an awareness of the latest trends. When possible, the well-dressed woman would wear garments created by elite designers. The most fashionable couturiers were in Paris, and rich Americans became some of their most important clients. As the art historian Debra Mancoff notes, Cassatt had expensive taste; she "seemed to prefer the couture houses particularly those of Worth and Paquin. When her sisters-in-law visited, she advised them on a couturier."[1]

Worth and Paquin were two of the leading design houses in Paris in the late nineteenth century. Given her family's wealth and, by the 1890s, the income she drew from lucrative sales by her dealer Paul Durand-Ruel, Cassatt could afford to commission dresses from couturiers like Worth, who charged on average 1,600 French francs (roughly $8,000 in today's dollars) for a day dress in 1868.[2] Yet one could dress in comparable elegance for far less. Charles Frederick Worth himself admitted that a respectable woman could dress on 1,500 francs a year—less than he charged for a single gown.[3]

Indeed, the nineteenth century witnessed an unprecedented democratization of fashion, made possible by industrialization, a growing middle class, the rise of

Mary Cassatt, *Peasant Mother and Child* (detail), c. 1894. Drypoint and aquatint on paper. Tenth (final) state. 17¼ x 11¼ in. (43.8 x 28.6 cm). Colby College Museum of Art, Waterville, Maine, The Lunder Collection, 2017.468

the department store, and the explosion of the fashion press. Although Cassatt was a consumer of designer clothes, her models were not all outfitted in such expensive frocks. Charged with depicting "The Modern Woman" in a mural for the Woman's Building at the 1893 Columbian Exposition in Chicago, she chose, of course, to present all the figures in contemporary dress, but in a letter to the pavilion's organizer, Bertha Palmer, she insisted they were not wearing designer fashions:

> Mr. Avery sent me an article from one of the New York papers this summer, in which the writer, referring to the order given me, said my subject was to be the "The Modern Woman as glorified by Worth"! That would hardly describe my idea, of course I have tried to express the modern woman in the fashions of our day and have tried to represent the fashions as accurately & as much in detail as possible.[4]

Contemporary critics praised her exactitude; a writer for the *New York Tribune* noted in 1895 that Cassatt's "spirit is essentially modern; she has that peculiar atmosphere of to-day that has been familiar chiefly since Manet's rise, and she retains that charm."[5] Yet despite general acknowledgment that Cassatt was knowledgeable about and was apparently a keen consumer of fashionable clothes, art historians have largely overlooked her choices in her art regarding fashion.[6] This essay examines Cassatt's fashion choices in her prints of the early 1890s, where she showcases mundane moments in women's lives with an attentive eye to the details of modern dress. Considering fashion in these prints not only affirms Cassatt's interest in the latest trends but also transforms our understanding of one her most important color prints, long known misleadingly as the *Peasant Mother and Child*—with a maternal figure who proves to be no peasant at all.

While interested, it seems, in fashion her entire life, Cassatt began to focus closely on fashion in her prints only in the late 1880s and early 1890s. Though the second print she made (c. 1878) was after a costume plate by the famed fashion illustrator Paul Gavarni, she altered his composition to elide all detail and create a hazy atmosphere. This sort of transformation is typical of her early prints. Whereas she often attended to details of dress and silhouette in her preparatory drawings, such details are often lost in the translation to print. *Lydia at Afternoon Tea* (p. 82) and *Before the Fireplace (No. 2)* (p. 83) indicate basic features of Lydia's two dresses, but Cassatt pays far more attention to the particulars of the setting, including a prominent tea set made for Cassatt's grandmother in 1813.[7] In the 1890s, however, Cassatt began to include more details related to fashion: she added prints to fabrics, experimented with different dress colors, and carefully recorded the changing shape of sleeves.

In *Tea* (p. 113), the young woman's dress features prominent bows on both shoulders, which Cassatt has carefully shaded to create a sense of dimension. The print is closely related to a pastel, *Girl in Pink with a Fan* (fig. 1), though in the print Cassatt has moved the flower vase so that both shoulder bows are visible. Pink evening dresses with bows at the shoulders were popular at the time, as indeed they had been for several years. Emphasizing the bows makes the print and pastel temporally specific—resonant with the particularities of young female adulthood in the late 1880s.[8]

In the different states of *The Mirror* (pp. 114–15), the volume of sleeve puffing at the upper arm becomes progressively more clearly delineated,

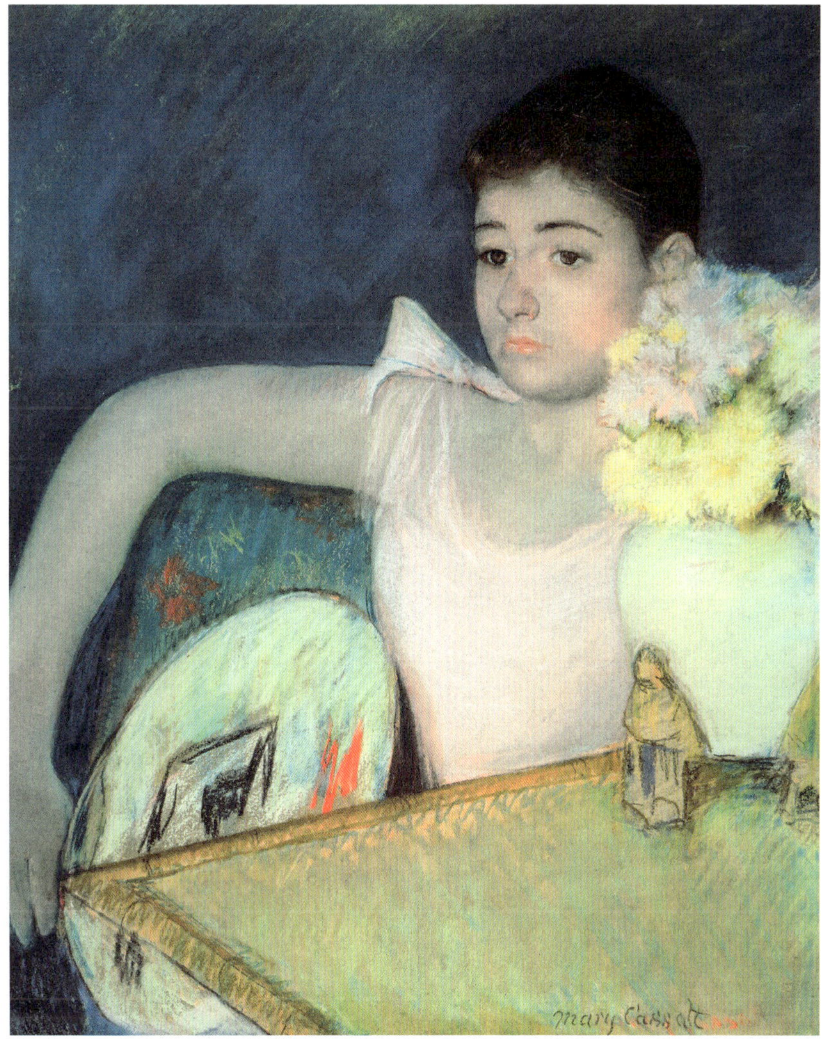

Fig. 1. Mary Cassatt, *Girl in Pink with a Fan*, c. 1889. Pastel on paper. 23½ x 19½ in. (59.8 x 49.5 cm). Tokyo Fuji Art Museum

revealing a Renaissance-revival-style sleeve, suggestive of sixteenth-century paning or slashing. This somewhat eccentric sleeve style was in vogue at the time and can be seen, for example, in a *La Mode illustrée* plate (no. 47) from late 1890. Cassatt's attention to such fashionable details makes the artworks historically specific, and her insistence on them in works that might otherwise seem to be timeless images of mothers and children demonstrates her commitment to depicting "the modern woman in the fashions of our day . . . as accurately & as much in detail as possible."

"Modern Woman" Mural (1892–93)

The twelve-by-fifty-eight-foot "Modern Woman" mural mentioned above centered on a scene depicting *Young Women Plucking the Fruits of Knowledge* with panels featuring *Young Girls Pursuing Fame* and *Art, Music, Dancing* on either side.[9] The mural itself is lost—presumed destroyed—but Cassatt reused many of the figures and the costumes in her paintings and prints, giving us an idea of the fashions involved.[10] For example, *The Banjo Lesson* features a young girl in a pink dress with bows at the shoulders, not unlike the garment in *Girl in Pink with a Fan*, and the same dress, and perhaps girl, featured in the central panel of the 1893 mural as well. A woman playing a banjo was also depicted in the *Art, Music, Dancing* panel, but the dress in the print was worn by the figure representing Art in the mural. In her garment choices, Cassatt focused on capturing what was trending at the moment.

Commentators at the time recognized the timeliness of the clothing, as Mariana Van Rensselaer, the art critic for Joseph Pulitzer's *The World,* related in a December 1892 column reporting on Cassatt's progress, relying on evidence from Sara Hallowell, who had been with the artist during the painting of the mural: "She very wisely determined to make her modern woman as truly modern as possible—to paint her in the most characteristic (which means, of course, the most fashionable) garments of the current year 1892."[11] This desire for contemporaneity accords with what Cassatt described in her letter to Bertha Palmer cited above, but Van Rensselaer goes on to insist that Cassatt was relying upon designer gowns for her models: "Costumes had to be secured and so the latest and loveliest summery 'creations' of Worth and Doucet were purchased, to be thrown about and dragged around in the studio."[12] One can only imagine Cassatt's indignation had she read this report. A Worth customer herself, she certainly knew what an 1892 Worth gown looked like, as indeed would any fashion-conscious American: Worth gowns appeared almost weekly on the cover of the leading US fashion magazine *Harper's Bazar.*

As Cassatt insisted, the dresses she chose to paint in the mural and include in prints after it are far simpler in their design and trimmings than those designed by Worth. Her rejection of Worth gowns has prompted some art historians to assume the dresses were not fashionable, but instead representations of aesthetic dress or dress reform garments.[13] As we will see, however, Cassatt's fashion choices were in tune with fashionable trends of the time, neither embracing the decorative exuberance of couture nor rejecting the silhouette and corseted styles of the day as advocated by dress reformers.

The Banjo Lesson (1893)

Cassatt created *The Banjo Lesson* in the fall of 1893 after shipping off the "Modern Woman" mural earlier that year.[14] Distinctively American instruments, banjos had been rising in popularity since the 1880s, making Cassatt's inclusion of one in the print quite a modish choice.[15] In late November of 1893, Cassatt exhibited *The Banjo Lesson* in three of its four states, including the final colored one (fig. 2), in her solo exhibition at the Durand-Ruel galleries in Paris.[16]

The second state (p. 117) carefully delineates the shape of the banjo player's sleeves and bodice, which closely reflect 1893 trends. The sleeve style, known as *bracelets aux manches*, has the large puff on the upper arm cinched in around the bicep and loosely hanging open around the elbow. Sleeve styles of the 1890s changed rapidly, and this sort of sleeve is not seen in fashion plates after 1893.[17] In the print's third

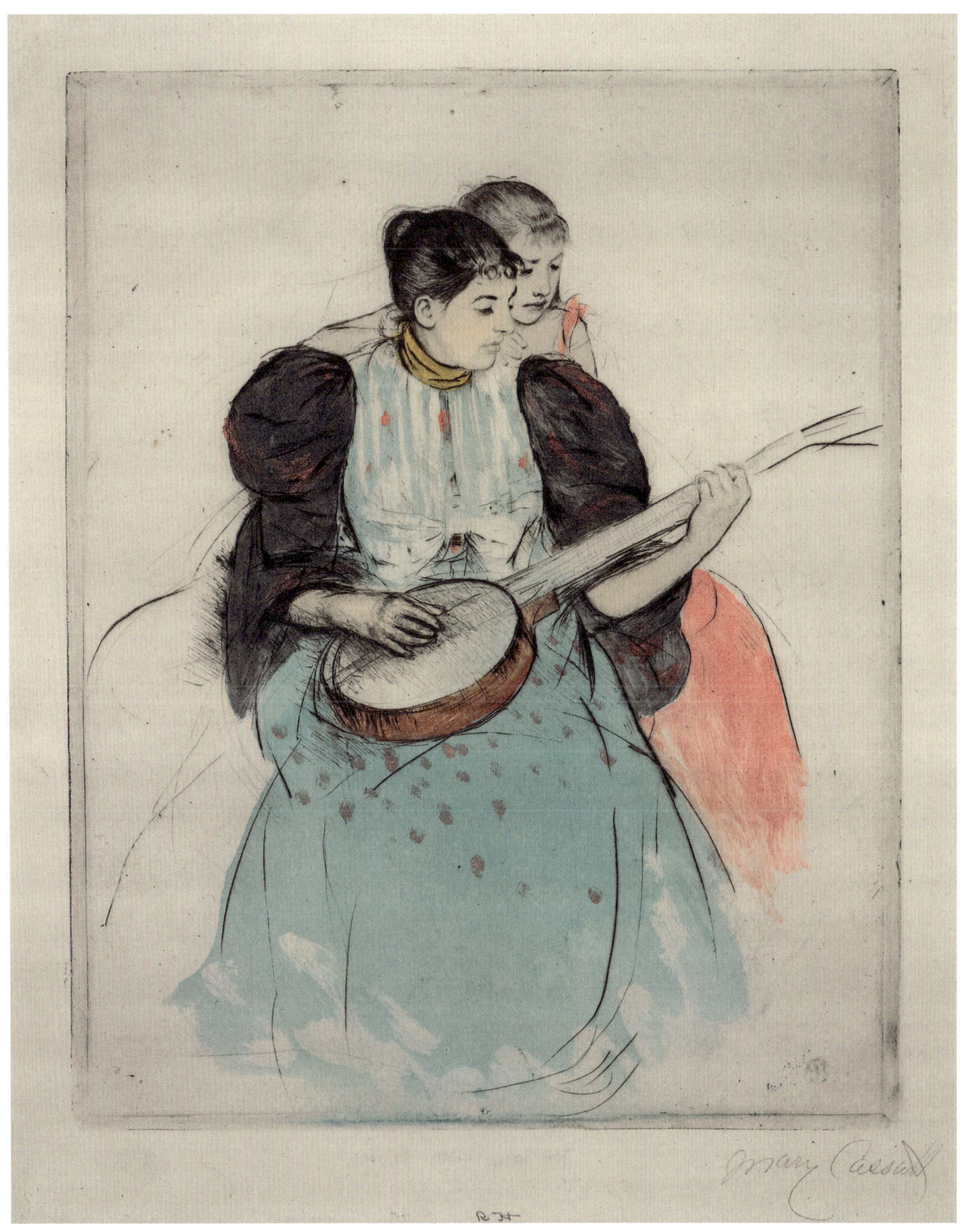

Fig. 2. Mary Cassatt, *The Banjo Lesson*, 1893. Hand-colored drypoint and aquatint on paper. Fourth (final) state. $11\frac{11}{16}$ x $9\frac{3}{8}$ in. (29.6 x 23.9 cm). Library of Congress, Washington, DC, LC-DIG-ppmsca-06604

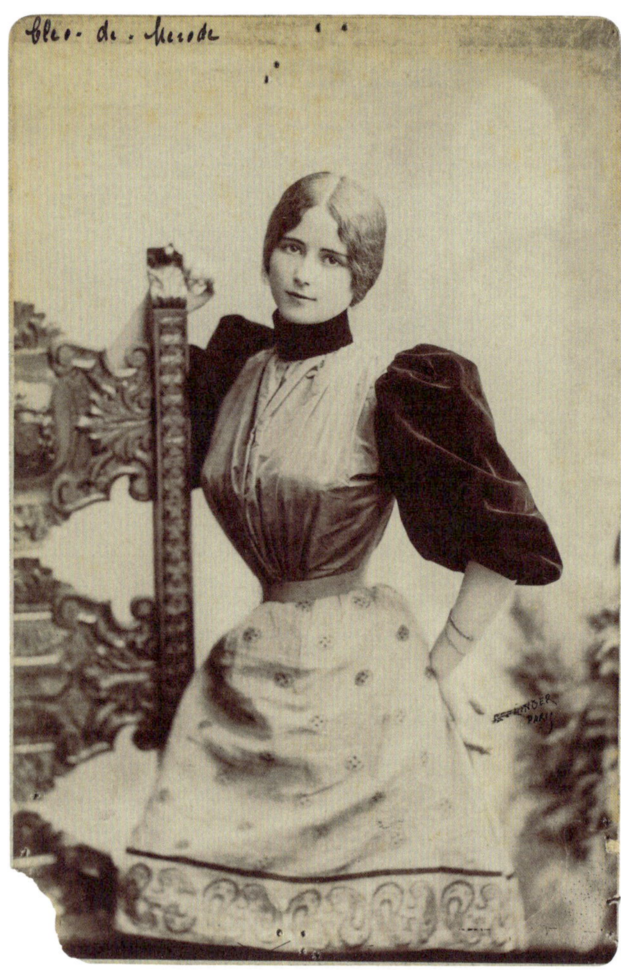

Fig. 3. Léopold Reutlinger, postcard of Cléo de Mérode, c. 1894. Bibliothèque nationale de France, Paris

state, Cassatt introduced light brown aquatint to create stripes on the bodice, implying pleating, as well as a dark collar and sleeves. The contrast between the paler bodice and the dark sleeves and high collar was commonly seen in 1893 and 1894. See, for example, the dress worn by the ballet dancer Cléo de Mérode (fig. 3), a renowned beauty frequently portrayed by leading photographers such as Léopold Reutlinger.[18] Mérode's bodice has the same high standing collar and a similar pleat pattern down the front, as well as the contrasting sleeves. That Cassatt's banjo player would be dressed similarly to a rising ballet star accords with Cassatt's commitment to depicting the fashions of the day. Though neither is likely wearing a dress by a famed couturier, each woman nonetheless appears in clothes at the height of style.

In the fourth state, in addition to the aquatint accenting the drypoint lines added in the prior state, Cassatt applied unique monotype inking to each plate; for each of the forty impressions, she painted the desired colors onto the plate before printing.[19] The resulting colored versions feature a light slate-blue skirt, yellow collar, and periwinkle blue sleeves, with pink dots on the skirt, blouse, and sleeves; the young girl is dressed in pink and the banjo is rendered in brown. The overall effect appears somewhat cacophonous to modern eyes but was not atypical of 1890s trends. In fact, a writer in the *New York Tribune* praised Cassatt's application of color in *The Banjo Lesson* when it was included in an 1895 Durand-Ruel exhibition in New York: "Subtlety of hand is perhaps most significantly apprehended in the drypoints, in such plates as No. 48, 'Le Banjo,' with its delightfully colored surfaces."[20]

The apparently haphazard arrangement of pink dots across not only the skirt but also the bodice and even sleeves may seem like a painterly invention, but it is faithful to a trend of 1893. See, for example, a plate from the May 1893 issue of *La Mode pratique* (fig. 4), which features a sheer tulle overlay sparkling with irregularly applied rose-colored sequins, with additional sequin detailing on the sleeves. Cléo de Mérode's skirt also features a sheer overlay with

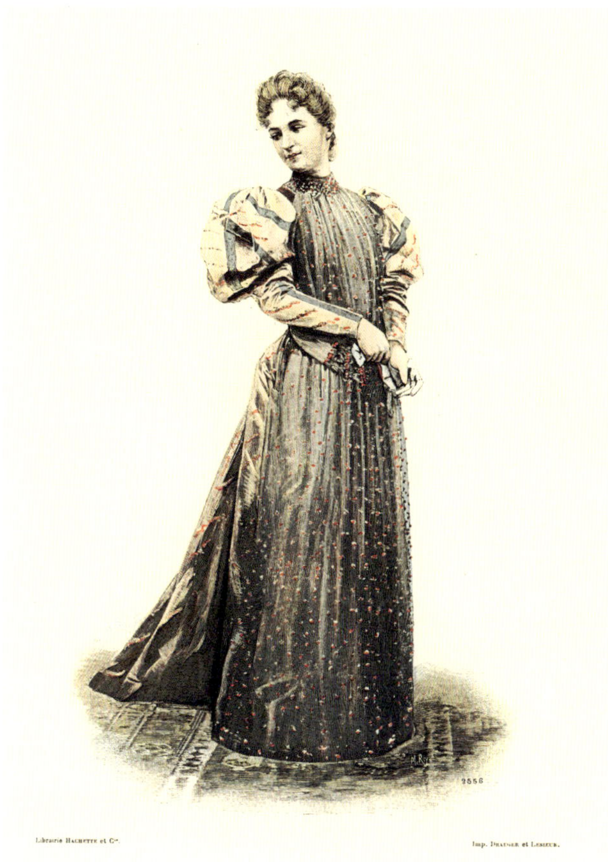

Fig. 4. Mme Moslard, *Dress*, 1893. *La Mode pratique* 2, no. 20 (May 20, 1893): plate 2556. Fashion Institute of Technology, New York, Special Collections, Gladys Marcus Library, TT500.M6

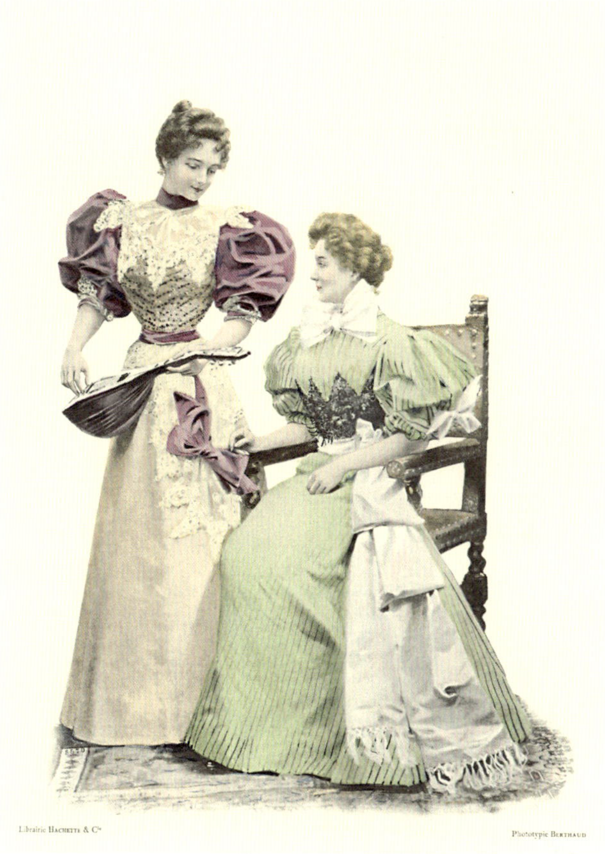

Fig. 5. Mme Moslard, *Dresses*, 1894. *La Mode pratique* 3, no. 37 (September 1894): plate 5570. Fashion Institute of Technology, New York, Special Collections, Gladys Marcus Library, TT500.M6

embroidered spotted circles. An 1894 *La Mode pratique* plate (fig. 5) includes sequin decorations on the bodice and a pale bodice contrasting with darker sleeves and collar. The model at left is also posed as a musician, though she holds a mandolin rather than a banjo. Cassatt had depicted a *Mandolin Player* (p. 98) around 1889 and included that print in the 1893 Durand-Ruel exhibition alongside *The Banjo Lesson*. In the print, drypoint lines trace the mandolin player's high collar and rounded sleeve cap. The different sleeve shapes of our three musicians highlight how quickly sleeve styles were evolving, from the narrow, tailored look of 1889 to the balloon-style fullness of 1894.

"Peasant" Mother and Child (1894)

Around 1894, Cassatt continued to make color prints, including a depiction of a mother and child (p. 120) that she exhibited as *Mère et Enfant* at the April 1895 Durand-Ruel exhibition in New York.[21] The related pastel, on which she likely based the print, was also included in the exhibition as *Mère et Enfant*.[22] Both have since come to be known as *Peasant Mother and Child*, a title which makes little sense given the luxury and modishness of the dress worn by the woman depicted. The title *Peasant Mother and Child* seems to have originated in the 1948 catalogue raisonné by Adelyn Breeskin. As the curators Judith Barter and Erica Hirshler remarked in their 1998 exhibition catalogue *Mary Cassatt: Modern Woman*:

> Titles are a particularly vexing problem in the study of Mary Cassatt's oeuvre. Adelyn Breeskin, in her 1948 and 1970 catalogues raisonné of Cassatt's prints and unique works, assigned largely descriptive titles that, for the most part, bear no relationship to those given by the artist herself.[23]

Mathews speculates that "the title, *Peasant Mother and Child*, may have been derived from the solemn coloration of the costumes that contrast with the decorative colors and leisure pursuits shown in *The Banjo Lesson*."[24] While the mother's golden green silk blouse lacks the decorative pink spangles of the banjo player, it is hardly drab, as "peasant" implies, and its high collar and leg-of-mutton sleeve shape were certainly à la mode at the time. The standing collar and large, exaggerated puffed upper sleeves resemble those seen on Mérode and in the two *La Mode pratique* plates discussed above. As in figure 4, the mother's expansive upper sleeve dramatically tapers and becomes extremely narrow along the forearm.

The reviewer for the New York newspaper *The Sun* praised the coloration of the pastel *Mère et Enfant* in particular when it was exhibited in 1895: "The four latest works by Miss Cassatt, indeed, are pastel harmonies, with this same mother and child for the subject. The 'Mere et Enfant' (No. 14) is most beautiful of these in color, the low-toned reds and greens being charmingly managed."[25] As the critic remarked, the models for this pastel (and related print) posed frequently for Cassatt in 1894 in a range of up-to-the-minute dress styles. They were depicted in at least eight pastel sketches and finished artworks (figs. 6 & 7). Several pastels show the same model in a white lace blouse with tiered lace sleeves and bands of green velvet at the neck and shoulder—an extremely chic style in the early 1890s.[26] Yet another pastel features the same model in a "mauve and pink" gown.[27]

This model also appears several times in a cantaloupe-hued blouse, its color quite fashionable at the time and referred to as "soie glacée nuance pelure d'oignon" (glazed silk the color of an onion peel) or "thon" (salmon).[28] Similar colors were frequently to be found in fashion magazines. In *Mother and Child* (fig. 6), Cassatt creates a luminous effect via the bold orange-toned blouse seeming to shimmer on the paper, the composition's greenish accents resembling those on the sleeves in figure 4. Here the interplay of pastel strokes suggests a variability in color likely due to the blouse's changeable silk material, which, depending on the light and angle at which it is viewed, reads as one of two different colors. Notably, Cassatt has the model dressed in separates, with a distinct skirt and blouse, rather than in a dress made of a single fabric—a fashion-forward choice

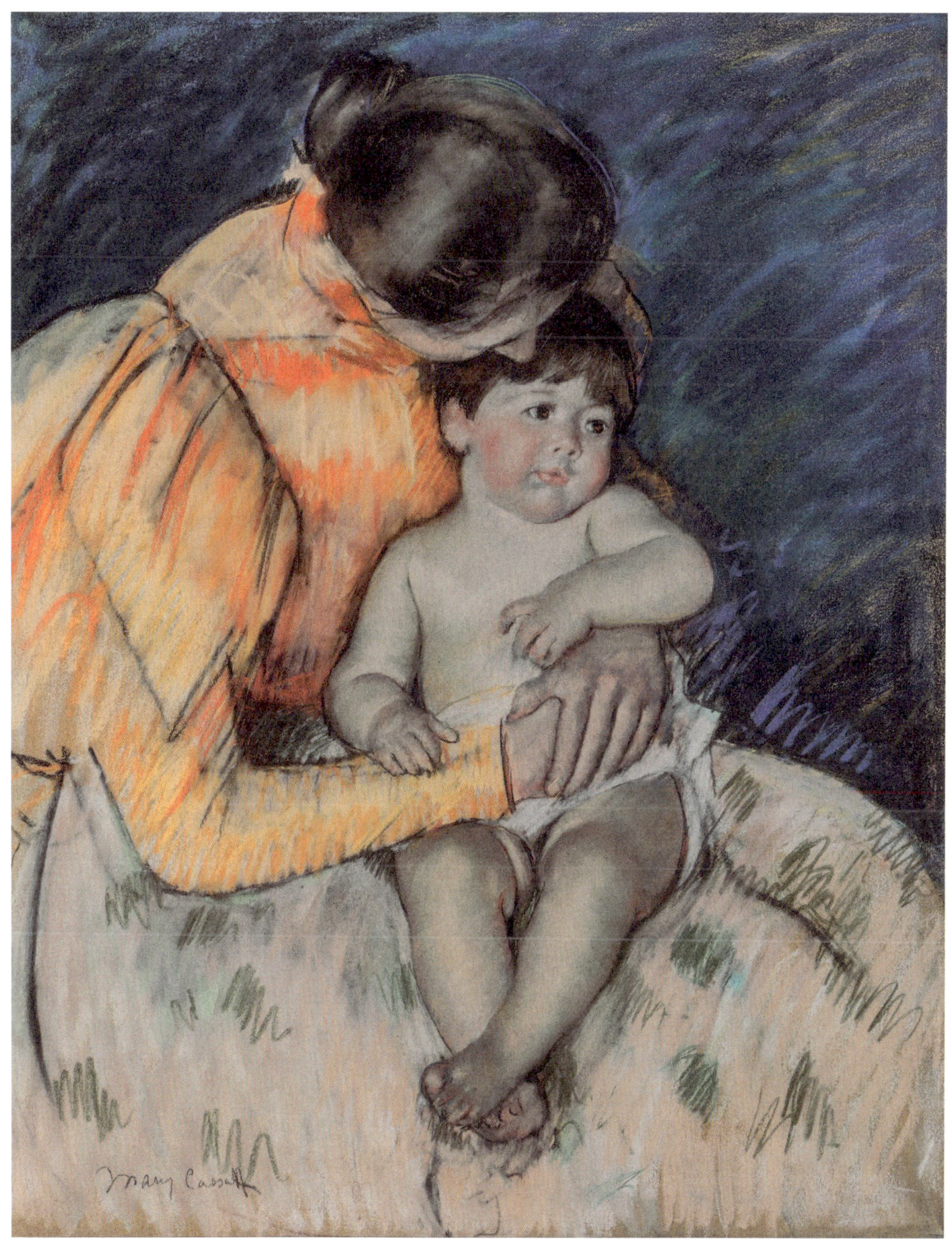

Fig. 6. Mary Cassatt, *Mother and Child*, c. 1895. Pastel on paper. 31½ x 25 in. (80.2 x 63.5 cm). The Pushkin State Museum of Fine Arts, Moscow

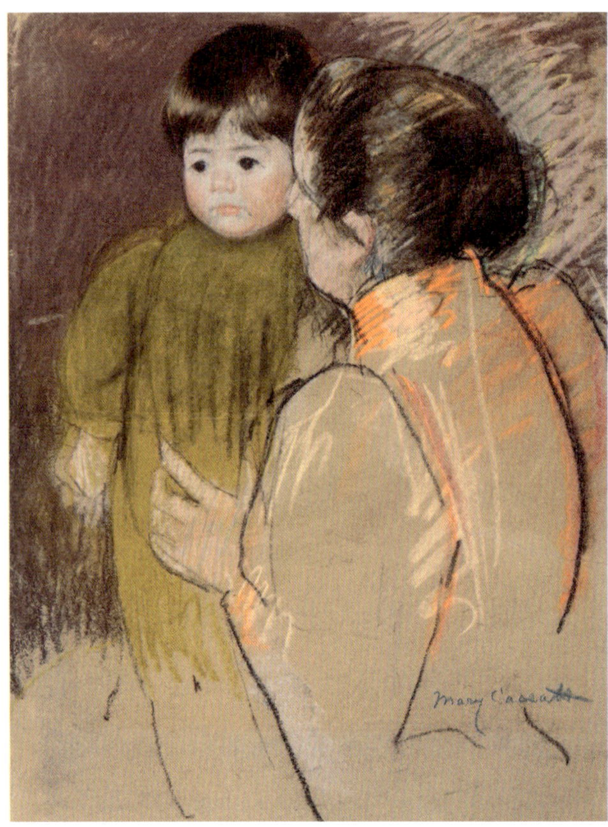

Fig. 7. Mary Cassatt, *Sketch of Peasant Mother and Child*, 1894–95. Pastel on gray paper. 27⅛ x 20½ in. (69 x 52 cm). National Museum, Belgrade, Serbia

that was being enthusiastically adopted by women for daytime wear, but was less frequently seen in haute couture and fashion magazines. Here we see Cassatt truly showcasing the modern woman, though not the sort of woman dressed by Worth or Paquin, who resisted this trend until later in the decade.

The same melon-colored blouse appears in a pastel sketch now known as *Sketch of Peasant Mother and Child* (fig. 7), which reveals Cassatt figuring out color harmonies as well as the composition for her print. The resulting drypoint and aquatint represents one of Cassatt's most varied experimentations with color, as she produced versions with the mother's blouse in salmon, in lilac, in golden green, and in reddish green.[29] Cassatt's creation of multiple blouse colors mirrors the way couturiers of the day would offer the same dress in different fabrics and colorways to suit clients' tastes. Across the different states, she adds greater detail to the clothing, with the shape of the skirt and the sleeve in particular gaining fuller definition between the fifth (fig. 8) and the tenth states (p. 120).

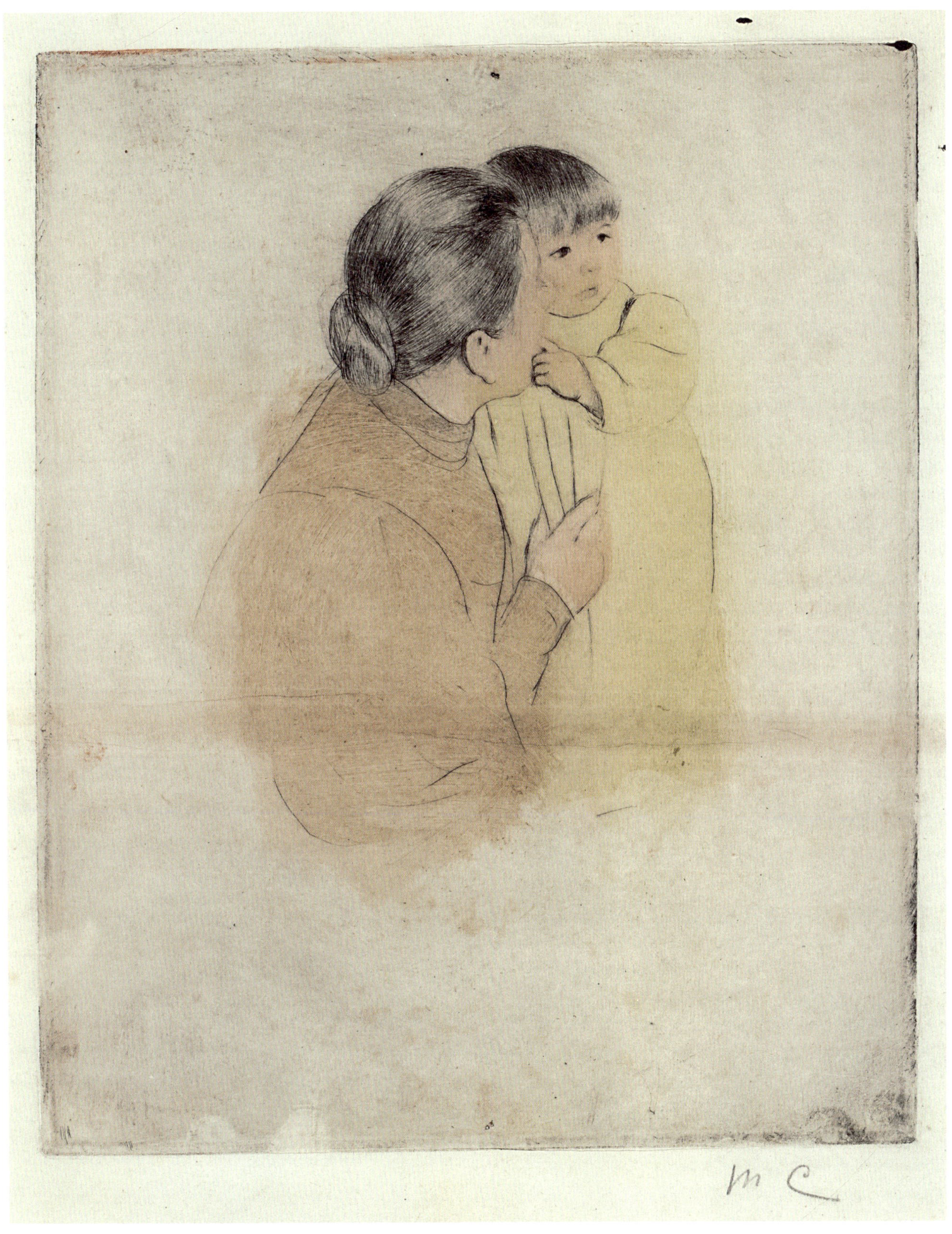

Fig. 8. Mary Cassatt, *Peasant Mother and Child*, c. 1894. Color drypoint and aquatint on paper. Fifth state (of ten). 11 11/16 x 9 5/8 in. (29.7 x 24.5 cm). National Gallery of Art, Washington, DC, Rosenwald Collection, 1943.3.2746

The blouse in the impression in the Colby College Museum of Art's collection shimmers in three shades of green and golden tones, suggesting it is also made of changeable silk, one of the most frequently seen fabrics in 1893. Art historians have often described the blouse as striped, but it should be noted that Cassatt was capable of producing distinct stripes in her color prints, as in her Japanese-inspired series of 1890–91, including *Woman Bathing* and *The Fitting*.[30] Here instead, as in the pastel, she seems to be attempting to capture the variability of this ultrafashionable dress textile.[31] The resulting play of color threatens to upstage the tender interaction between mother and child, but such a tension was clearly intentional as Cassatt worked the print through ten states. The final print harmonizes the dress of the mother and child, capturing an intimate moment but also the fashionability of the pair. Although fashion had become more accessible in the nineteenth century, peasants of the 1890s, it need hardly be said, were not wearing changeable silk blouses with leg-of-mutton sleeves. The present title hinders our understanding of Cassatt's intentions.

The themes of Cassatt's works were often universal in the 1890s. But Cassatt was careful to make the clothing of her sitters temporally specific, devoting close attention to the latest trends. By dedicating herself to modern dress, Cassatt was insisting upon the modernity of her art. Adopting this emphasis, she aligned herself with Édouard Manet and other Impressionists and their commitment to depicting the details of modern fashion. They believed that modernity encompassed, as Charles Baudelaire had famously written in "The Painter of Modern Life" in 1863, "the ephemeral, the fugitive, the contingent, the half of art whose other half is the eternal and the immutable."[32] To appreciate Cassatt's art, we must honor its eternal and ephemeral aspects alike, which for the 1890s prints means looking closely at Cassatt's use of fashion.

Notes

1. Debra N. Mancoff, *Mary Cassatt: Reflections of Women's Lives* (London: F. Lincoln, 1998), 64.

2. Diana De Marly, *Worth: Father of Haute Couture* (London: Elm Tree Books, 1980), 101–2. This essay calculates the historic conversion at £1 = 25 francs; historic francs to modern dollars: 1 franc = $5.

3. Ibid., 100.

4. Mary Cassatt to Bertha Palmer, October 11, 1892, in *Cassatt and Her Circle: Selected Letters*, ed. Nancy Mowll Mathews (New York: Abbeville Press, 1984), 237–38.

5. "The Chronicle of Arts," *New York Tribune*, April 21, 1895, 25.

6. Griselda Pollock quotes the above letter to Palmer and then remarks simply: "Clothes again." Though she discusses the Impressionists' interest in fashion, the history of Worth, and the dress reform movement, she does not address the specifics of Cassatt's fashion choices. Griselda Pollock, *Mary Cassatt: Painter of Modern Women* (London: Thames & Hudson, 1998), 54.

7. Mancoff, *Mary Cassatt: Reflections of Women's Lives*, 50.

8. See, for example, the color plate for January 1889 in the *Journal des demoiselles*. For an earlier instance, see the January 1886 color plate in *Journal des demoiselles*.

9. Nancy Mowll Mathews and Barbara Stern Shapiro, *Mary Cassatt: The Color Prints* (New York: Abrams, 1989), 49; Sally Webster, *Eve's Daughter/Modern Woman: A Mural by Mary Cassatt* (Urbana: University of Illinois Press, 2008).

10. Several photographs and contemporary accounts of the mural suggest the overall composition and effect. See Webster, *Eve's Daughter/Modern Woman*.

11. Mariana G. Van Rensselaer, "Current Questions of Art," *The World* (New York), December 18, 1892, 24.

12. Ibid.

13. Nancy Mowll Mathews and Pierre Curie, *Mary Cassatt: An American Impressionist in Paris* (New Haven, CT: Yale University Press, 2018), 125; Webster, *Eve's Daughter/Modern Woman*, 81.

14. Mathews and Shapiro, *Mary Cassatt: The Color Prints*, 49.

15. Judith A. Barter, "Mary Cassatt: Themes, Sources, and the Modern Woman," in *Mary Cassatt: Modern Woman*, ed. Judith A. Barter (Chicago: The Art Institute of Chicago, 1998), 95–96.

16. Michel Melot, *The Impressionist Print*, trans. Caroline Beamish (New Haven, CT: Yale University Press, 1996), 228.

17. It can be seen on a model in a May 1893 fashion plate from *La Mode pratique*. Some women, of course, continued to wear the style in daily life after it had peaked in fashion.

18. Michael D. Garval, *Cléo de Mérode and Rise of Modern Celebrity Culture* (Burlington, VT: Ashgate, 2012), 46.

19. Marc Rosen et al., *Mary Cassatt: Prints and Drawings from the Collection of Ambroise Vollard* (New York: Adelson Galleries, 2008), 117; Kimberly A. Jones, ed., *Degas/Cassatt* (Washington, DC: National Gallery of Art, 2014), 111.

20. "The Chronicle of Arts," 25.

21. Thanks to Rick Sieber, librarian for reader services at the Philadelphia Museum of Art, for scanning the catalogue. Durand-Ruel Galleries, *Exposition of Paintings, Pastels and Etchings by Miss Mary Cassatt: From the 16th to the 30th of April, 1895* (New York, 1895).

22. Adelyn Dohme Breeskin, *Mary Cassatt: A Catalogue Raisonné of the Oils, Pastels, Watercolors, and Drawings* (Washington, DC: Smithsonian Institution Press, 1970), no. 232, current location unknown; Durand-Ruel Galleries, *Exposition of Paintings, Pastels and Etchings by Miss Mary Cassatt*.

23. Adelyn Dohme Breeskin, *The Graphic Work of Mary Cassatt: A Catalogue Raisonné* (New York: Bittner, 1948); Barter, *Mary Cassatt: Modern Woman*, 315. Prior to Breeskin's catalogue raisonné, the pastel had been simply known in English as *Mother and Child*. See, for example, a reproduction courtesy of Durand-Ruel in *The International Studio* 78 (March 1924): 485, or *The Arts* 10, no. 1 (July 1926): 2.

24. Mathews and Shapiro, *Mary Cassatt: The Color Prints*, 168.

25. "Miss Cassatt's Paintings," *The Sun* (New York), April 19, 1895, 7.

26. Breeskin, *Mary Cassatt: A Catalogue Raisonné of the Oils, Pastels, Watercolors, and Drawings*, nos. 226–28. For fashion plates depicting this dress style, see *La Mode française* 1891, no. 44; *La Mode illustrée* 1892, no. 23; and *La Mode illustrée* 1893, no. 49.

27. Breeskin, *Mary Cassatt: A Catalogue Raisonné of the Oils, Pastels, Watercolors, and Drawings*, no. 229, current location unknown.

28. *La Mode pratique*, no. 52 (December 1894).

29. Breeskin writes: "The color of the mother's striped blouse varies. In some impressions the stripes are red and green. In others, different shades of green or brown and green." I have been unable to locate any of the red and green versions. Adelyn Dohme Breeskin, *Mary Cassatt: Pastels and Color Prints* (Washington, DC: Smithsonian Institution Press, 1978), 66. See also Mathews and Shapiro, *Mary Cassatt: The Color Prints*. For the lilac version, see Rosen et al., *Mary Cassatt: Prints and Drawings from the Collection of Ambroise Vollard*, 104.

30. See Breeskin quoted above, also Rosen et al., *Mary Cassatt: Prints and Drawings from the Collection of Ambroise Vollard*, 128.

31. Breeskin describes the pastel (now unlocated) as depicting a "dark, changeable green and brown dress." Breeskin, *Mary Cassatt: Pastels and Color Prints*, 113.

32. Charles Baudelaire, "The Painter of Modern Life" (1863), in *The Painter of Modern Life and Other Essays*, ed. and trans. Jonathan Mayne (London: Phaidon, 1964), 12.

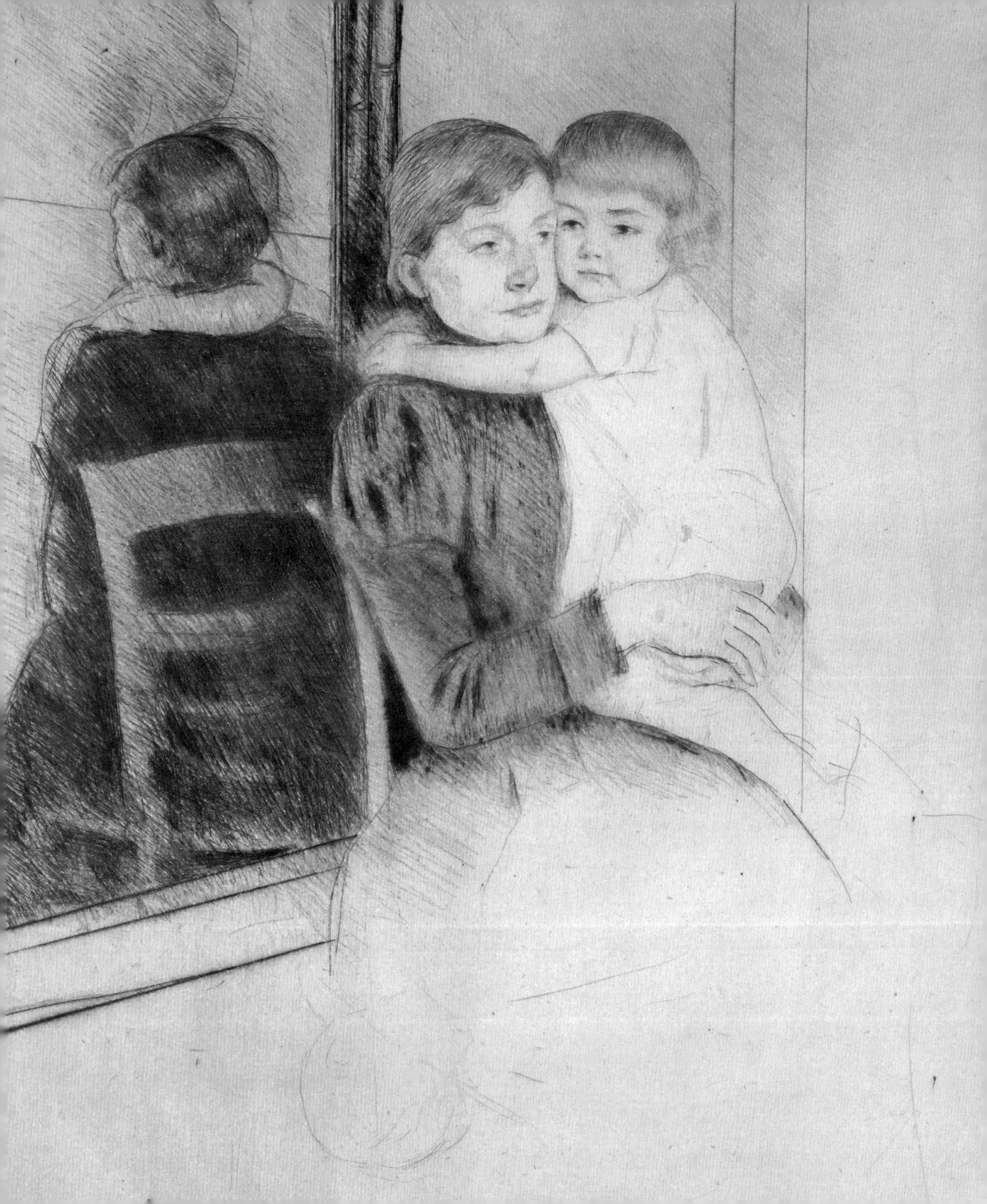

Intimacy and Privacy in Cassatt's Prints

Daniel Harkett

I write at five in the morning these days. Six months into a global coronavirus pandemic, my house is chaos when everyone is awake. Two children—a one-year-old and a teenager—home from daycare and school, my wife and I trying to meet their clashing needs, keep everyone safe, and remember our professional lives. (She works late at night; someone is almost always up.) It has been a privilege for us to work at home during this profoundly challenging time, but it is a privilege we've also experienced as a constriction. Activities and identities have collapsed together, yielding attentional fragmentation and exhaustion. Inside, finding a moment alone—an interior, interior space—is difficult. Outside, we're still inside: behind a mask, socially distanced, separated from friends and strangers.

Inside Out, Outside In

Mary Cassatt knew all too well the challenges of navigating complex relationships between inside and outside, private and public. As a female artist working in late nineteenth-century France, with ambitions to respond pictorially in innovative ways to the particular experiences of modernity, Cassatt had to contend with restrictions on how a bourgeois woman could engage with the world. The influential poet and critic Charles Baudelaire had set the terms for the radical artists of Cassatt's generation, a cohort that came of age in the 1860s. In a widely read essay published in 1863, he urged them to represent modern life, which he identified with Paris's busy boulevards and its spaces of illicit or barely licit pleasure, such as brothels and dance halls.[1] As the art historian Griselda Pollock has argued, Baudelaire's conception of the modern artist as an anonymous urban stroller or *flâneur* was structurally

Mary Cassatt, *The Mirror* (detail), c. 1891. Drypoint on paper. Sixth state (of seven). 8⅞ x 6¹¹⁄₁₆ in. (22.5 x 17 cm). Colby College Museum of Art, Waterville, Maine, The Lunder Collection, 2012.322

masculine.[2] Bourgeois women artists, like Cassatt, could neither freely wander the streets without becoming the focus of unwanted male attention nor easily visit the sites of sexually charged leisure that so fascinated Baudelaire and male avant-garde painters such as Édouard Manet and Edgar Degas. "What I long for is the freedom of going about alone," wrote Marie Bashkirtseff, another female artist living in Paris in the late nineteenth century. "Do you imagine that I get much good from what I see, chaperoned as I am, and when, in order to go to the Louvre, I must wait for my carriage, my lady companion, my family?"[3]

Cassatt, like many other young people before and since, found ways to evade some of the restrictions imposed upon her while she was training to be an artist in Paris in the 1860s. She and her friend Eliza Haldeman visited the louche outdoor dance venue the Jardin Mabille and met male acquaintances at the Louvre when they couldn't at their hotel.[4] What mattered in art, though, was not so much what a woman artist did as, in the art historian Aruna D'Souza's elegant phrase, what she could be "seen to see."[5] Racy scenes at a dance hall or flirtatious interactions with men were not subjects Cassatt could represent and at the same time maintain her respectability—and the social and economic advantages that came with it.

When Cassatt takes us outside the home in her prints, she often draws attention to the restrictive conditions that shaped the life of a bourgeois woman in nineteenth-century Paris while marking out spaces where her female subjects could be protected from the predatory male gaze. In a series of etchings representing a woman in an auditorium (pp. 74–77), for example, Cassatt imagines a private space within the public space of spectacle. A woman holds a fan open in front of her, visually compressing her body into a shallow area between the fan and a rhymingly curved seat back. The gesture feels constrictive and speaks of a culture in which women's capacity for acting in public was limited, but it's also protective, a choice that blocks the view of others and creates a small zone of autonomy within a large, open theater.[6] Likewise, in *Woman Driving in a Victoria* (pp. 70–73), Cassatt imagines a trip out as staying in. A diagonal separates the carriage interior from the world beyond, which even in the print's most detailed version is present only as a filmy blur. Inside the carriage, the female figure sits almost expressionless, her hands gently crossed on her lap. She is, we might say, lost in her thoughts. But to suggest that someone is "lost" in their thoughts is to adopt an outsider's perspective; the figure seems lost only to us, her viewers. For her, the moving interior of the Victoria would offer an opportunity to find something—an interior life—unbothered by others.

If Cassatt represents public spaces as private enclaves, she conversely imagines bourgeois domestic interiors as open to the world in complicated ways. Figures—men and women—read newspapers, compendia of modern life that brought events near and far to a comfortable chair in the parlor.[7] In *Reading the Newspaper (No. 1)* (p. 90), a woman reads by the light of a globular lamp, which, the art historian Hollis Clayson has argued, represents a "displaced evocation" of the forms of the modern streetlights that illuminated Paris's new boulevards and were the focus of much contemporary discussion.[8] Cassatt's figures drink tea, cultural theorist Stuart Hall's drink of empire, its leaves and sugar the products of exploitative colonial economies.[9] In *The Banjo Lesson* (p. 117), a woman teaches her younger companion an instrument that had long been associated with the cultural traditions of enslaved African Africans as well as wildly popular blackface minstrel shows. Cassatt's print stages a version of what the art historian Sarah Burns has called "whiteface," as a symbol of Blackness is appropriated and assimilated into bourgeois white domestic life, where it becomes, through its use in a ritual of instruction, a sign of elite social reproduction.[10]

Like representations of the newspaper, the lamp, the cup of tea, and the banjo, Cassatt's depiction of her pet Coco in *The Parrot* (p. 116) comes freighted with meaning from the outside world. In Europe, parrots were and remain generalized signs of the exotic, as Cassatt's friend Degas made clear when he began a poem about Coco with a reference to Robinson Crusoe on his desert island.[11] Parrots also carried associations with femininity and intimacy, associations worked into erotic fantasy in two paintings by artists Cassatt admired, Manet and Gustave Courbet.[12] In *Woman with a Parrot* (fig. 1), Courbet represents a nude female figure engaged in sensual play with her parrot, while in his version of the same subject made the same year Manet imagines a scene of coy flirtation using his model Victorine Meurent, who was connected in the public mind with the frank sexuality of the artist's scandalous *Olympia* (1863).[13] Cassatt reaffirms connections joining parrots, intimacy, and femininity in her print, which portrays her maid Mathilde contemplating Coco. But she doesn't trade in the eroticism of the paintings by her male avant-garde contemporaries. Instead, she invites us to think about the strangeness of the parrot from the point of view of a white, Western woman. The bird, though engaged through touch and sight and described in great detail, remains other. Indeed it's the very closeness of Coco and Mathilde, beak almost brushing nose, that heightens our sense of the gulf that separates animal from human. As in the images of tea and the banjo, the print acknowledges the presence of difference within the private sphere, but the living presence of the parrot is less easily absorbed than the other commodities Cassatt depicts. She leaves us with—alongside—the other and opens the door for us to ask: How would things look through Coco's eyes?[14]

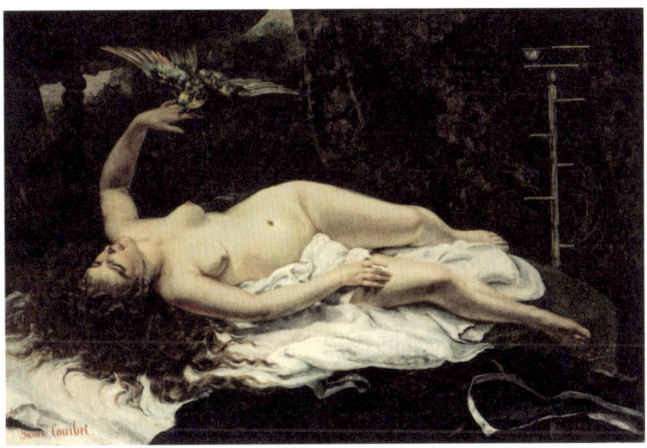

Fig. 1. Gustave Courbet, *Woman with a Parrot*, 1866. Oil on canvas. 51 x 77 in. (129.5 x 195.6 cm). Metropolitan Museum of Art, New York, H. O. Havemeyer Collection, bequest of Mrs. H. O. Havemeyer, 1929, 29.100.57

Like many other writers discussing Cassatt's life and work, the author of the catalogue raisonné of the artist's prints, Adelyn Breeskin, characterizes Cassatt's world as a "sheltered orbit, refined and limited."[15] While Cassatt's images of public spaces do create protective environments for the women represented in them, we should, following the work of feminist scholars like Griselda Pollock, see such sheltering as a strategic choice made within a patriarchal context. In Cassatt's domestic scenes, although the atmosphere might be quiet, we're introduced to the interior as a bourgeois, white technology of assimilation, one in dynamic contact with modern media, global commodity flows, and discourses of race and empire.

Together, Alone

In Cassatt's images of domestic life, whether painted or printed, sociability is a constant. Figures take tea together, read together, and play together. Even when Cassatt represents people alone, tight cropping brings the viewer in, suggesting the proximity of another. To be inside, she suggests, is to be with others, others who know you. Yet in this dense domestic world, physical connections are often offset by moments of disconnection. In images of women and children, such as *The Mirror* (pp. 114–15) and *Repose* (pp. 108–9), closeness is established through touch but resisted by vision as adults and children look away from one another. When figures are shown alone, they can seem mentally far away, with expressions—like that of the young woman riding in the Victoria—that are difficult to read.

For a long time, I've wondered how to interpret these visual breaks. Are they markers of comfort—the comfort of familiarity that does not necessitate constant engagement among family members? Do they speak of contented presence, of what the nineteenth-century novelist and critic Joris-Karl Huysmans described as "the joyous quietude, the tranquil goodwill of an interior" to be found in Cassatt's works?[16] Or are these moments of disconnection signs of boredom, small rebellions against the routines of bourgeois domestic life?

Recently I've been sitting with the difficulty of interpreting what Cassatt's figures are thinking or feeling, with what the art historian Norma Broude has called the "strange ambiguity of meaning and mood and intention" in Cassatt's interior scenes.[17] By populating her images with figures whose expressions are hard to decipher, Cassatt set her work decisively apart from earlier moments in the tradition of French art she was joining. In the seventeenth century, for example, the head of France's art academy, the Académie royale de peinture et de sculpture, which was to become the dominant art institution in Europe for more than a century, attempted to map the relationship between interior states of feeling and exterior signs. In a lecture that was published in many editions and in widely reproduced drawings, Charles Le Brun proposed and illustrated clear connections between emotional experience and the disposition of facial features.[18] Sadness, for instance, was to be signified with drooping eyes and lips (fig. 2). Le Brun

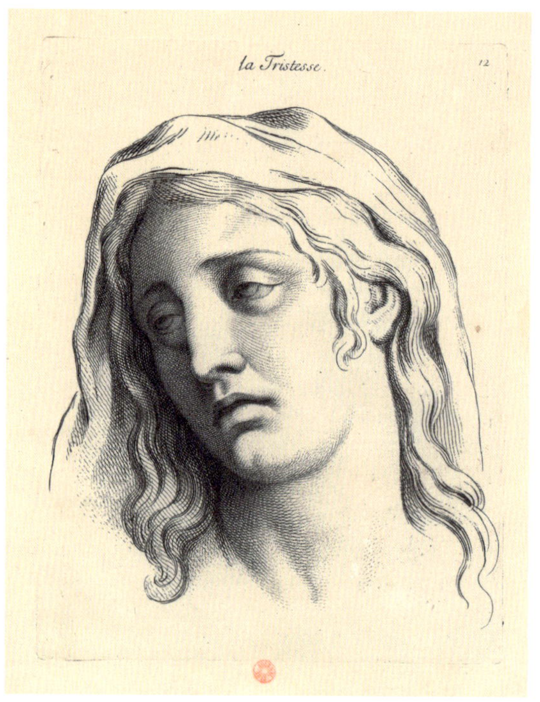

Fig. 2. Jean Audran after Charles Le Brun, *La Tristesse (Sadness)*, from *Les expressions des passions de l'âme, représentées en plusieurs testes gravées d'après les dessins de feu M. Le Brun* (Expressions of the Passions of the Soul, Represented in Several Heads Engraved from the Drawings of the Late M. Le Brun), 1727. Engraving with etching on paper. 9 15/16 x 7 3/4 in. (25.2 x 19.7 cm). Bibliothèque nationale de France, Paris

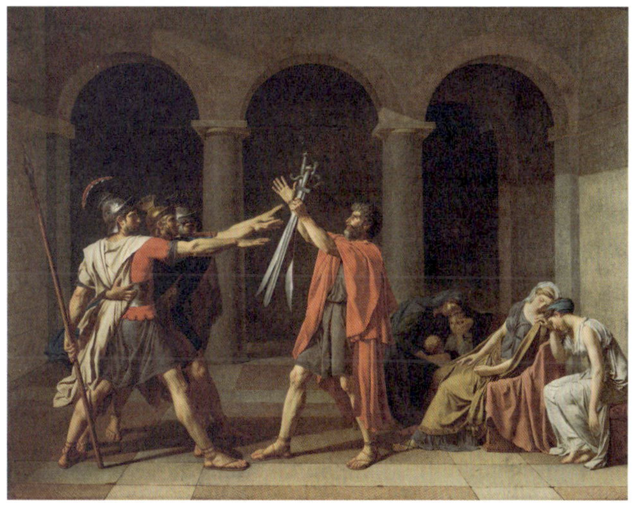

Fig. 3. Jacques-Louis David, *Oath of the Horatii*, 1784. Oil on canvas. 129¹³⁄₁₆ x 167³⁄₁₆ in. (329.8 x 424.8 cm). Museé du Louvre, Paris

created, in short, a visual code to help artists make easily legible narrative pictures. By using this code, the idea was, artists would ensure that viewers understood exactly how the component parts of a story fit together; who is doing what to whom; what their motivations are; what the effects of those actions are. Such a narrative system made a virtue of transparency, but this kind of transparency tended to fix protagonists into one-dimensional social roles. The weeping women in one of the best-known narrative paintings of the eighteenth century, Jacques-Louis David's *Oath of the Horatii*, weep because their male family members might die in an imminent conflict, but they are also shown behaving this way because weeping, in David's conception, is what women are supposed to do when the domestic sphere is threatened (figs. 3 & 4).

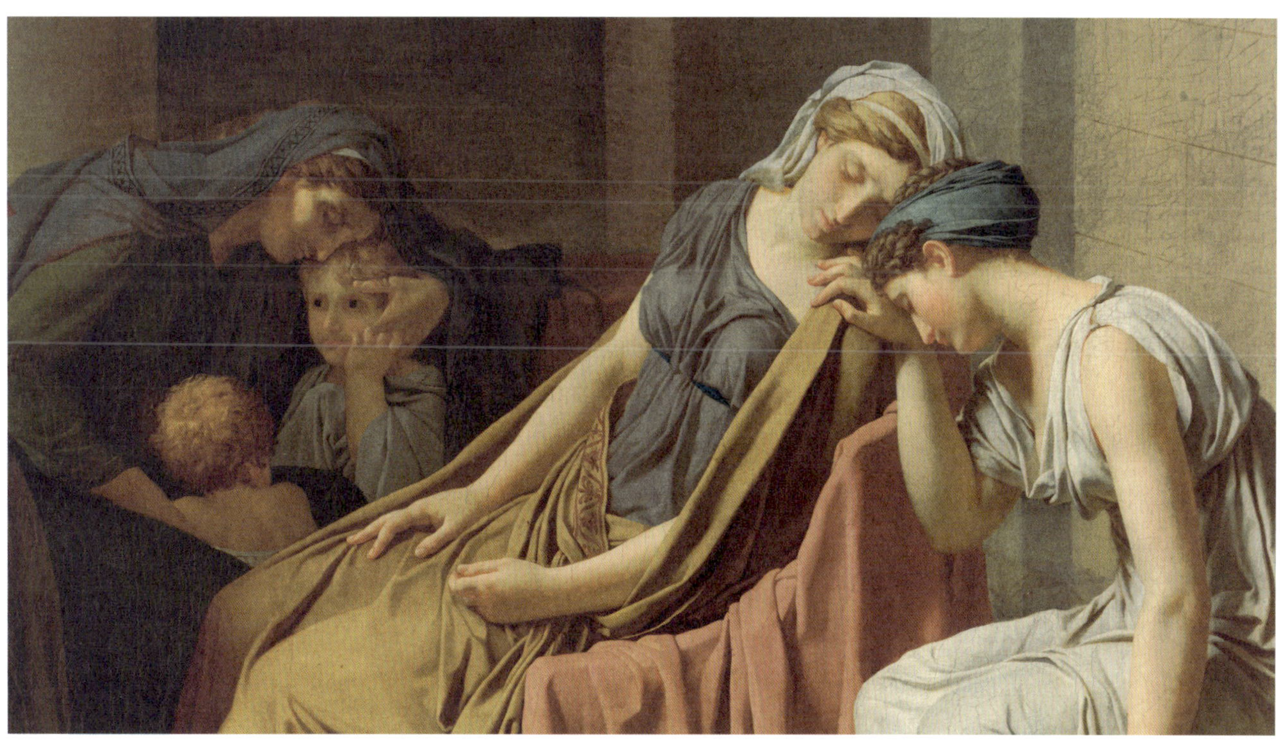

Fig. 4. Jacques-Louis David, *Oath of the Horatii* (detail), 1784. Oil on canvas. 129¹³⁄₁₆ x 167³⁄₁₆ in. (329.8 x 424.8 cm). Museé du Louvre, Paris

Though she trained early in her career with Jean-Léon Gérôme, an artist devoted to maintaining the academic tradition, Cassatt likely wasn't entering into conscious dialogue with Le Brun and his expressive system. But the contrast between Le Brun's commitment to precisely translating interior feeling into external appearance and Cassatt's embrace of indeterminacy underscores the resistant qualities of her art. (What I find fascinating about Cassatt is that she can reinforce bourgeois norms and undermine them at the same time.) If Le Brun's investment in narrative clarity often locks figures into gendered stereotypes, Cassatt's ambiguous images disrupt certain myths of womanhood. It's not that Cassatt doesn't show us women doing the things that women typically would do in the nineteenth century, such as take care of children. It's that when she depicts them in these pursuits, she gives her figures an individual presence that exceeds these social practices. "Whether child or adult," Pollock says, "figures are represented in her pictures to convey a psychological interiority—a combination of thoughts and feelings that intimate an 'inner life.'"[19] Key here, I think, is that what is inside remains unknown to the viewer. In *Lydia at Afternoon Tea* (p. 82), Cassatt represents her sister sitting quietly, cup of tea in hand, looking ahead at nothing in particular, absorbed in reflection. What is she thinking? It could be anything—these thoughts might be happy or sad, trivial or deep—and that's the beauty of it, we just don't know. On the table next to Lydia stands a large and well-defined teapot—almost another figural presence—and two more cups. Along with the tabletop, these cups tilt toward the viewer, their near-white interiors appearing as open voids, visual metaphors not of subjective emptiness but perhaps of interior autonomy amid the social demands of domestic life.

Scenes like *Lydia at Afternoon Tea*, with figures whose inner lives are kept apart from the work's viewers, repeat across Cassatt's interconnected oeuvre—in her paintings, pastels, and prints—but in her prints they are allied with an economy of means that pushes the indeterminacy furthest. Consider a print known as *The Map* (p. 107). Two young women sit close, heads together, hair, facial features, and a sleeve carefully defined by thin lines of drypoint. They look intensely at a sheet laid out on a table, a sheet given form only by a single line marking its edge. Usually identified by art historians as a map, it contains no information or indicators of specificity—to us at least, the print's viewers. If it is a map, it is unlike the famous maps that feature in the domestic settings painted by a seventeenth-century Dutch artist Cassatt esteemed, Johannes Vermeer.[20] In Vermeer's works such as *The Art of Painting* (fig. 5), detailed maps operate as signs of a broader cultural commitment to describing the world clearly, what art historian Svetlana Alpers has characterized as "the mapping impulse in Dutch art."[21] Vermeer demonstrates such a commitment, Alpers suggests, by giving his represented maps "an astonishing material presence," by supplying us with enough visual information that we can easily identify what they represent and even appreciate the qualities of the paper they have fictively been printed on.[22] In *The Art of Painting*, Vermeer signs his name on the map, claiming an identity as a painter-mapmaker. That identity is clearly gendered, with the "art of painting" imagined as a domestic scene in which a male artist surveys, while a woman is among the things surveyed. What Cassatt gives us, in contrast, is an image of two young women looking, exploring together, with the focus of their exploration conspicuously blank. As elsewhere in her domestic scenes, Cassatt takes us

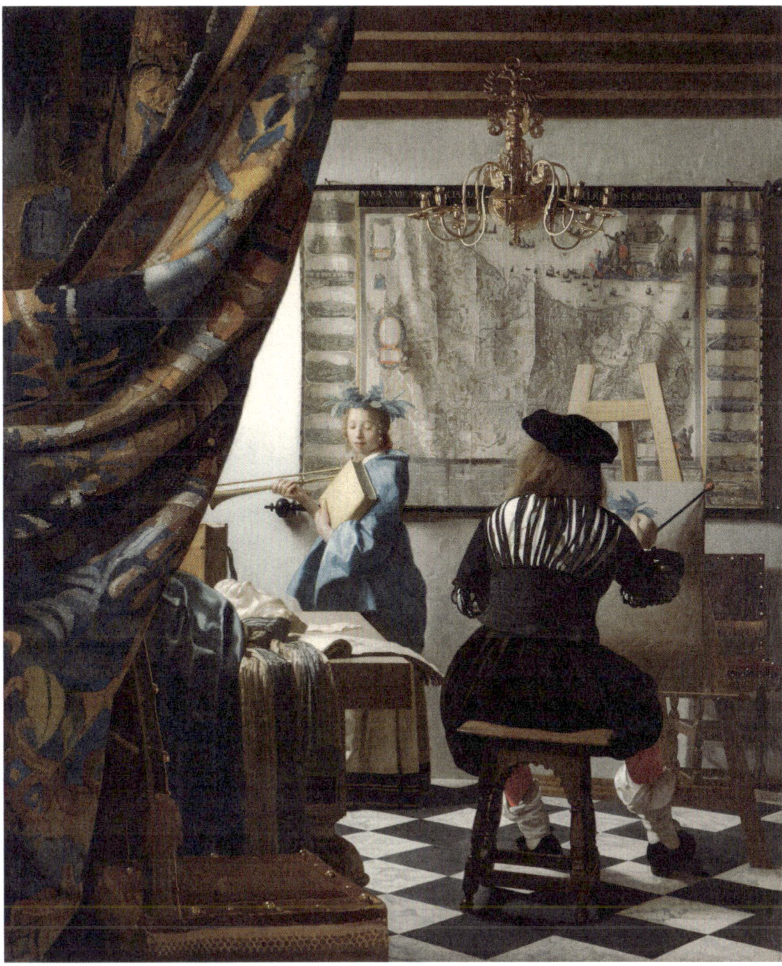

Fig. 5. Johannes Vermeer van Delft, *The Art of Painting*, 1666–68. Oil on canvas. 47¼ x 39⅜ in. (120 x 100 cm). KHM-Museumsverband, Vienna

in close but in such a way as to preserve the privacy of her subjects. She sets limits on her surveying, and by doing so imagines a way of being together in the intimate spaces of a home that doesn't require surrendering to the gaze of others.

For me, looking at Cassatt's images through a pandemic, which I have experienced so far as domestic pandemonium framed by generalized anxiety, has offered an odd form of solace. With their figures who look elsewhere, guard their thoughts and feelings, and absorb themselves in matters unknown, the pictures model the holding open of space for reflection and daydreaming. Cassatt shows us how, even when we're deeply embedded in social relations—social relations that we value—we might still be able to find sustaining space for the self.

Notes

1. Charles Baudelaire, "The Painter of Modern Life" (1863), in *The Painter of Modern Life and Other Essays*, ed. and trans. Jonathan Mayne (London: Phaidon, 1964), 1–40.

2. Griselda Pollock, "Modernity and the Spaces of Femininity," in *Vision and Difference: Feminism, Femininity, and the Histories of Art* (London: Routledge, 2003), 94.

3. Quoted in Pollock, "Modernity and the Spaces of Femininity," 98.

4. Nancy Mowll Mathews, *Mary Cassatt: A Life* (New Haven, CT: Yale University Press, 1998), 53. Mathews quotes Haldeman in a letter: "But as gentlemen cannot come to see us at the Hotel, we [Haldeman and Cassatt] are obliged to receive them at the Louvre."

5. Aruna D'Souza, "Why the Impressionists Never Painted the Department Store," in *The Invisible Flâneuse? Gender, Public Space, and Visual Culture in Nineteenth-Century Paris*, ed. Aruna D'Souza and Tom McDonough (Manchester: Manchester University Press, 2006), 137.

6. On the complexity of the fan's relationship to femininity in nineteenth-century France, see Susan Hiner's chapter "Fan Fetish: Gender, Nostalgia, and Commodification," in her *Accessories to Modernity: Fashion and the Feminine in Nineteenth-Century France* (Philadelphia: University of Pennsylvania Press, 2010), 145–77.

7. On the role of the mass-circulation newspaper in constructing an idea of modernity for its readers, see Richard Terdiman, "Newspaper Culture: Institutions of Discourse; Discourse of Institutions," in his *Discourse/Counter-Discourse: The Theory and Practice of Symbolic Resistance in Nineteenth-Century France* (Ithaca, NY: Cornell University Press, 1985), 117–48.

8. Hollis Clayson, "Mary Cassatt's Lamp," in *Is Paris Still the Capital of the Nineteenth Century? Essays on Art and Modernity, 1850–1900*, ed. Hollis Clayson and André Dombrowski (London: Routledge, 2016), 272.

9. Stuart Hall, "Old and New Identities, Old and New Ethnicities," in *Culture, Globalization, and the World-System: Contemporary Conditions for the Representation of Identity*, ed. Anthony D. King (Minneapolis: University of Minnesota Press, 1997), 48–49.

10. Sarah Burns, "Whiteface: Art, Women, and the Banjo in Late-Nineteenth-Century America," in *Picturing the Banjo*, ed. Leo G. Mazow (University Park: Pennsylvania State University Press, 2005), 82.

11. For a translation of Degas's poem "Parrots," see George T. M. Shackelford, "*Pas de deux*: Mary Cassatt and Edgar Degas," in *Mary Cassatt: Modern Woman*, ed. Judith A. Barter (Chicago: The Art Institute of Chicago, 1998), 131.

12. On the associations evoked by parrots in nineteenth-century France, see Mona Hadler, "Manet's *Woman with a Parrot* of 1866," *Metropolitan Museum Journal* 7 (1973): 115–22. Recalling the moment when she joined the Impressionist group in the 1870s, Cassatt said to her biographer Achille Ségard, "I admired Manet, Courbet and Degas." Quoted in Adelyn Dohme Breeskin, "Mary Cassatt: Her Life and Her Art," in *Mary Cassatt: A Catalogue Raisonné of the Graphic Work* (Washington, DC: Smithsonian Institution Press, 1979), 13. Cassatt's friends Louisine and Henry Osborne Havemeyer, whom Cassatt advised on art purchases, bought Courbet's *Woman with a Parrot* in 1898, several years after Cassatt executed her print and during which year Cassatt visited the United States. Gary Tinterow, "The Havemeyer Pictures," in *Splendid Legacy: The Havemeyer Collection* (New York: Metropolitan Museum of Art, 1993), 22.

13. Manet, *Young Lady in 1866 (Woman with a Parrot)* (1866), Metropolitan Museum of Art, New York.

14. For further discussion of *The Parrot*, which situates the work in relation to Cassatt's investment in drawing, see Whitney Kruckenberg, "Degas, Cassatt, Pissarro and the Making and Marketing of the *Belle Épreuve*" (PhD diss., Temple University, 2014), 181–84.

15. Breeskin, "Mary Cassatt: Her Life and Her Art," 19.

16. Quoted in Clayson, "Mary Cassatt's Lamp," 265.

17. Norma Broude, "Mary Cassatt: Modern Woman or the Cult of True Womanhood?," *Woman's Art Journal* 21, no. 2 (2000–2001): 40.

18. On Le Brun's *Conférence sur l'expression* (Lecture on Expression) and his drawings, see Linda Walsh, "Charles Le Brun, 'Art Dictator of France,'" in *Academies, Museums and Canons of Art*, ed. Gill Perry and Colin Cunningham (New Haven, CT: Yale University Press, 1999), 108–12.

19. Griselda Pollock, *Mary Cassatt: Painter of Modern Women* (London: Thames & Hudson, 1998), 16. See also Pollock's discussion of Cassatt's use of the "non-aggressive look away" to secure her figures' individual presence in her *Differencing the Canon: Feminist Desire and the Writing of Art's Histories* (London: Routledge, 1999), 210–13.

20. For discussion of Cassatt's interest in Vermeer, which emphasizes affinities between the two artists' works, see Judith A. Barter, "Mary Cassatt: Themes, Sources, and the Modern Woman," in Barter, *Mary Cassatt: Modern Woman*, 62; and Pollock, *Mary Cassatt: Painter of Modern Women*, 172–73. My suggestion here is that a contrast with Vermeer helps us discern something significant in Cassatt's print.

21. Svetlana Alpers, *The Art of Describing: Dutch Art in the Seventeenth Century* (Chicago: University of Chicago Press, 1983), 119–68.

22. Ibid., 122.

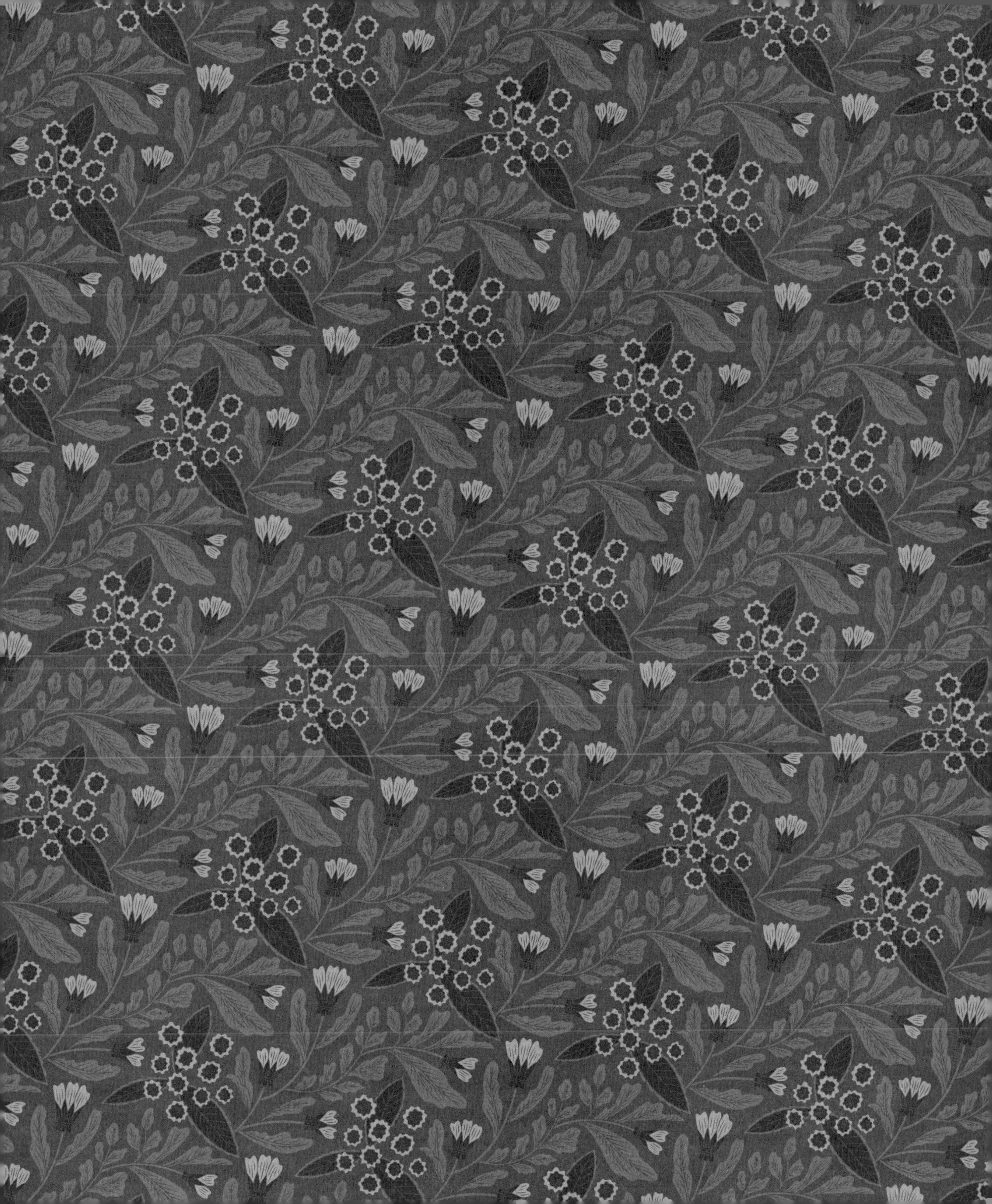

The Lunder Collection of Mary Cassatt

Colby College Museum of Art

Mary Cassatt, *Knitting in the Library* (detail), c. 1881. Softground etching and aquatint on paper. Second state (of three). 10⅞ x 8⁹⁄₁₆ in. (27.6 x 21.8 cm). Colby College Museum of Art, Waterville, Maine, The Lunder Collection, 2012.296

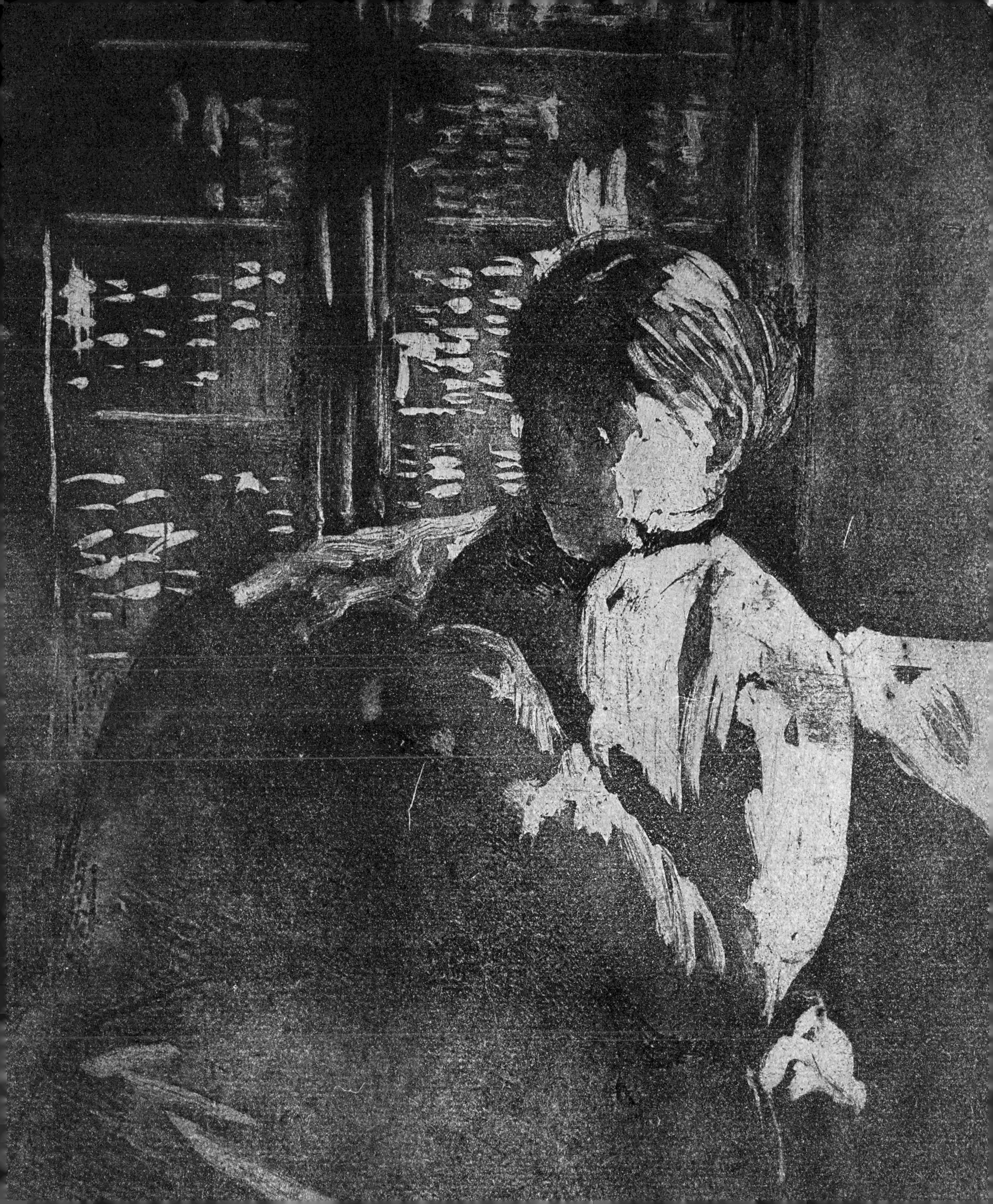

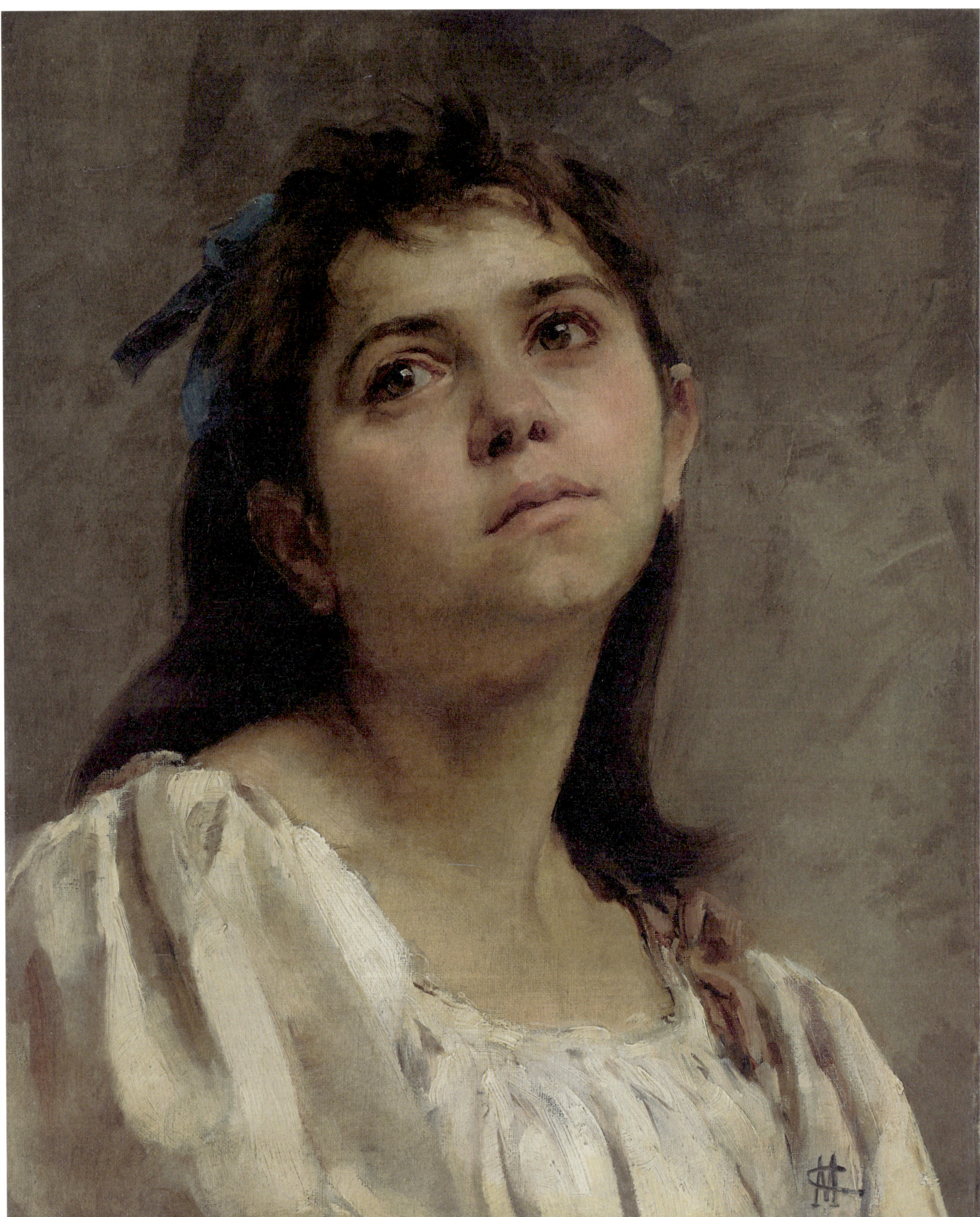

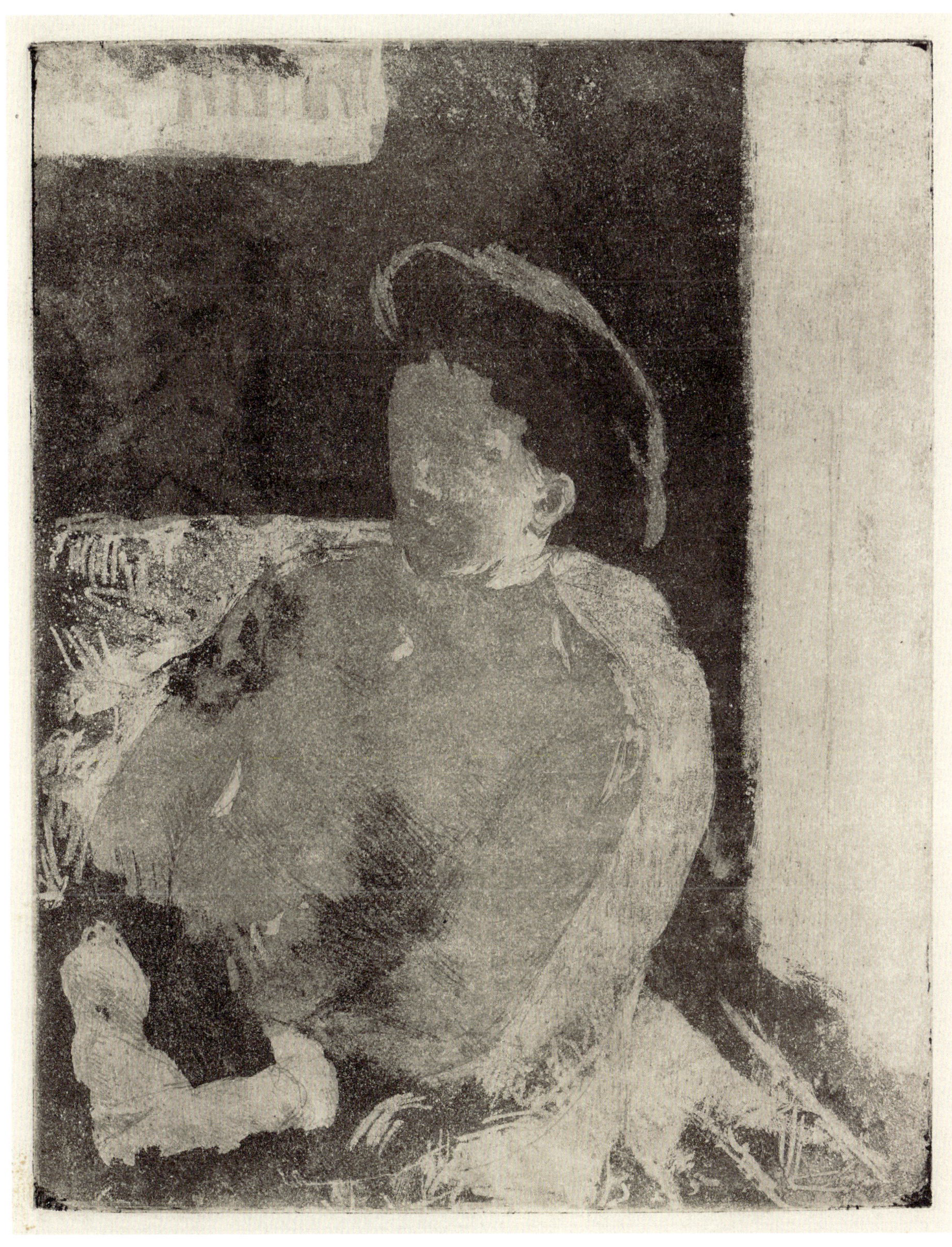

Pensive Roman Girl, c. 1872. Oil on canvas. 18¼ x 15 in. (46.4 x 38.1 cm). The Lunder Collection, 2013.038

The Corner of the Sofa (No. 2), c. 1879. Softground etching on paper. Second state (of three). 8⅛ x 6 7/16 in. (20.6 x 16.4 cm). The Lunder Collection, 2012.290

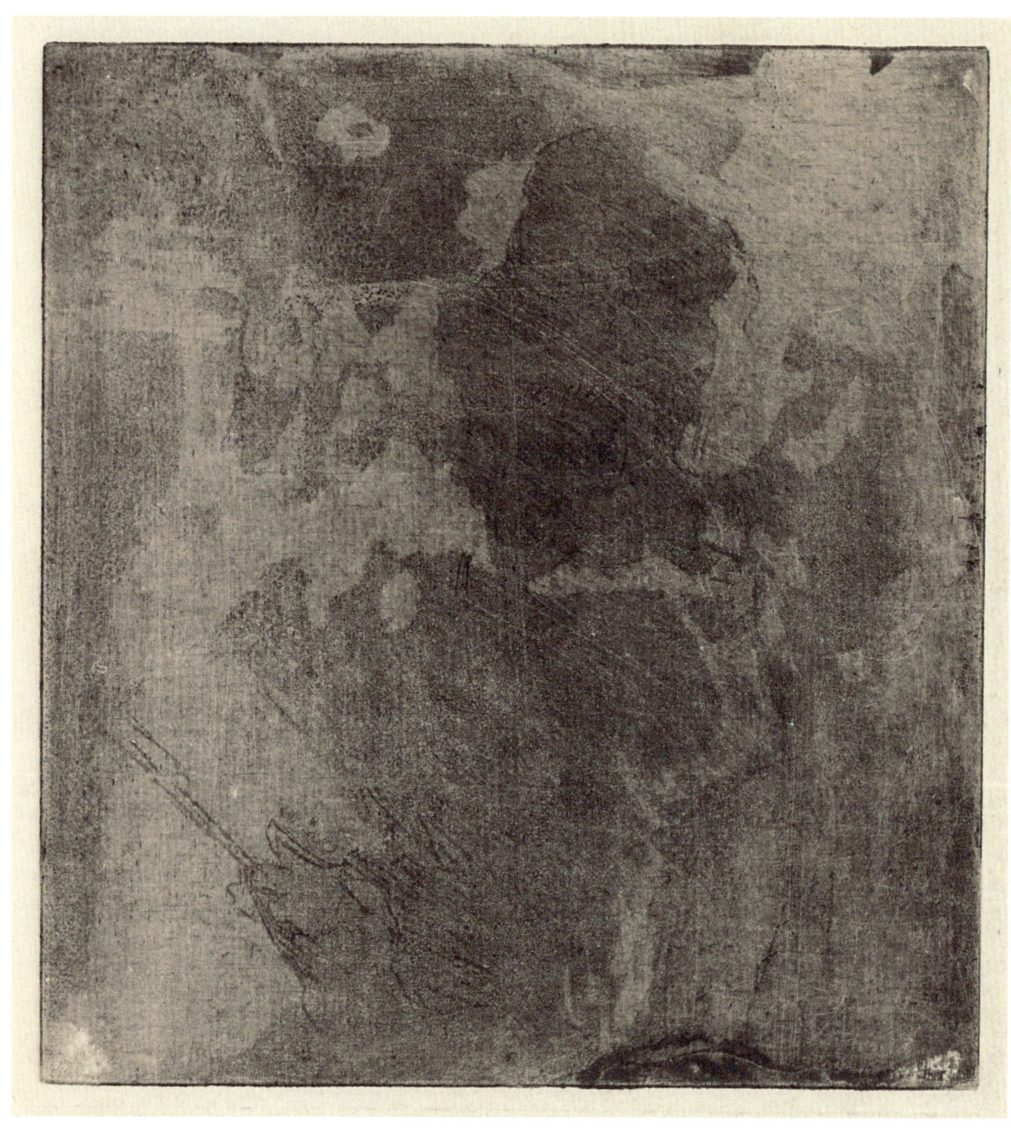

In the Shade, c. 1879. Softground etching on paper. Only known state. 5⅜ x 5¹⁄₁₆ in. (13.7 x 12.8 cm). The Lunder Collection, 2012.283

Standing Nude with a Towel, c. 1879. Softground etching and aquatint on paper. First state (of four). 10¹⁵⁄₁₆ x 8⅝ in. (27.8 x 21.9 cm). The Lunder Collection, 2012.284

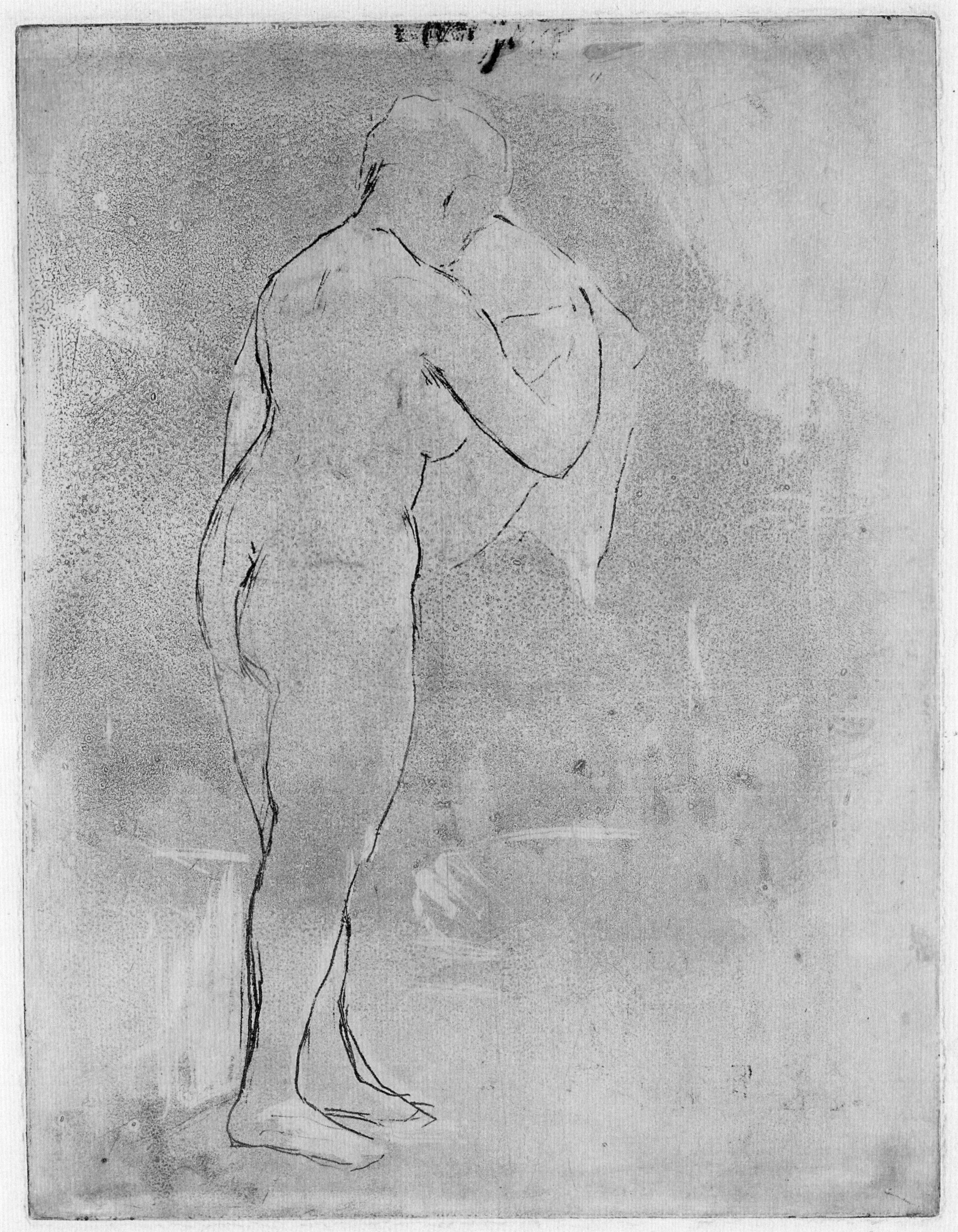

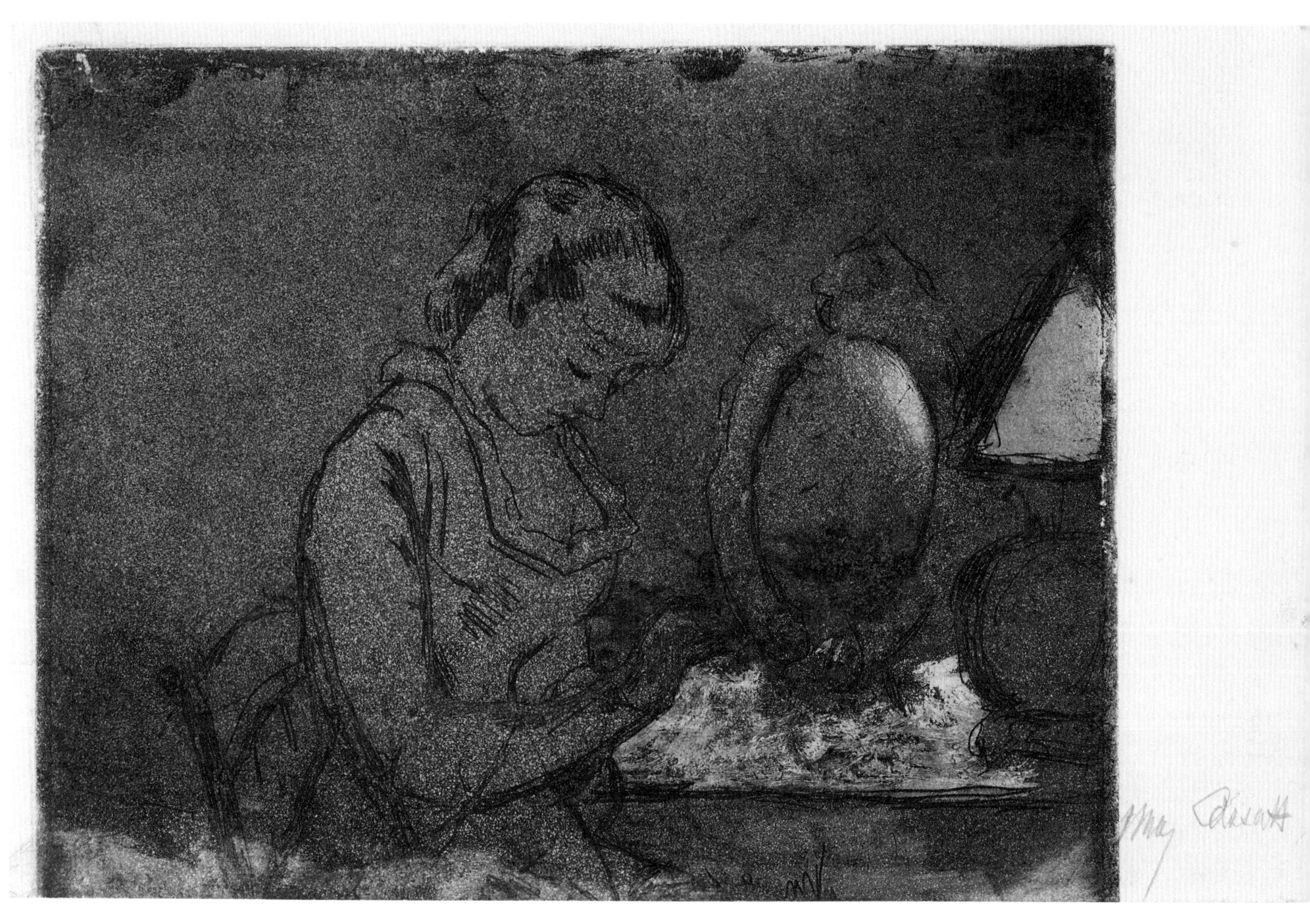

At the Dressing Table, c. 1879. Softground etching, aquatint, and etching on paper. Trial proof of third state (of four). 6¼ x 8¼ in. (15.9 x 21 cm). The Lunder Collection, 2012.285

Waiting, c. 1879. Softground etching and aquatint on paper. Third state (of four). 8⅝ x 5¹³⁄₁₆ in. (21.9 x 14.8 cm). The Lunder Collection, 2012.286

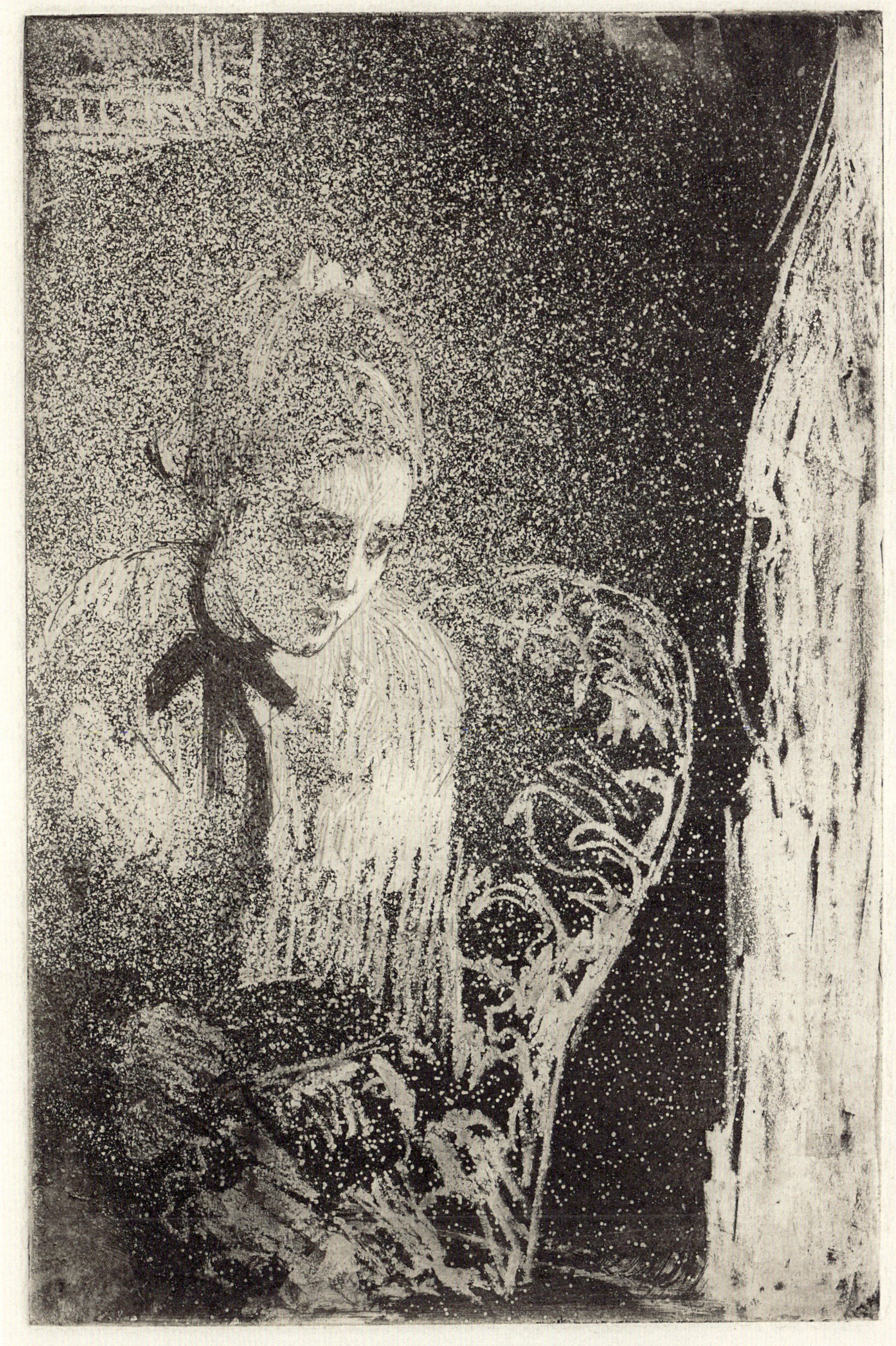

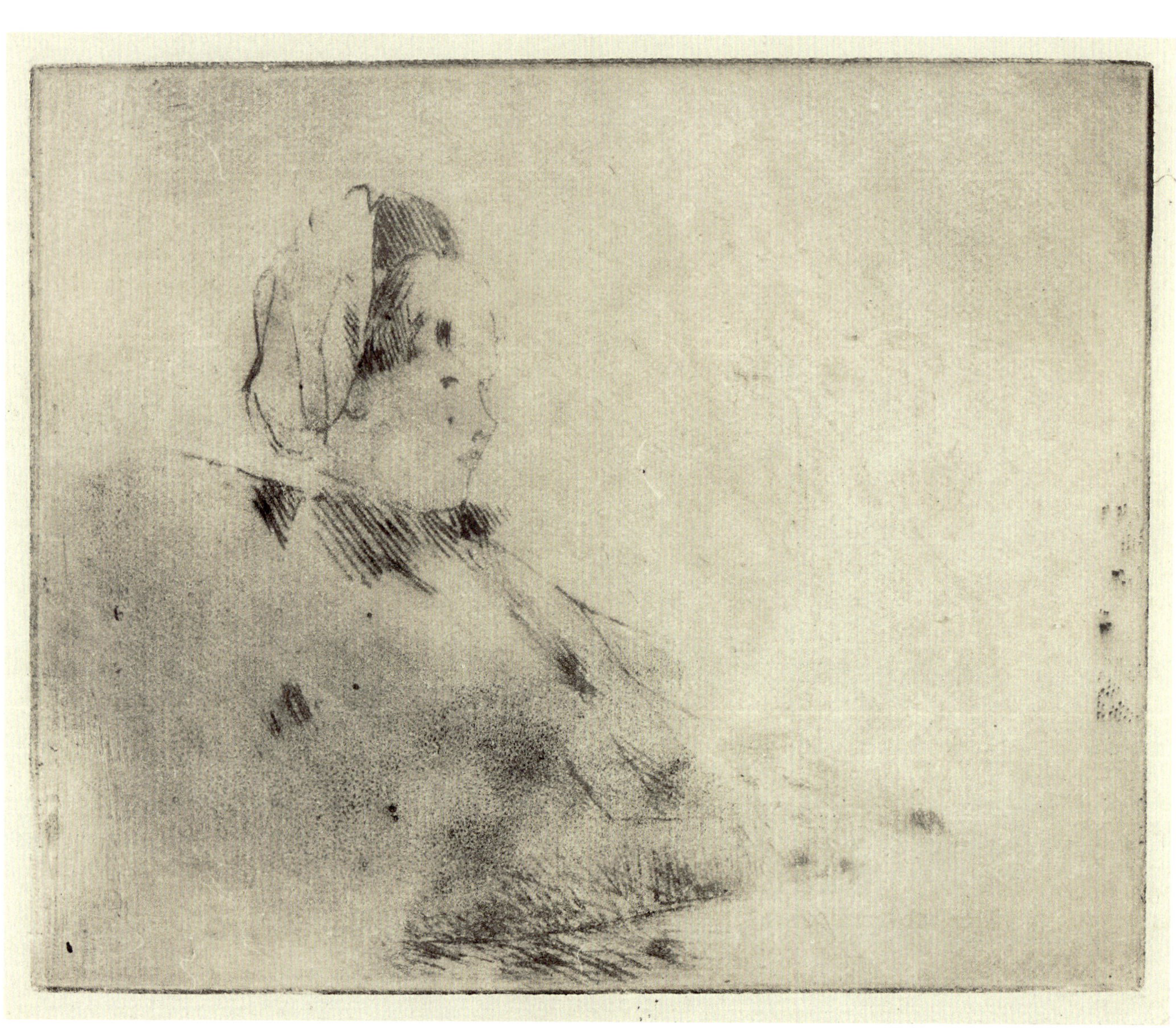

Woman Driving in a Victoria, c. 1879. Softground etching on paper. First state (of three). 5¼ x 6½ in. (13.3 x 16.5 cm). The Lunder Collection, 2012.287

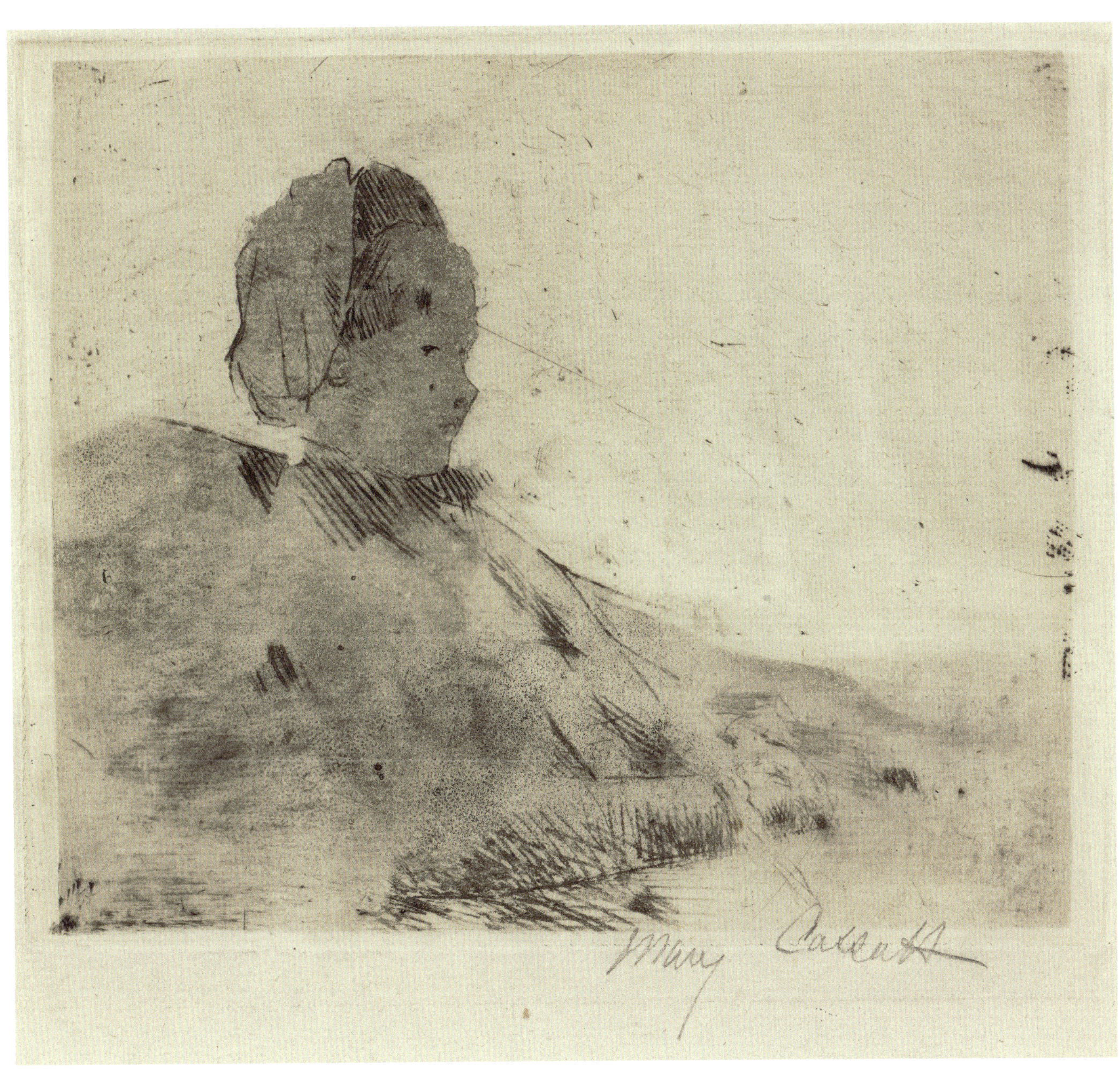

Woman Driving in a Victoria, c. 1879. Softground etching on paper. Second state (of three). 6 x 6½ in. (15.2 x 16.5 cm). The Lunder Collection, 2012.288

Woman Driving in a Victoria, c. 1879. Softground etching on paper. Third (final) state. 5¼ x 6½ in. (13.3 x 16.5 cm). The Lunder Collection, 2012.289

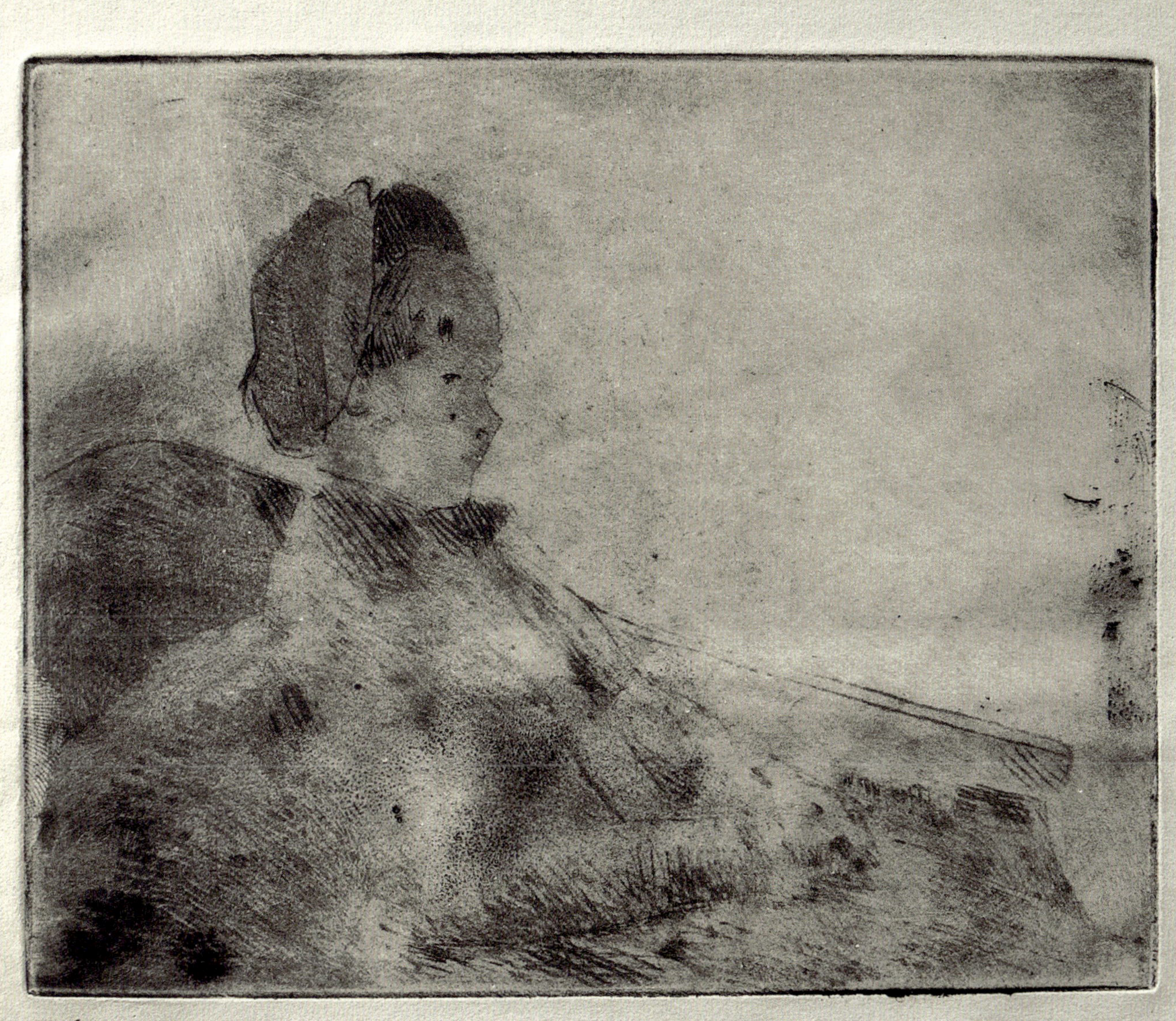

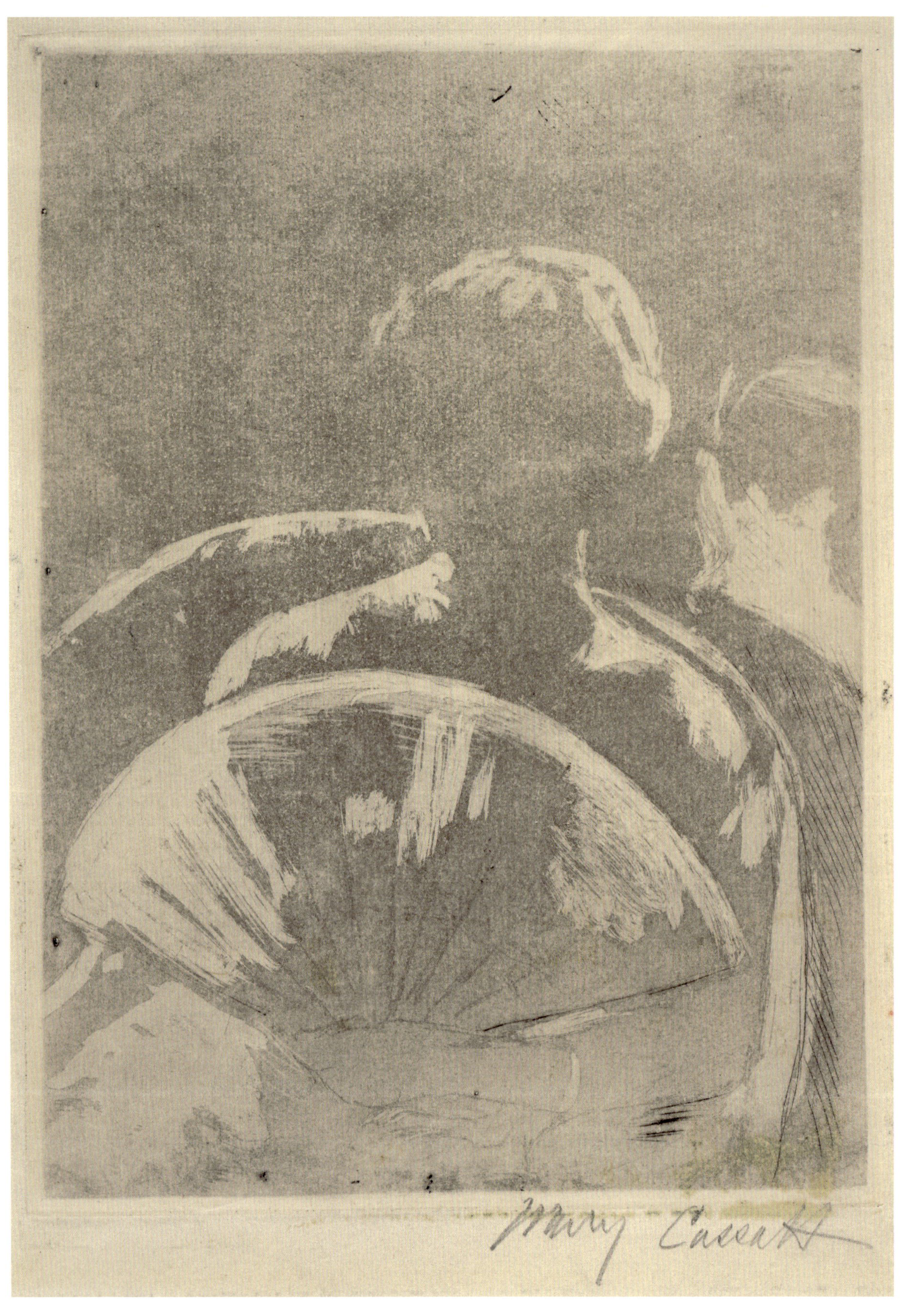

In the Opera Box (No. 2), 1879–80. Softground etching on paper. First state (of three).
12$\frac{3}{16}$ x 9$\frac{3}{16}$ in. (31 x 23.3 cm). The Lunder Collection, 2012.292

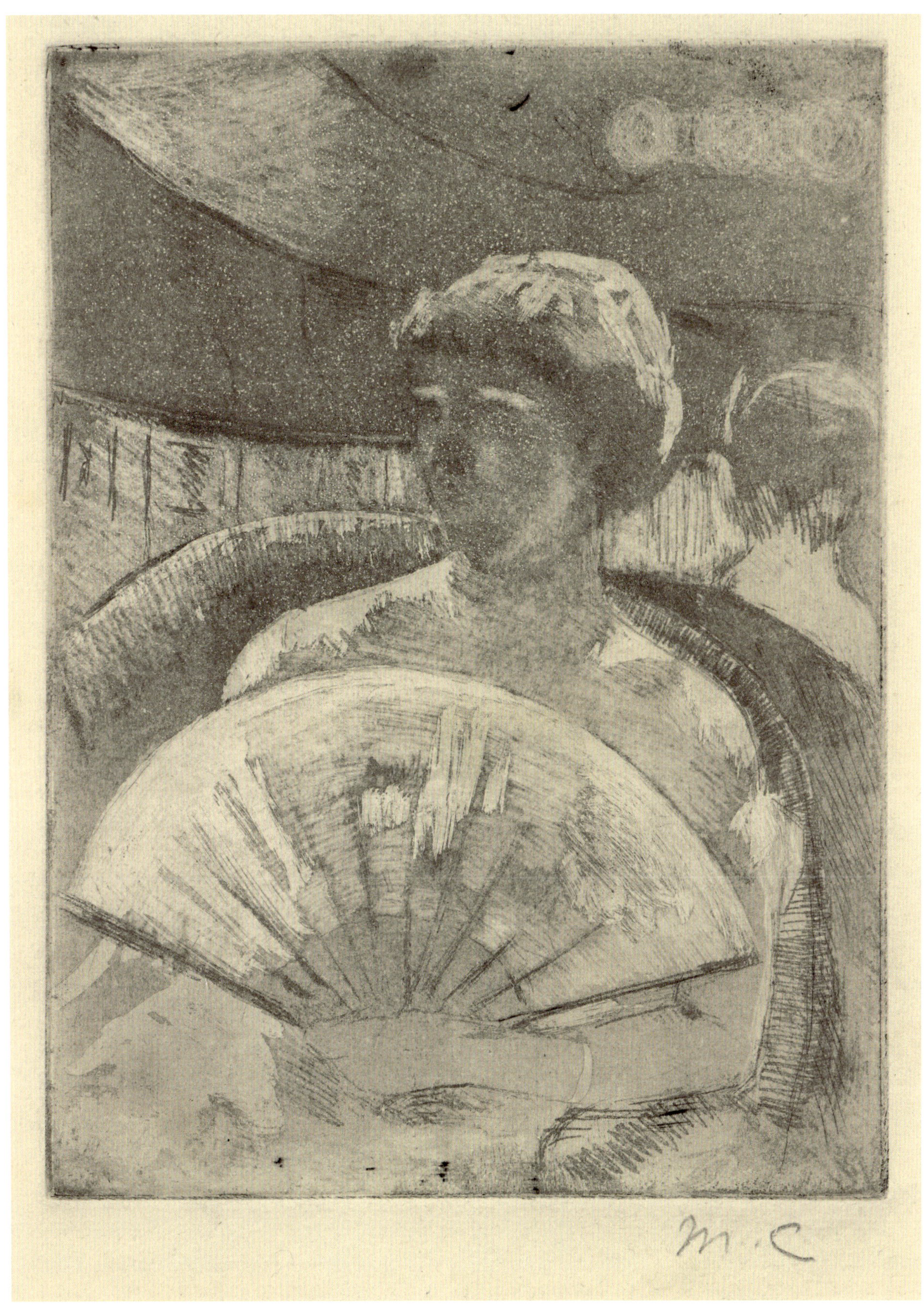

In the Opera Box (No. 2), 1879–80. Softground etching and aquatint on paper. Second state (of three). 12¾⁄16 x 9⅝⁄16 in. (31 x 23.7 cm). The Lunder Collection, 003.2010

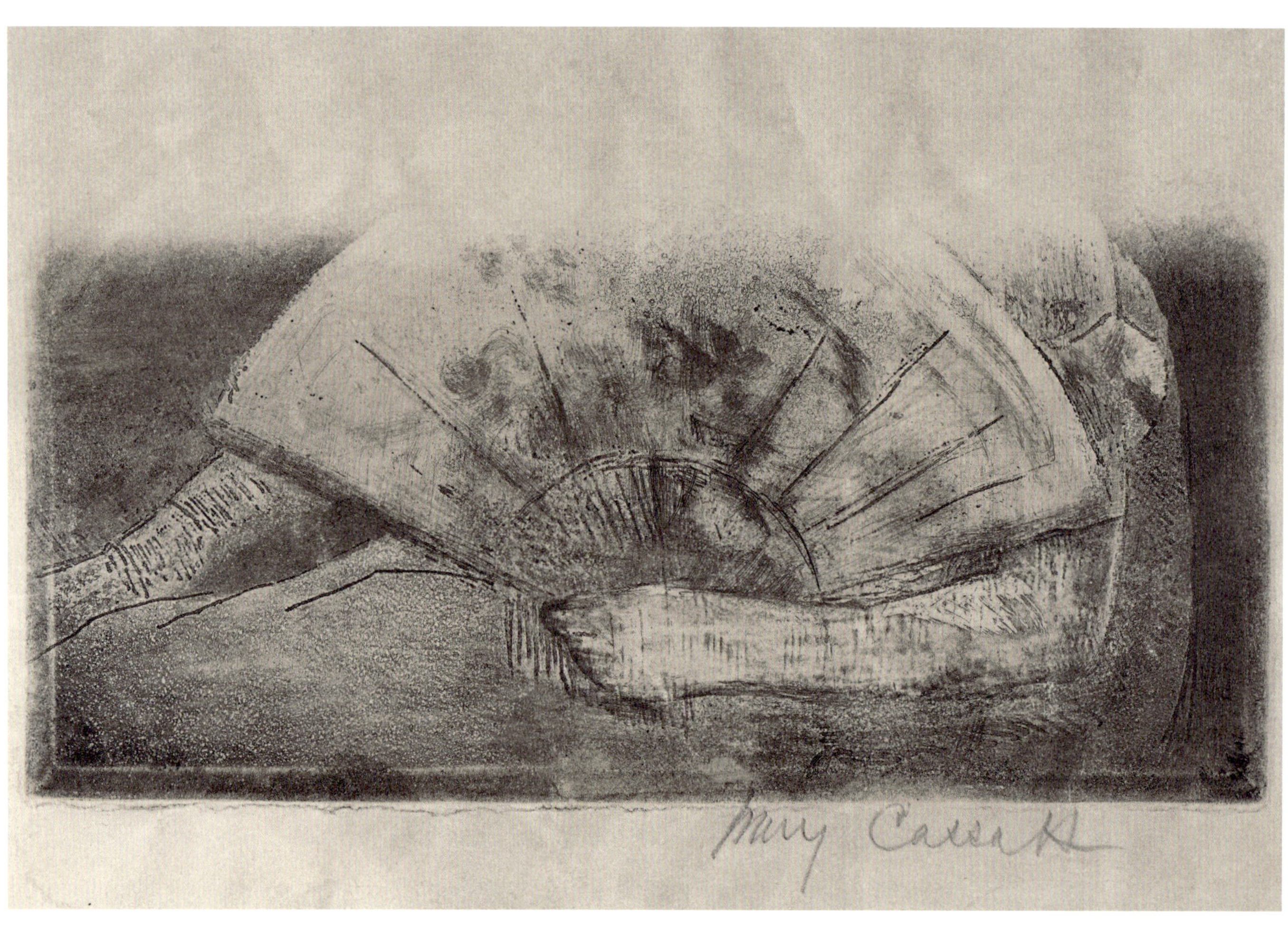

In the Opera Box (No. 3), 1879–80. Softground etching and aquatint on paper. Trial proof of fourth (final) state. 3⅜ x 7⅜ in. (8.6 x 18.7 cm). The Lunder Collection, 2012.293

In the Opera Box (No. 3), 1879–80. Softground etching, aquatint, and etching on paper. Fourth (final) state. 14 1/16 x 10⅝ in. (35.7 x 27 cm). The Lunder Collection, 2012.294

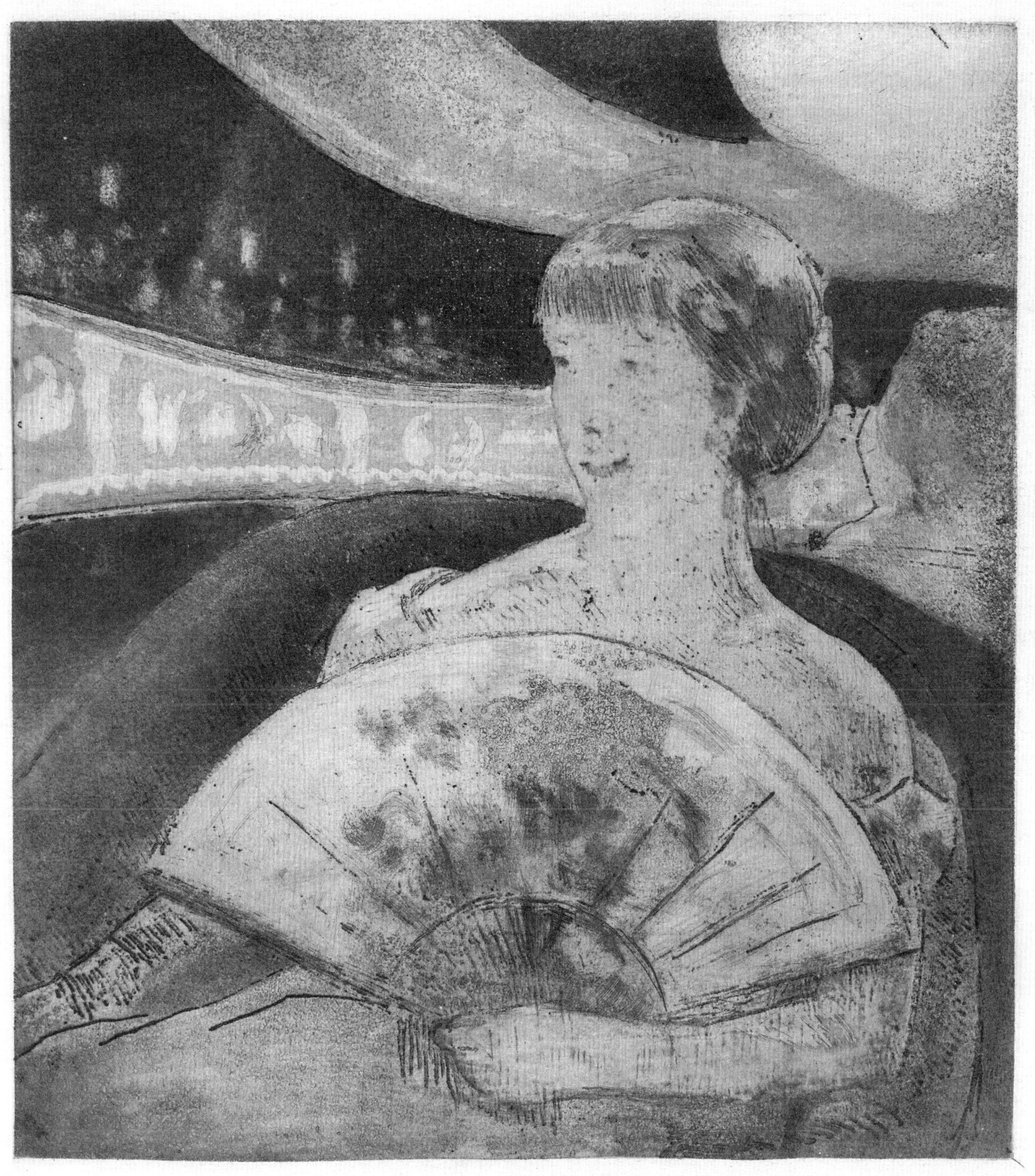
Mary Cassatt

The Bouquet, c. 1880. Softground etching and aquatint on paper. First state (of three). 9⁹⁄₁₆ x 6½ in. (24.3 x 16.5 cm). The Lunder Collection, 2012.291

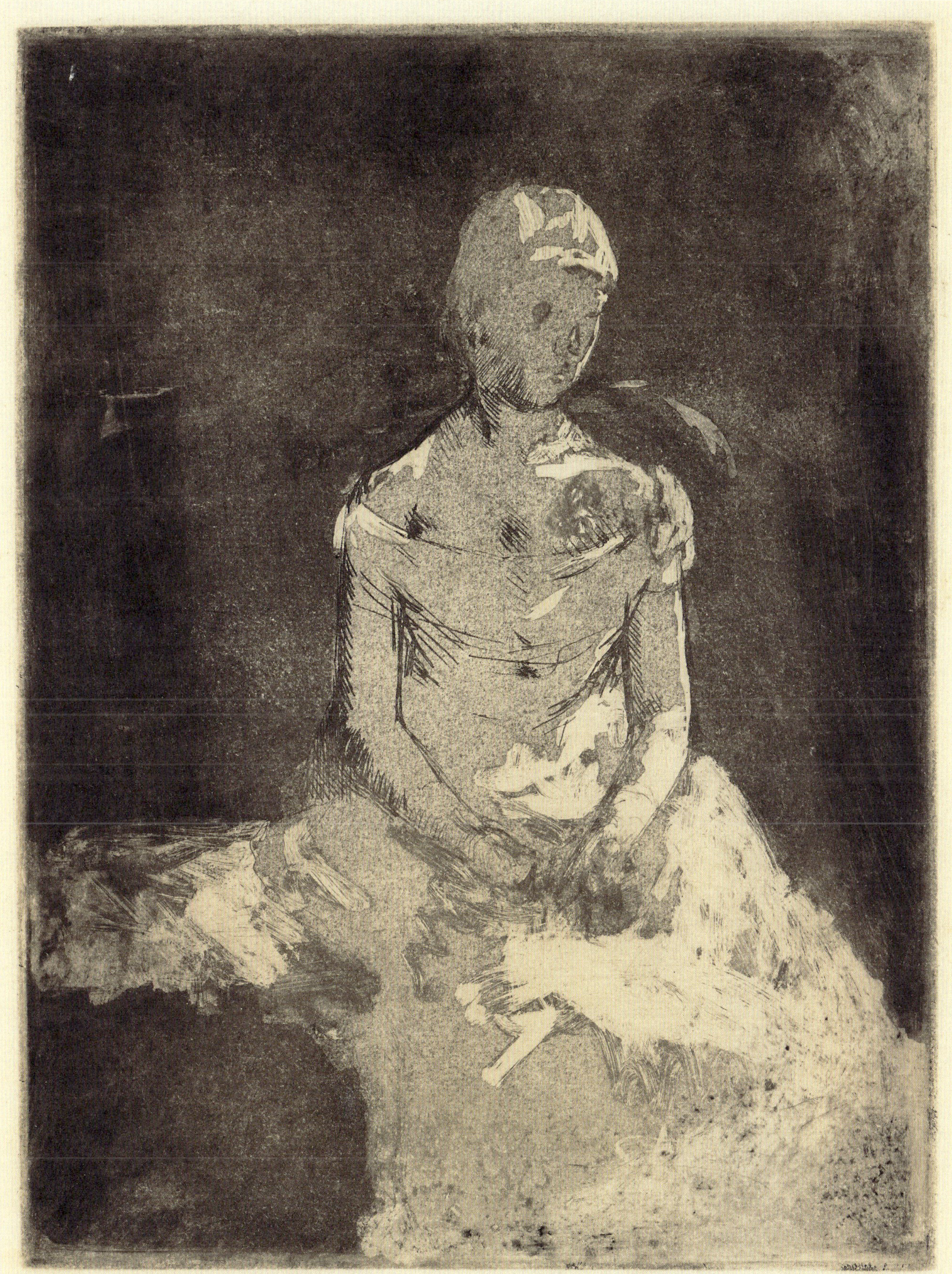

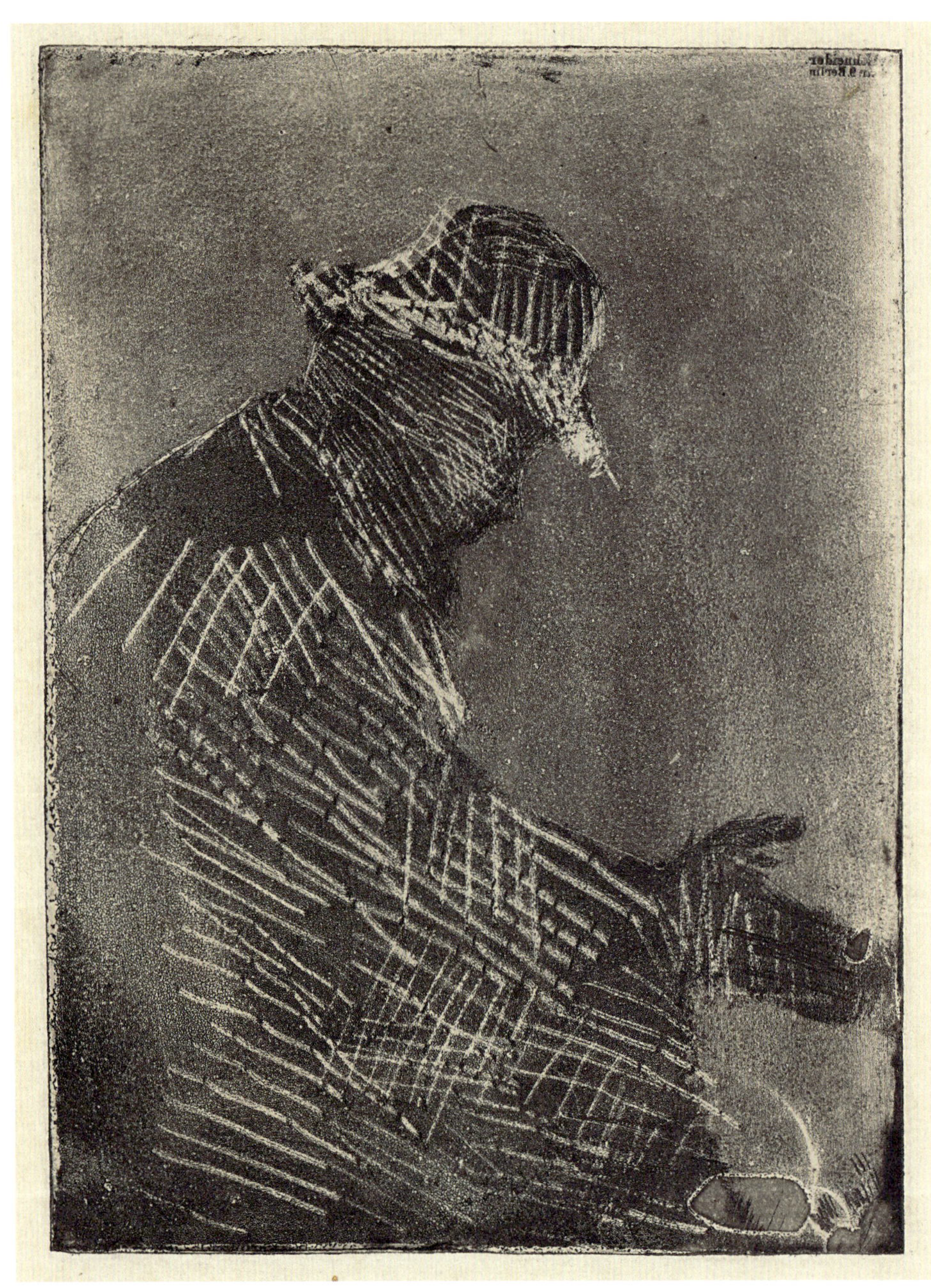

Warming His Hands, c. 1880. Softground etching on paper. Only known state. 6⁵⁄₁₆ x 4⁹⁄₁₆ in. (16 x 11.6 cm). The Lunder Collection, 2012.295

The Visitor, c. 1880. Softground etching, aquatint, etching, drypoint, burnishing and fabric texture on paper. Second state (of six). 15½ x 12³⁄₁₆ in. (39.4 x 31 cm). The Lunder Collection, 2012.297

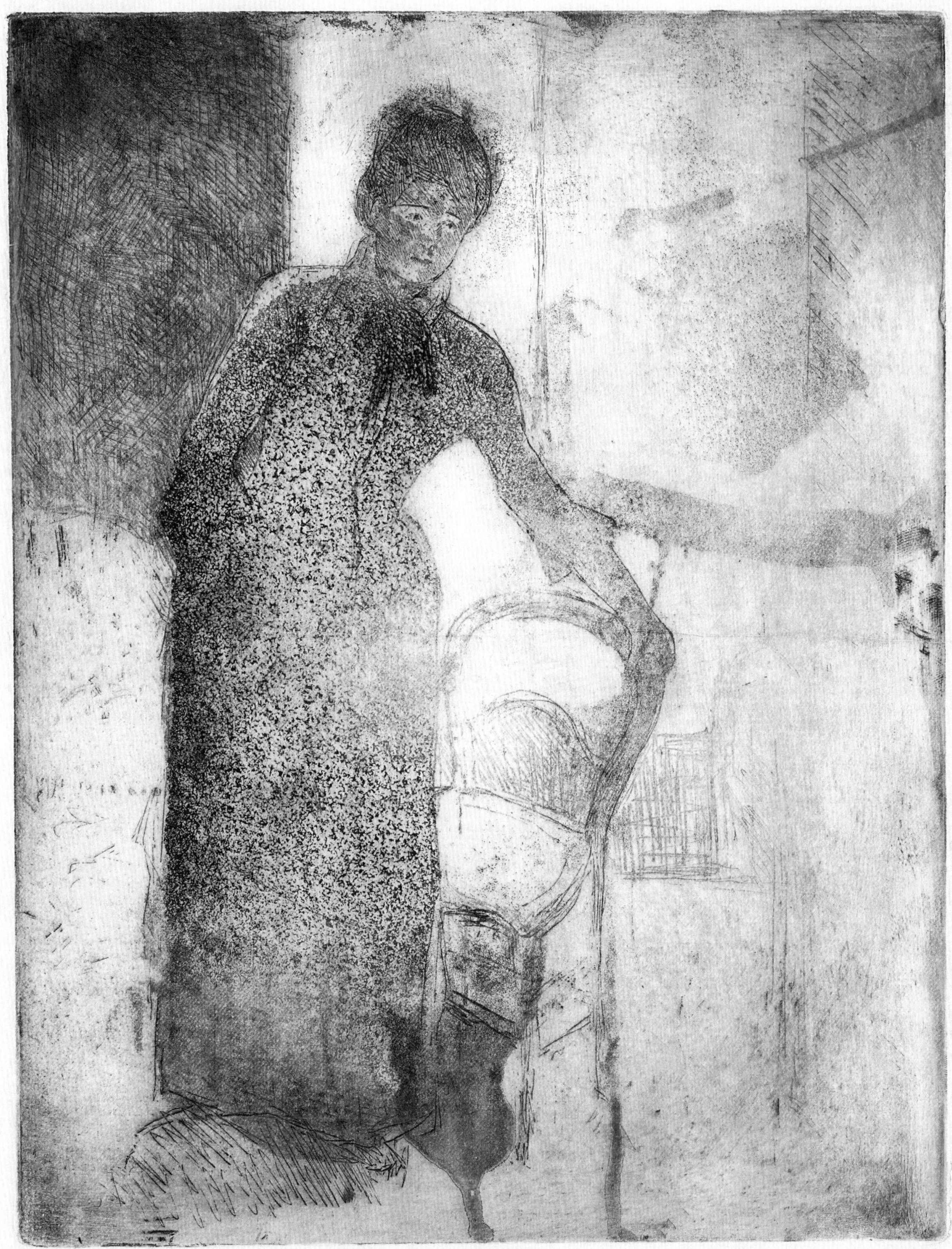

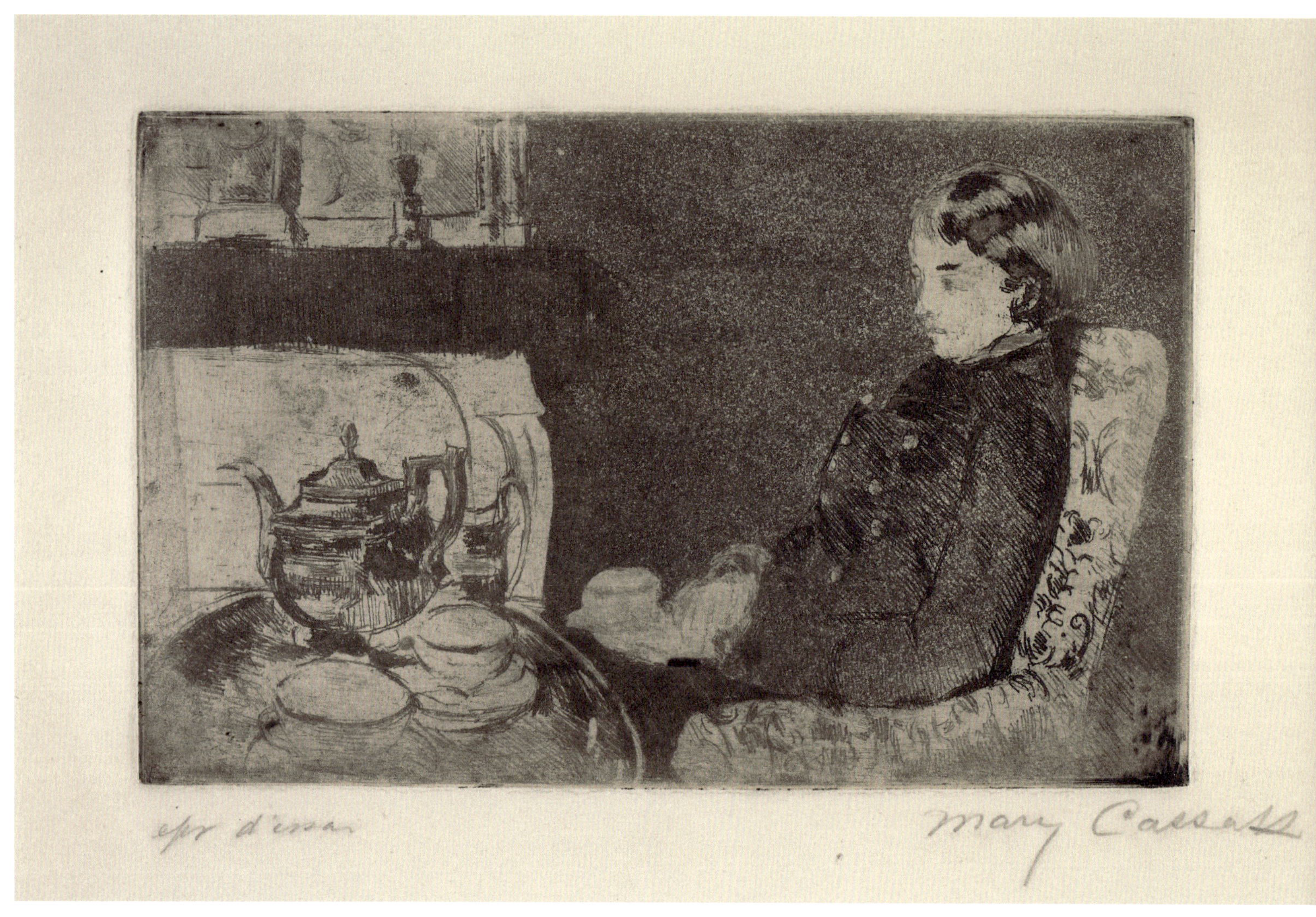

Lydia at Afternoon Tea, 1880–82. Softground etching and aquatint on paper. Trial proof of third state (of five). $5\frac{1}{2}$ x $8\frac{13}{16}$ in. (14 x 22.4 cm). The Lunder Collection, 2012.306

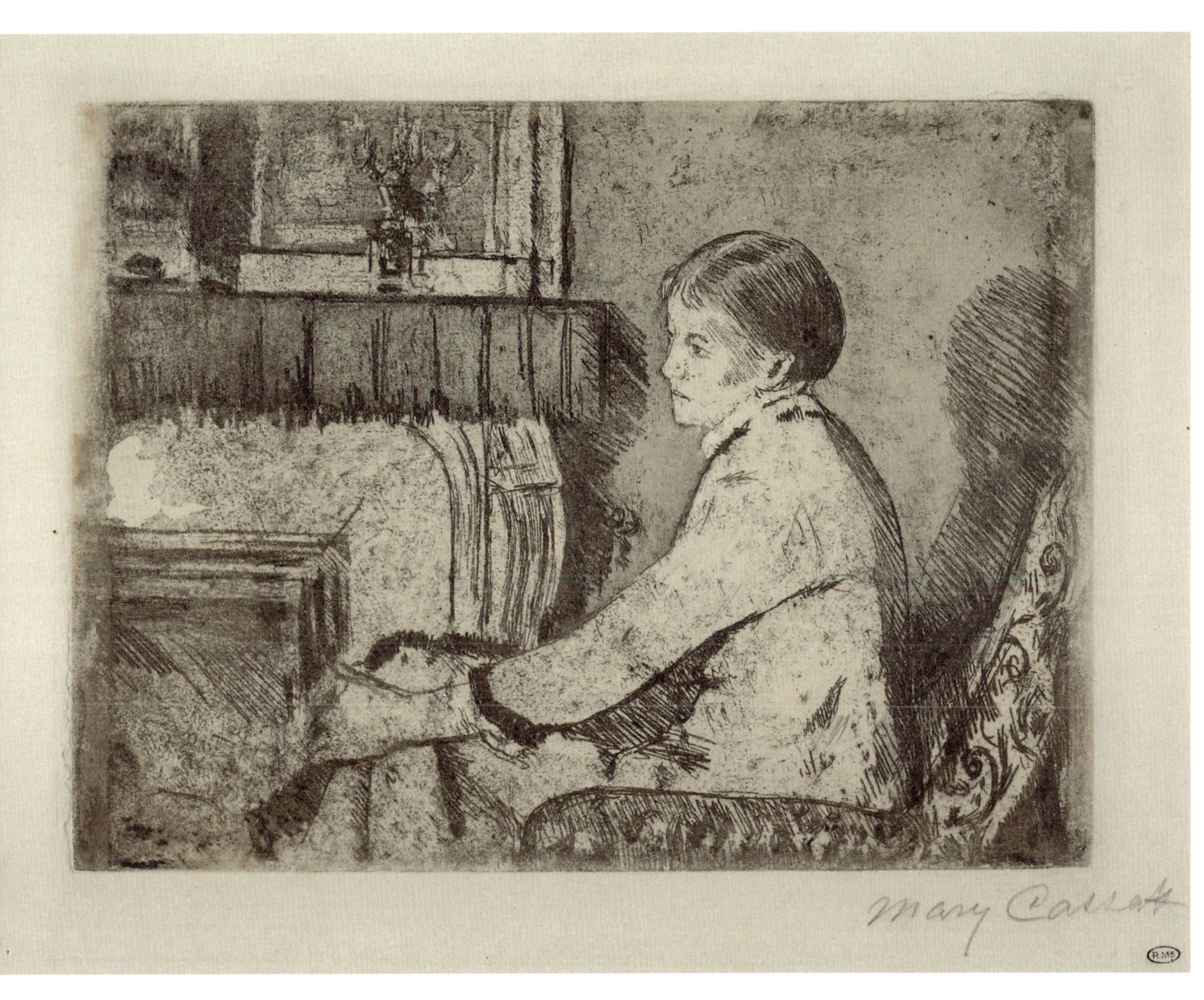

Before the Fireplace (No. 2), c. 1882. Softground etching and aquatint on paper. Only known state. $6\frac{5}{16}$ x $8\frac{5}{8}$ in. (16 x 21.9 cm). The Lunder Collection, 2012.305

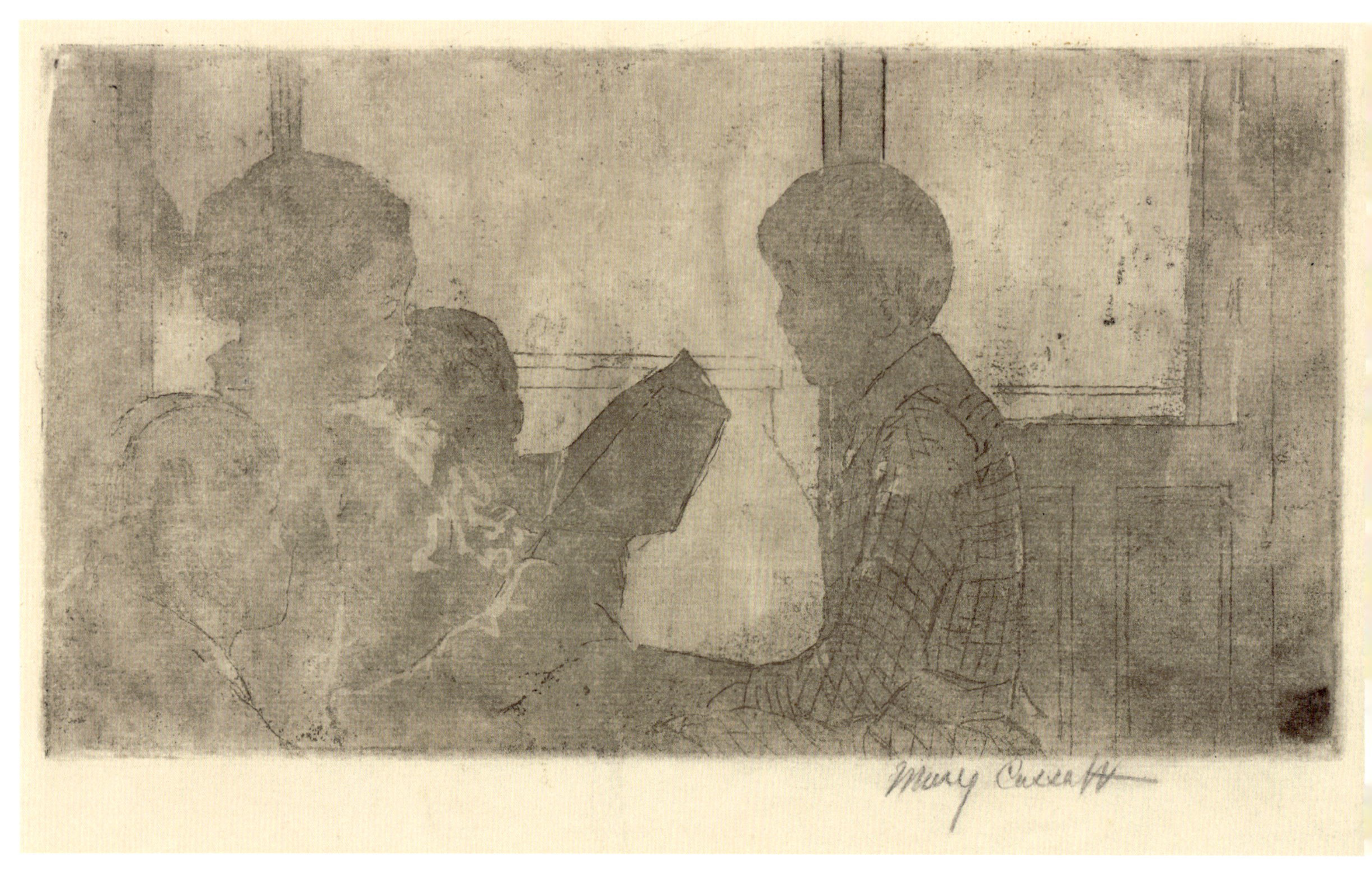

Mrs. Cassatt Reading to Her Grandchildren (No. 1), c. 1880. Softground etching on paper. First state (of three). $6\frac{1}{8}$ x $11\frac{3}{4}$ in. (15.6 x 29.9 cm). The Lunder Collection, 2012.302

Knitting in the Library, c. 1881. Softground etching and aquatint on paper. Second state (of three). $10\frac{7}{8}$ x $8\frac{9}{16}$ in. (27.6 x 21.8 cm). The Lunder Collection, 2012.296

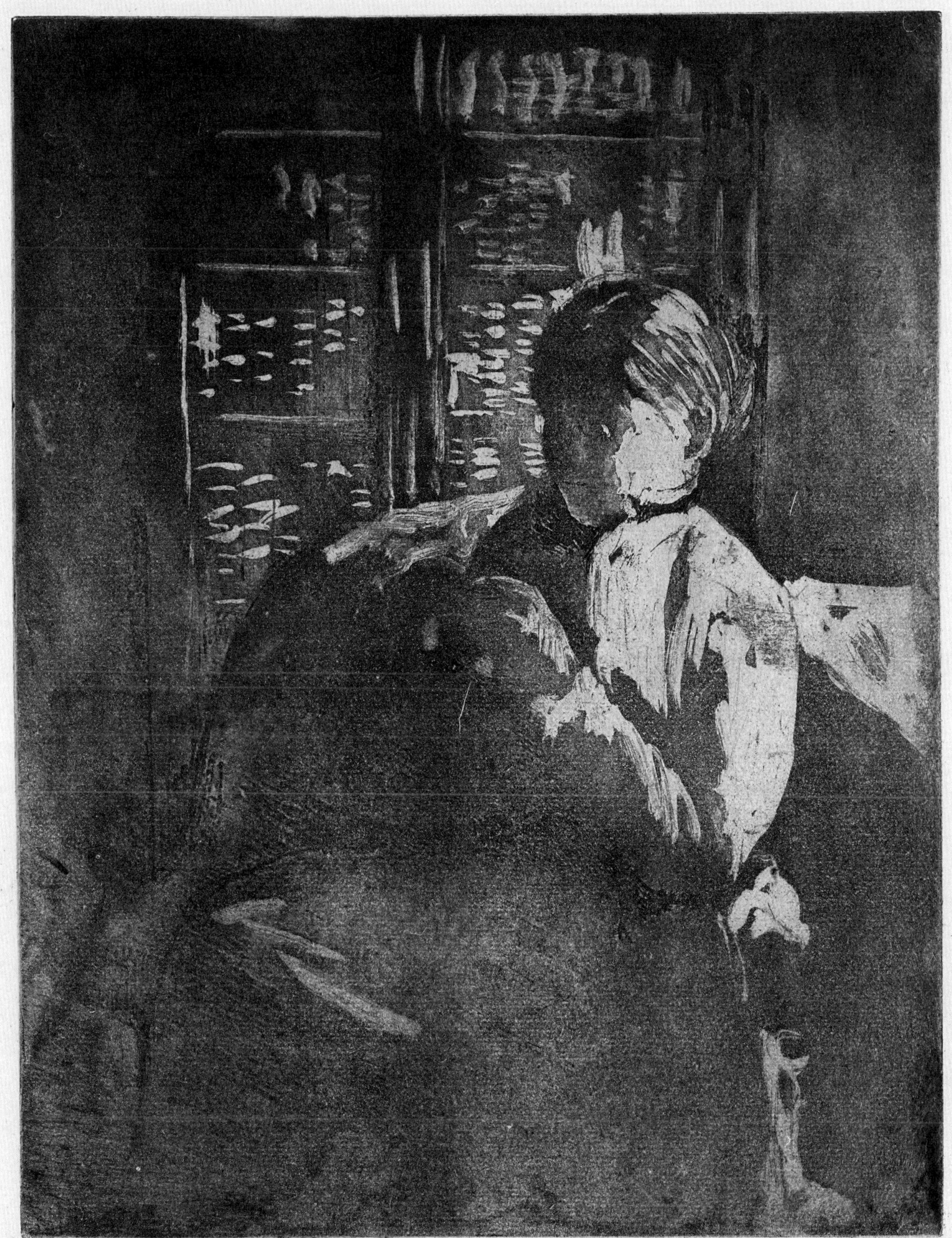
Mary Cassatt

Lydia Reading, Turned Toward Right, c. 1881. Softground etching and aquatint on paper. Second (final) state. 7¹⁄₁₆ x 4³⁄₈ in. (17.9 x 11.1 cm). The Lunder Collection, 2012.304

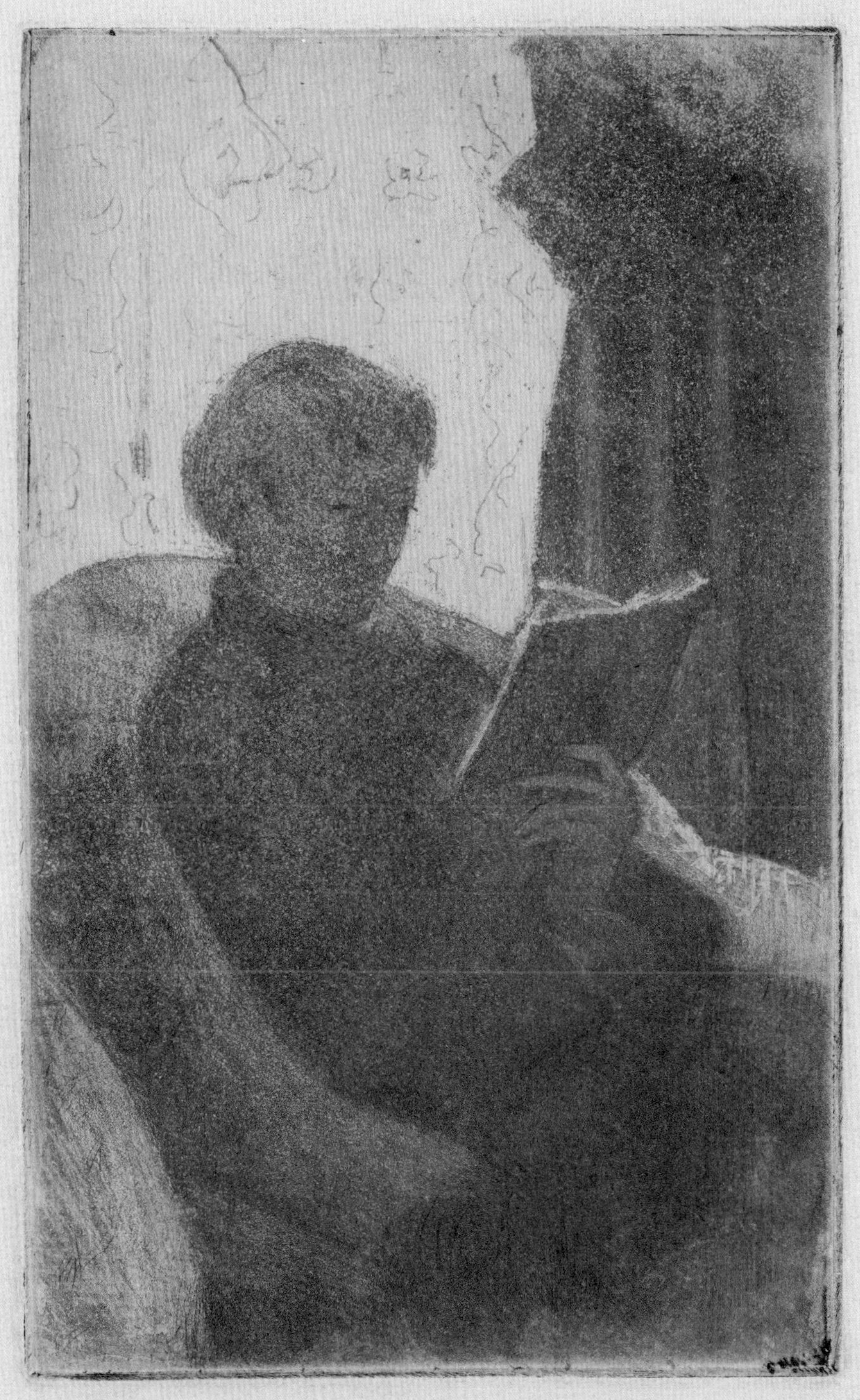
Mary Cassatt

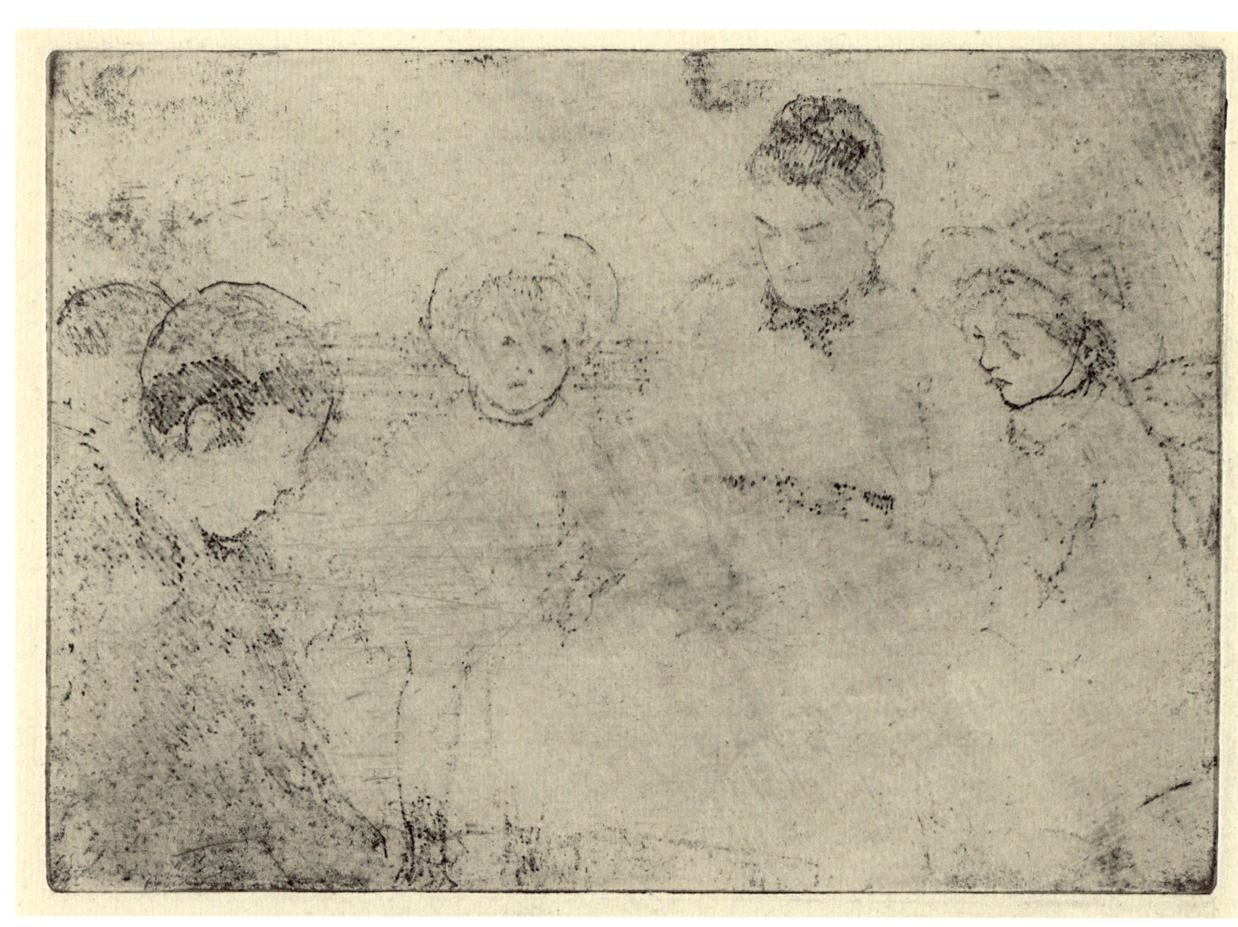

Mathilda Reading to the Children, 1881. Softground etching on paper.
Only known state. 4⅚₁₆ x 6¼ in. (11 x 15.9 cm). The Lunder Collection, 2012.303

Profile of Mrs. Cassatt Reading, with Glasses, c. 1881. Pencil on paper.
8¼ x 5¼ in. (21 x 13.3 cm). The Lunder Collection, 2013.035

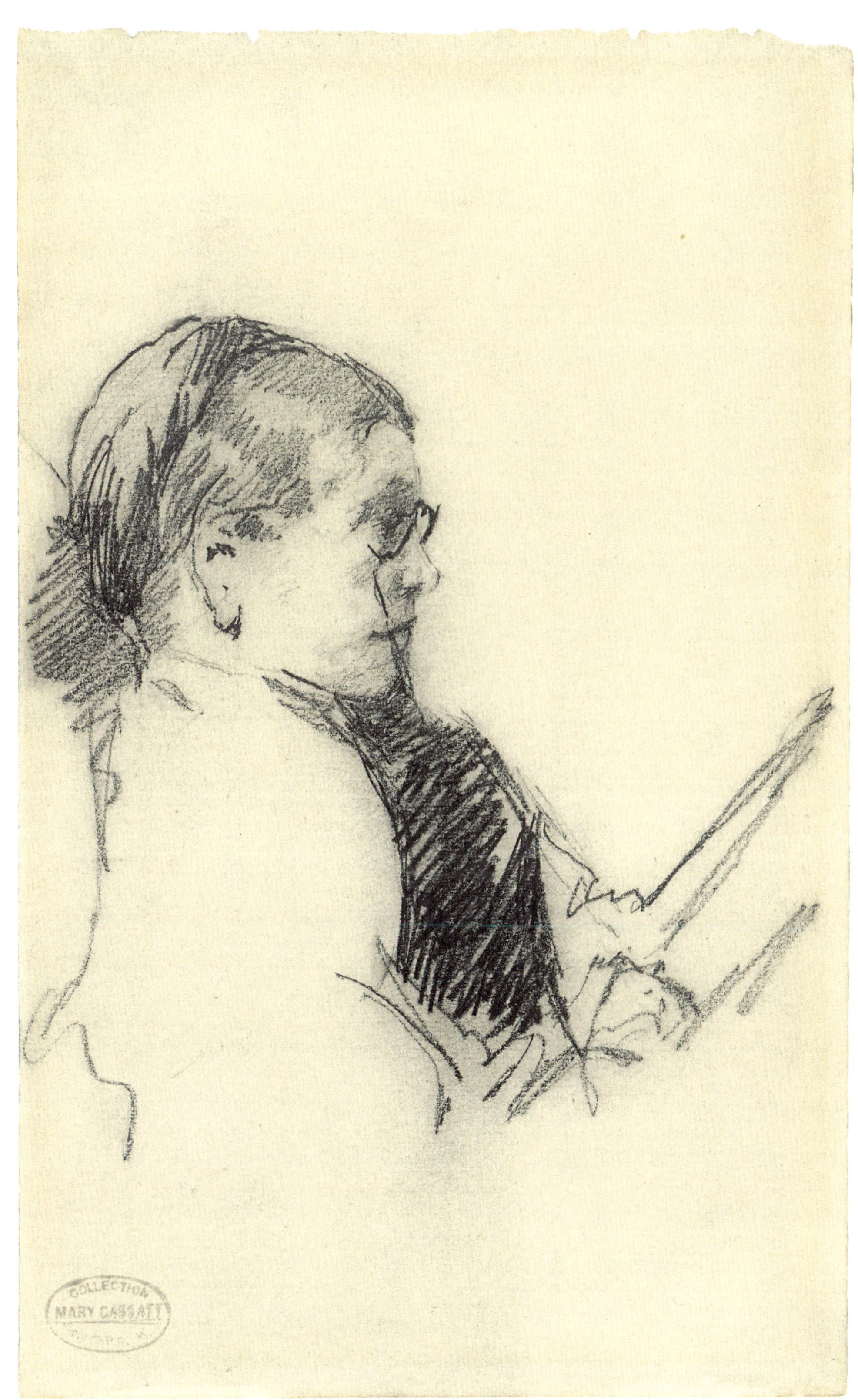
COLLECTION
MARY CASSATT

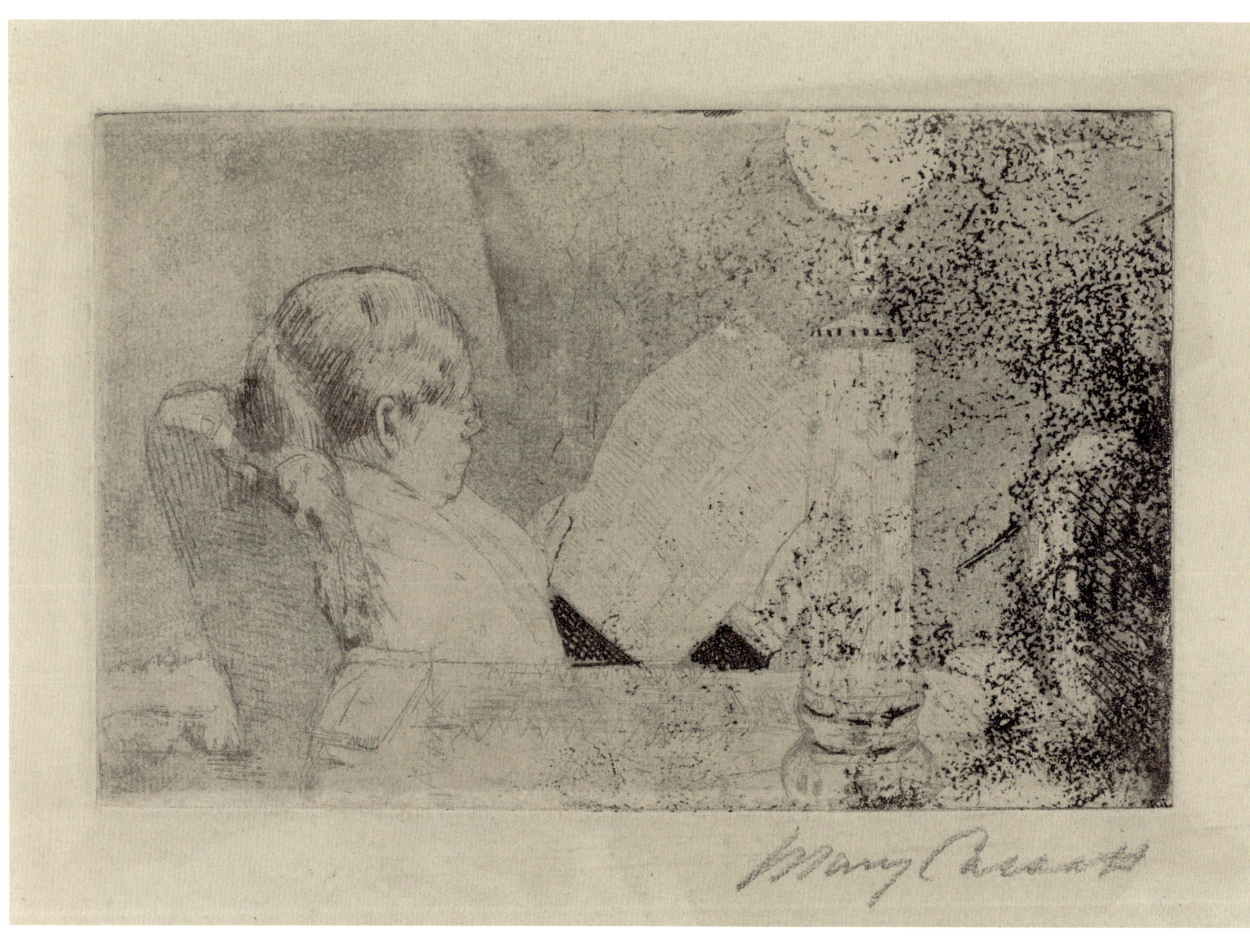

Reading the Newspaper (No. 1), c. 1882. Softground etching with fabric texture on paper. First state (of two). 5½ x 8¾ in. (14 x 22.2 cm). The Lunder Collection, 002.2010

The Round-Backed Armchair, c. 1881. Softground etching and aquatint on paper. Only known state. 11 x 7$\frac{1}{16}$ in. (27.9 x 17.9 cm). The Lunder Collection, 2012.298

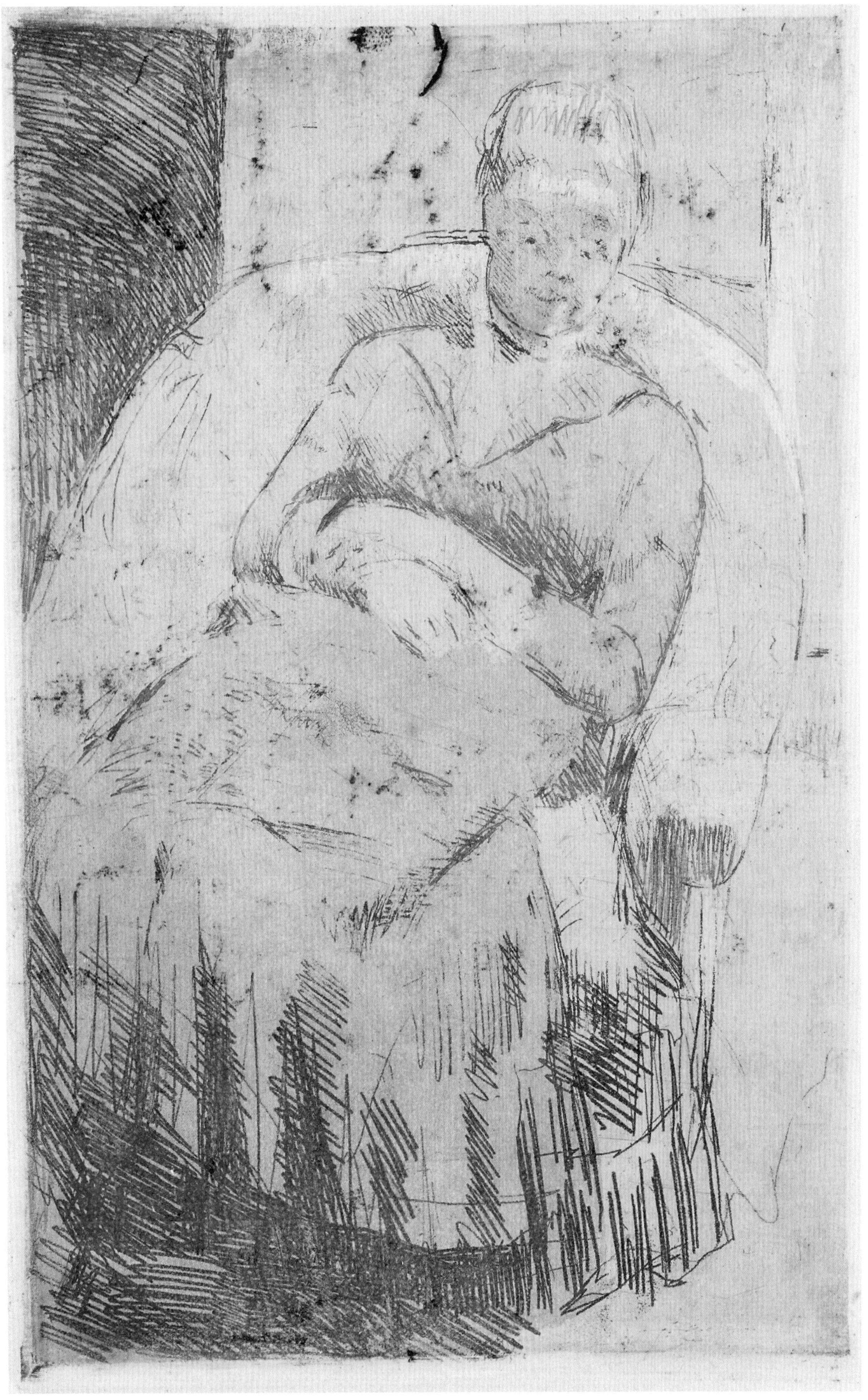

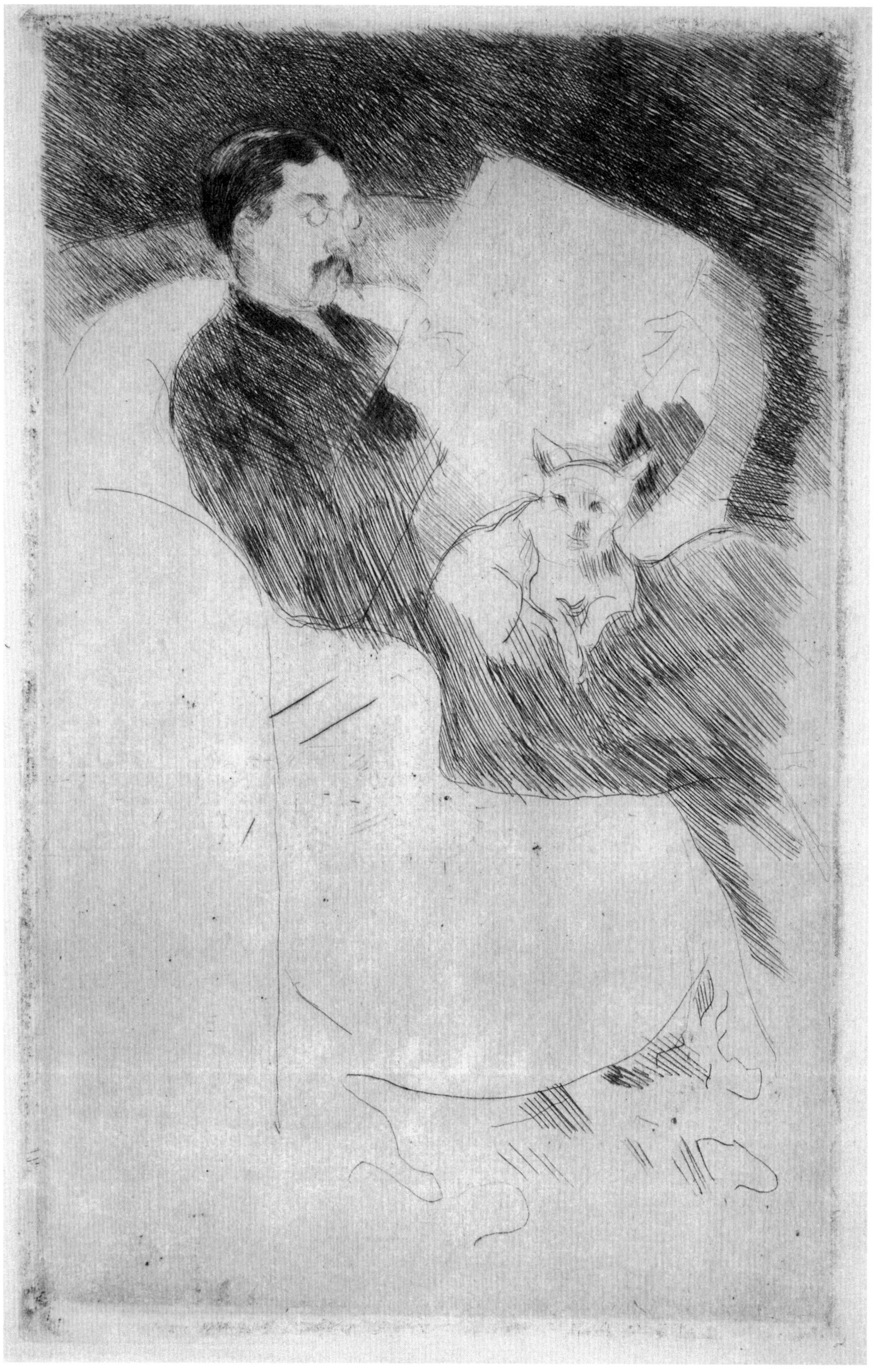

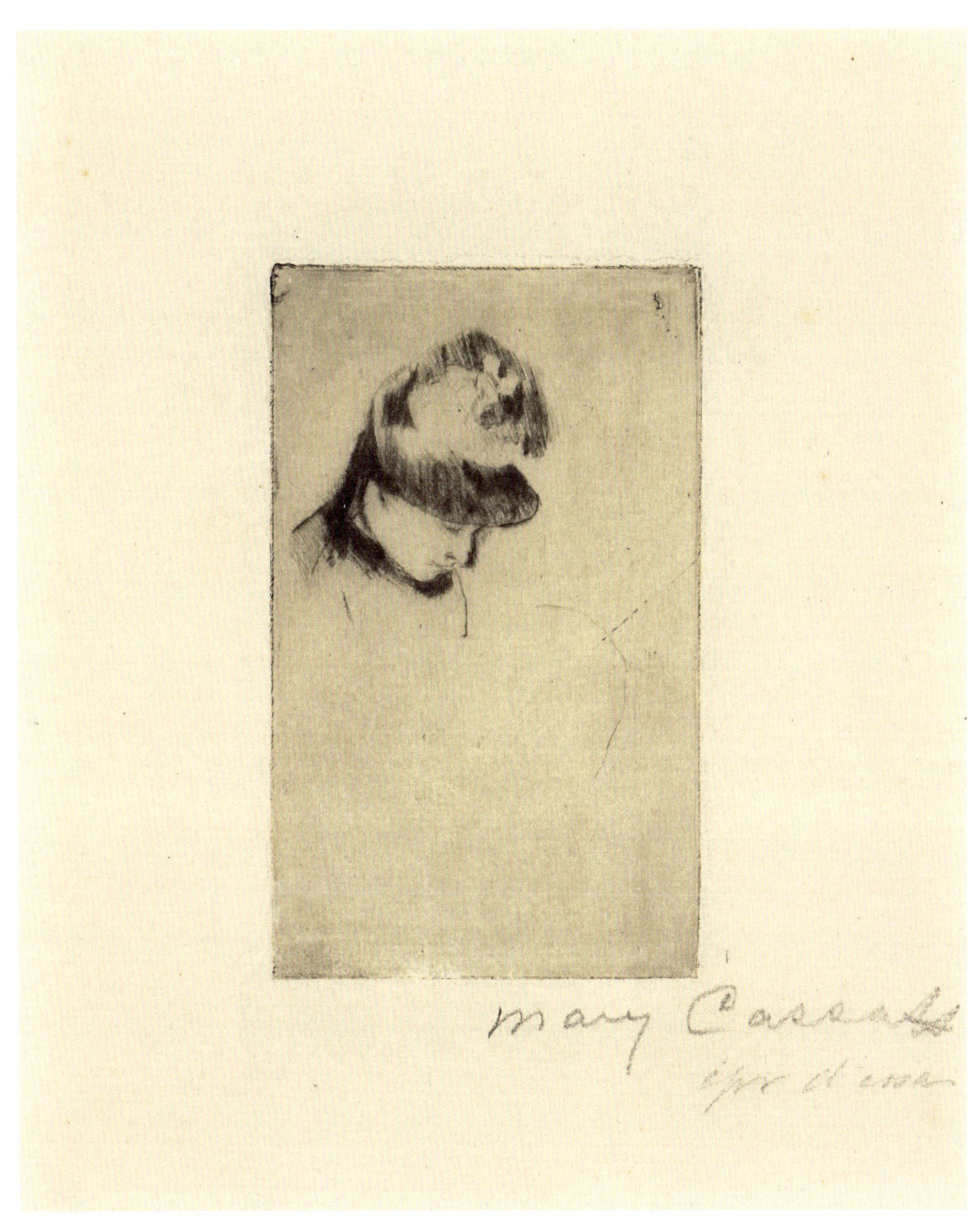

Mr. Gardner Cassatt Reading the Paper, c. 1883. Etching and drypoint on paper. Only known state. $10\frac{7}{8}$ x $6\frac{7}{8}$ in. (27.6 x 17.5 cm). The Lunder Collection, 2012.307

Sketch of the Black and Green Bonnet, c. 1883. Drypoint on paper. Trial proof of only known state. $3\frac{13}{16}$ x $2\frac{5}{16}$ in. (9.7 x 5.9 cm). The Lunder Collection, 2012.299

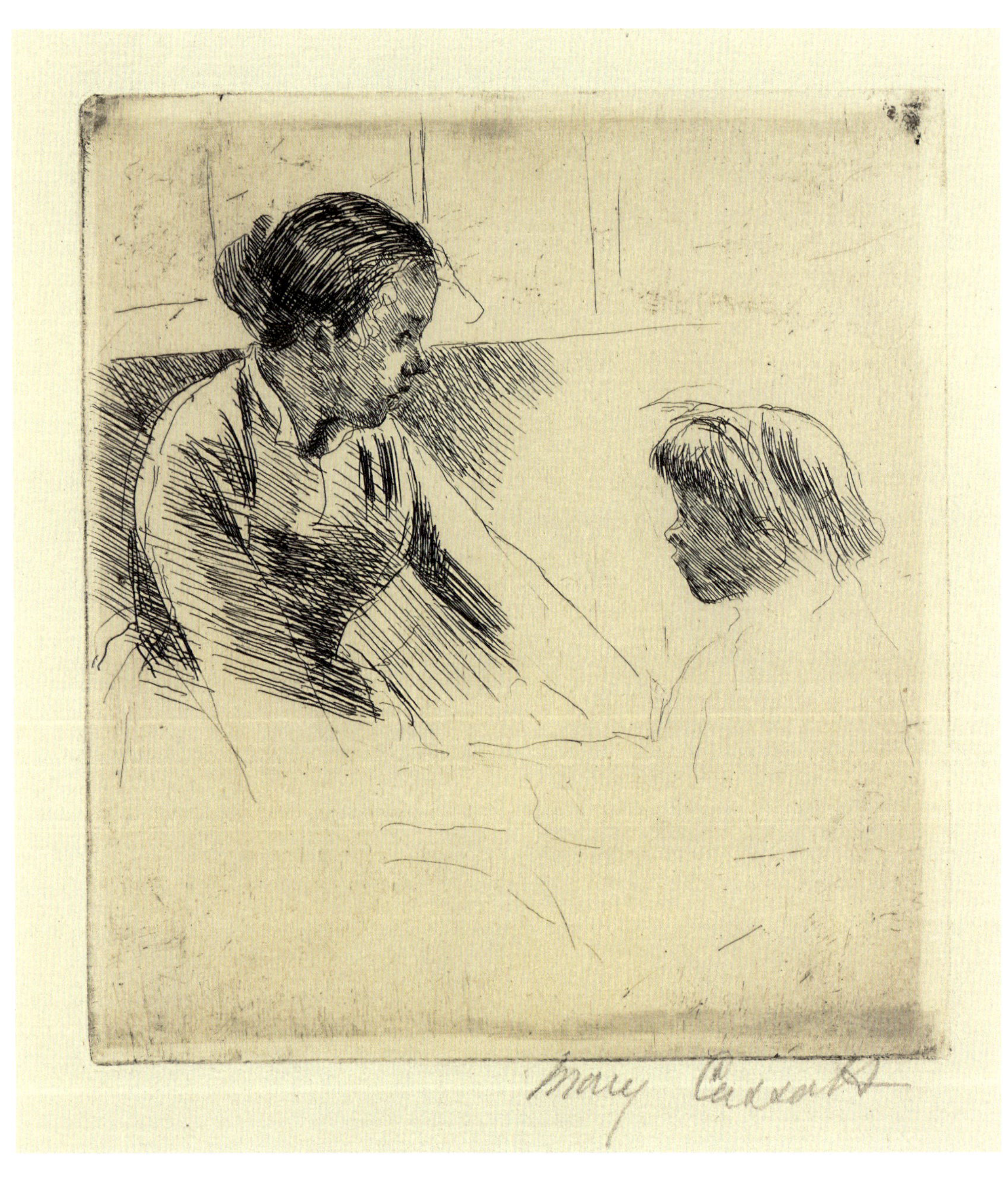

Susan and Child Facing Each Other, c. 1883. Etching on paper. Only known state. 5½ x 5 in. (14 x 12.7 cm). The Lunder Collection, 2012.300

Susan Looking Down at Her Hands, c. 1883. Drypoint on paper. Only known state. 8¾ x 5½ in. (22.2 x 14 cm). The Lunder Collection, 2012.301

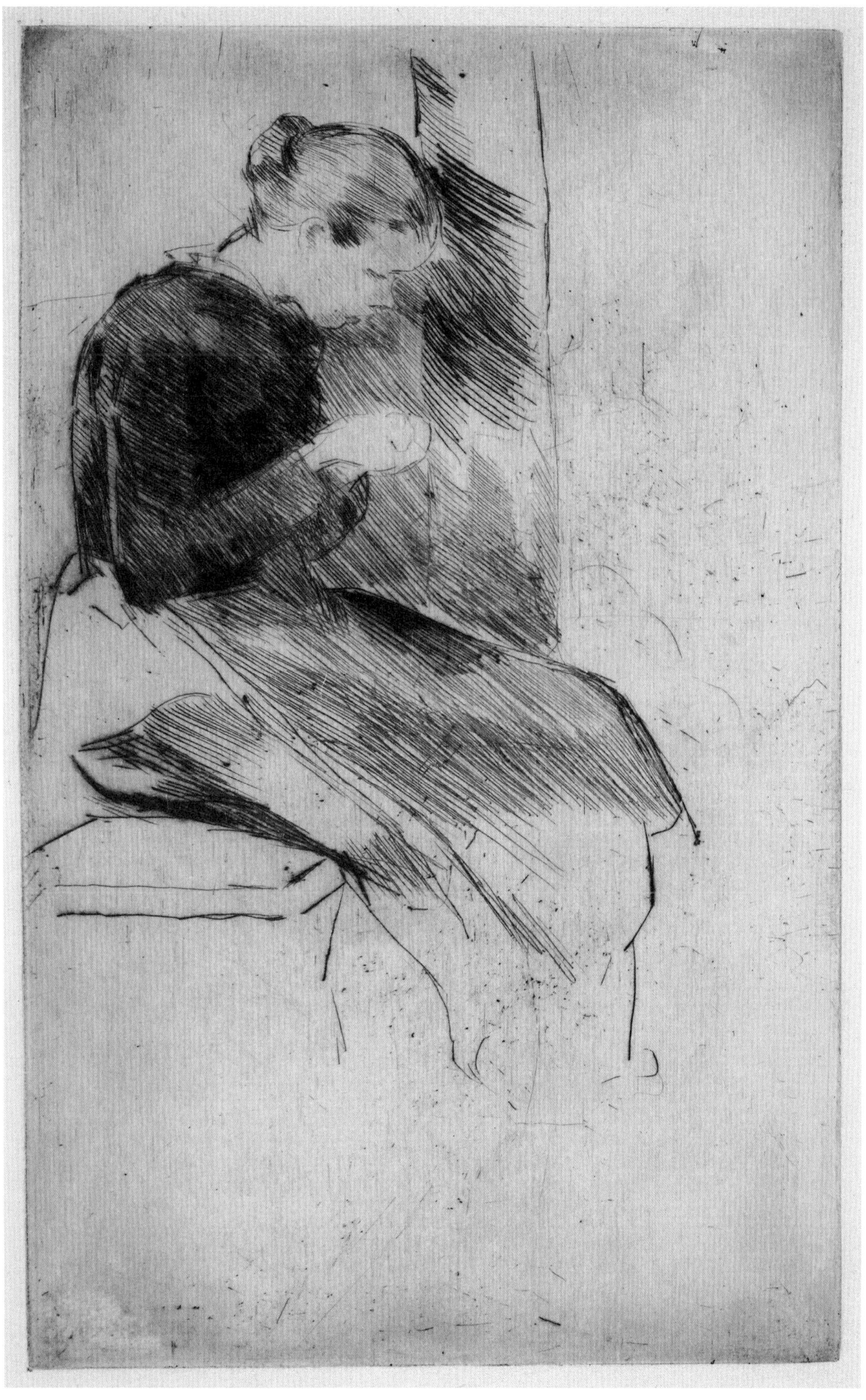

Emmie and Her Child, c. 1889. Softground etching, aquatint, and drypoint on paper. Only known state. 8⅜ x 6⅛ in. (21.3 x 15.6 cm). The Lunder Collection, 2012.309

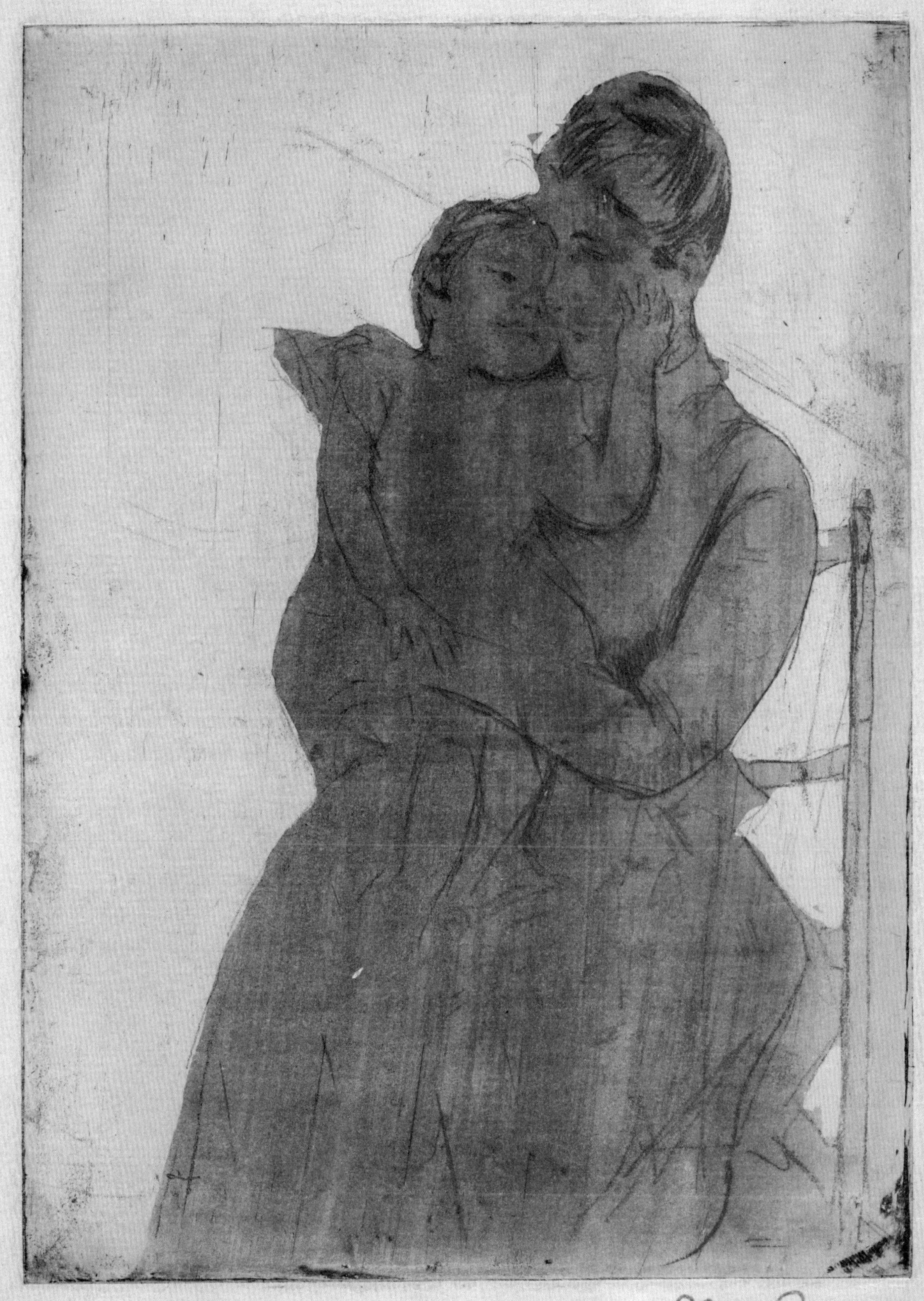

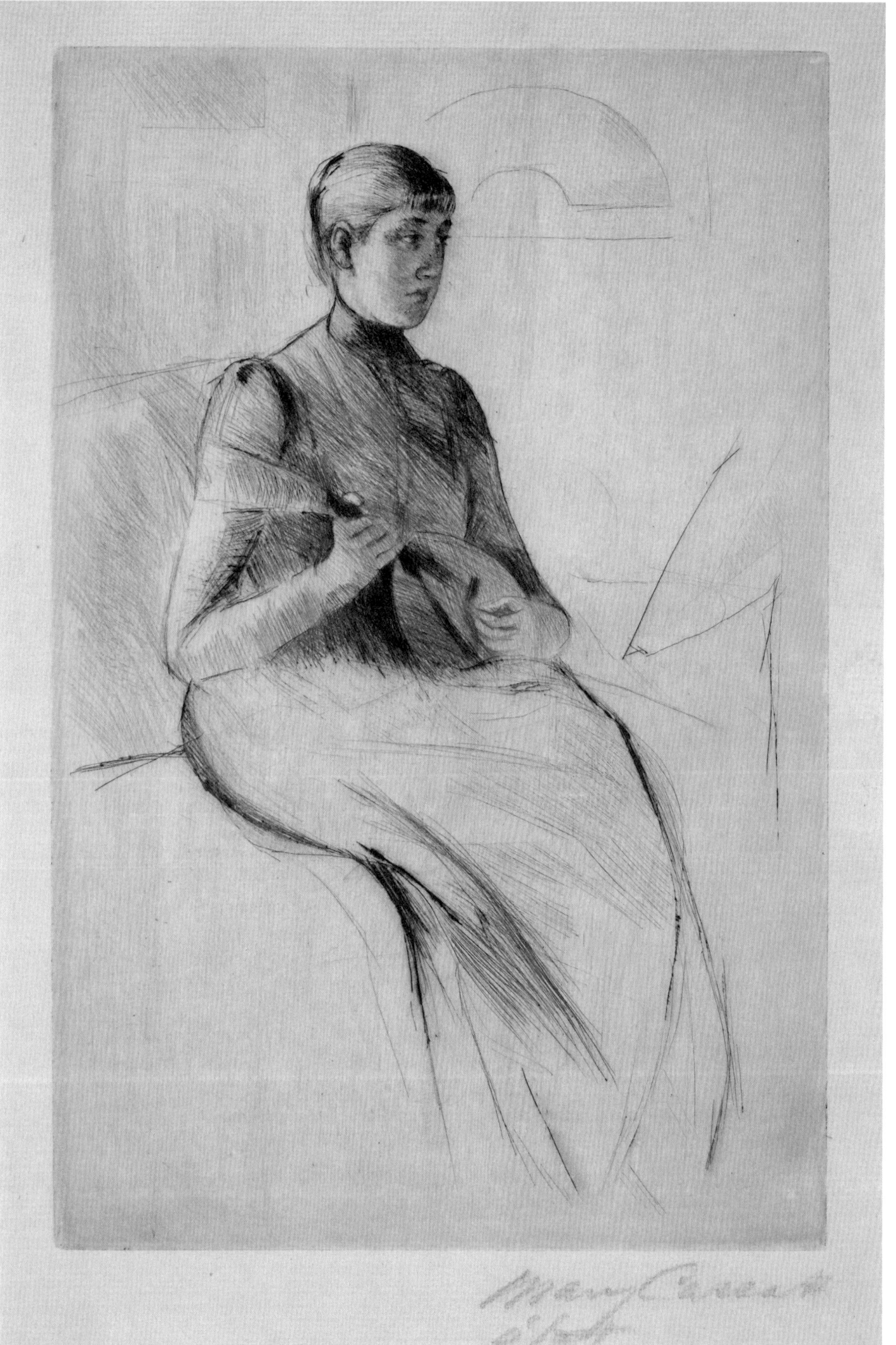
Mary Cassatt

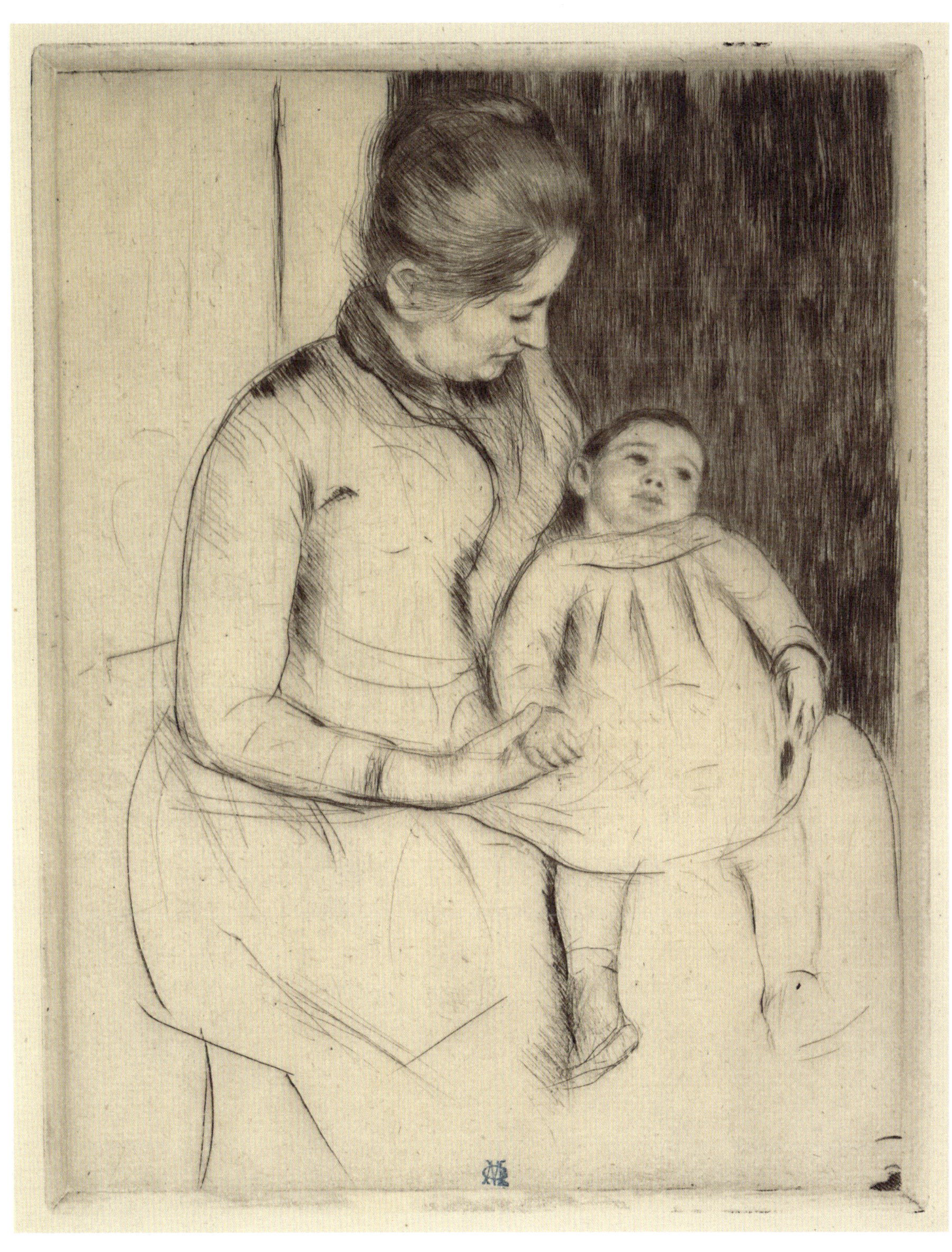

The Mandolin Player, c. 1889. Drypoint on paper. Fifth state (of seven). 9⅛ x 6⅜ in. (23.2 x 16.2 cm). The Lunder Collection, 2012.317

Solicitude, c. 1889. Drypoint on paper. Fourth (final) state. 7⅜ x 5¹³⁄₁₆ in. (18.7 x 14.8 cm). The Lunder Collection, 2012.308

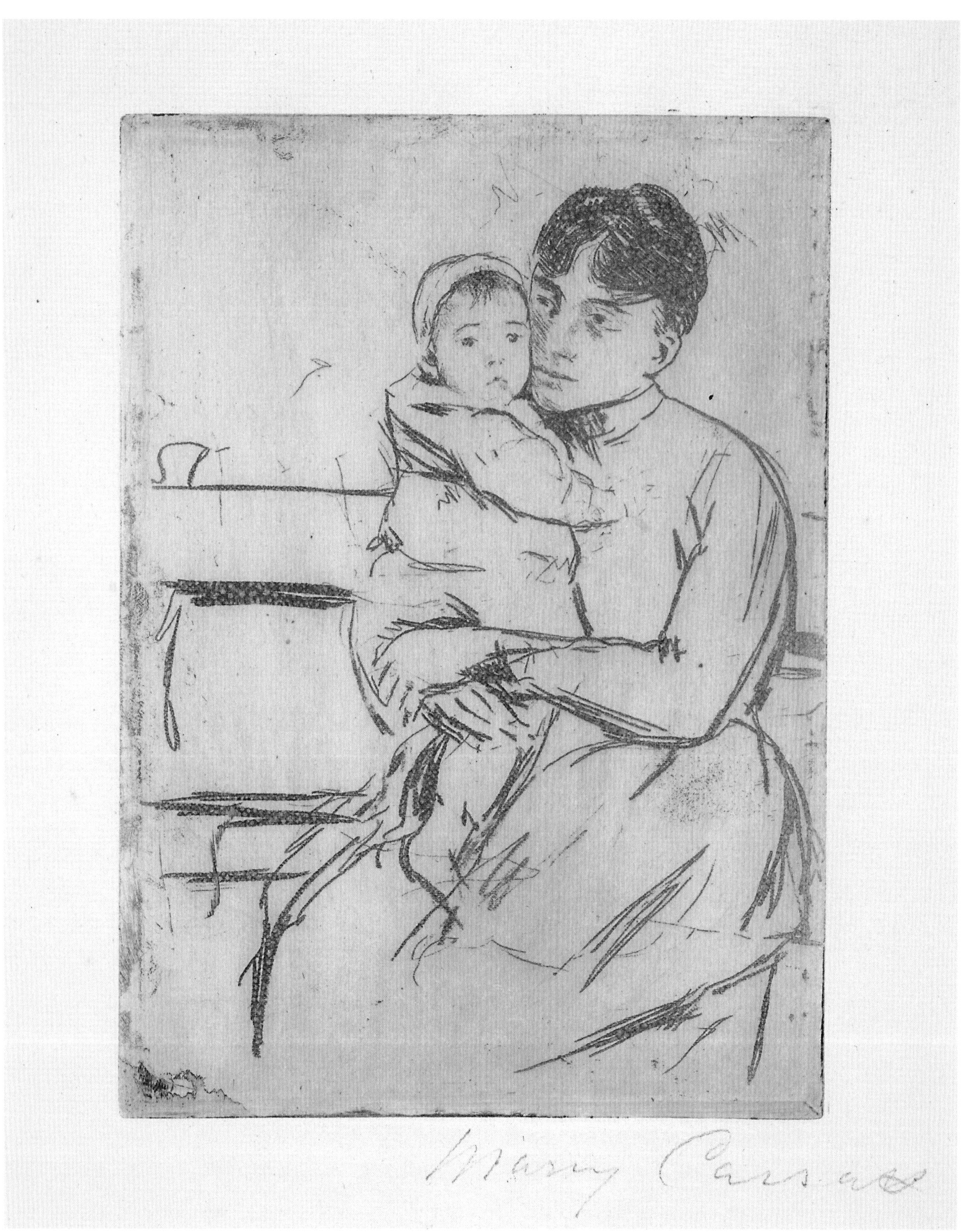

On the Bench, c. 1889. Softground etching on paper. Only known state.
7 3/8 x 5 5/16 in. (18.7 x 13.5 cm). The Lunder Collection, 2012.310

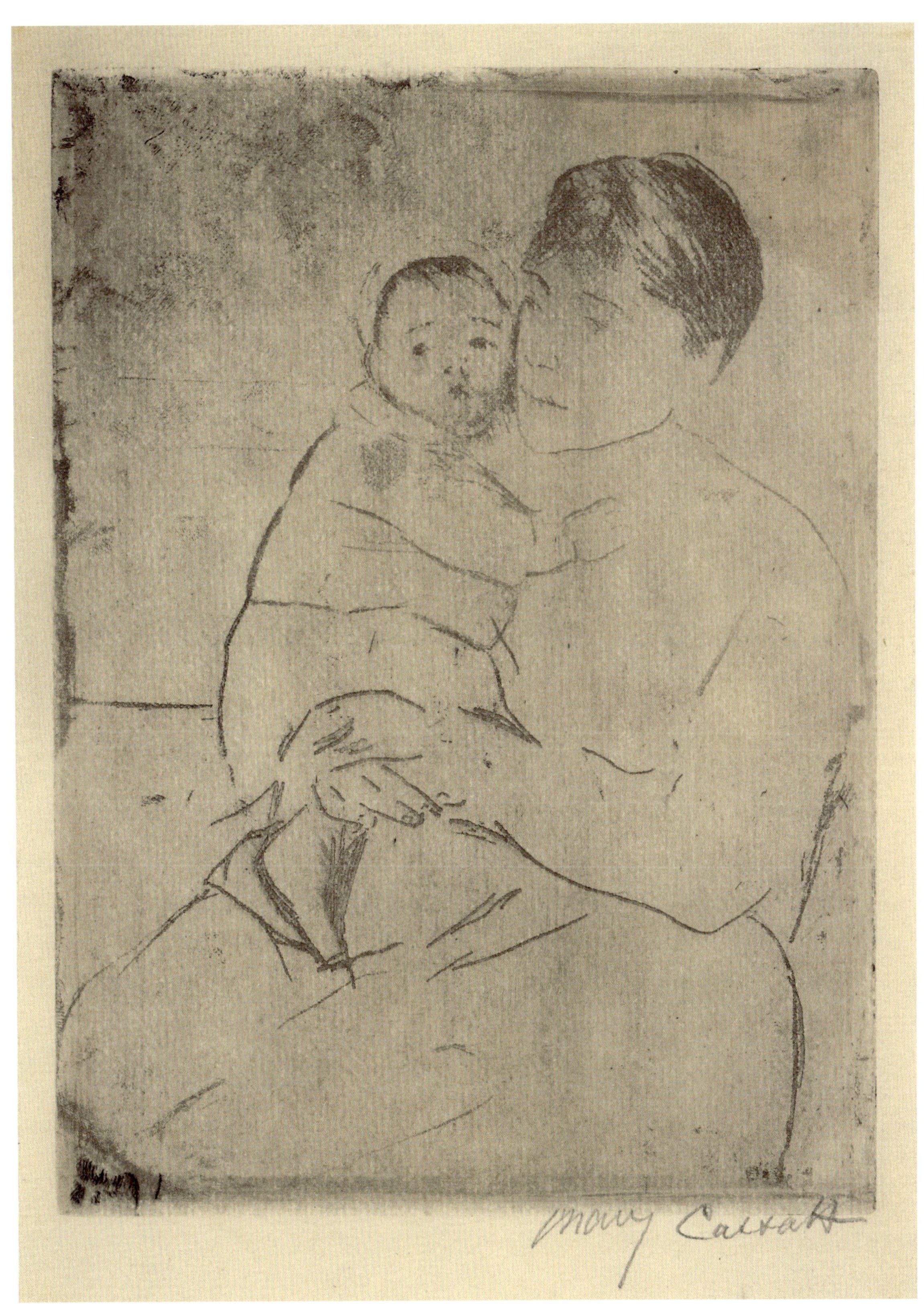

Nurse and Baby Bill (No. 1), c. 1889. Softground etching, aquatint, and netting texture on paper. Intermediate state between first and second state (of four). $7\frac{3}{8}$ x $5\frac{5}{16}$ in. (18.7 x 13.5 cm). The Lunder Collection, 2012.311

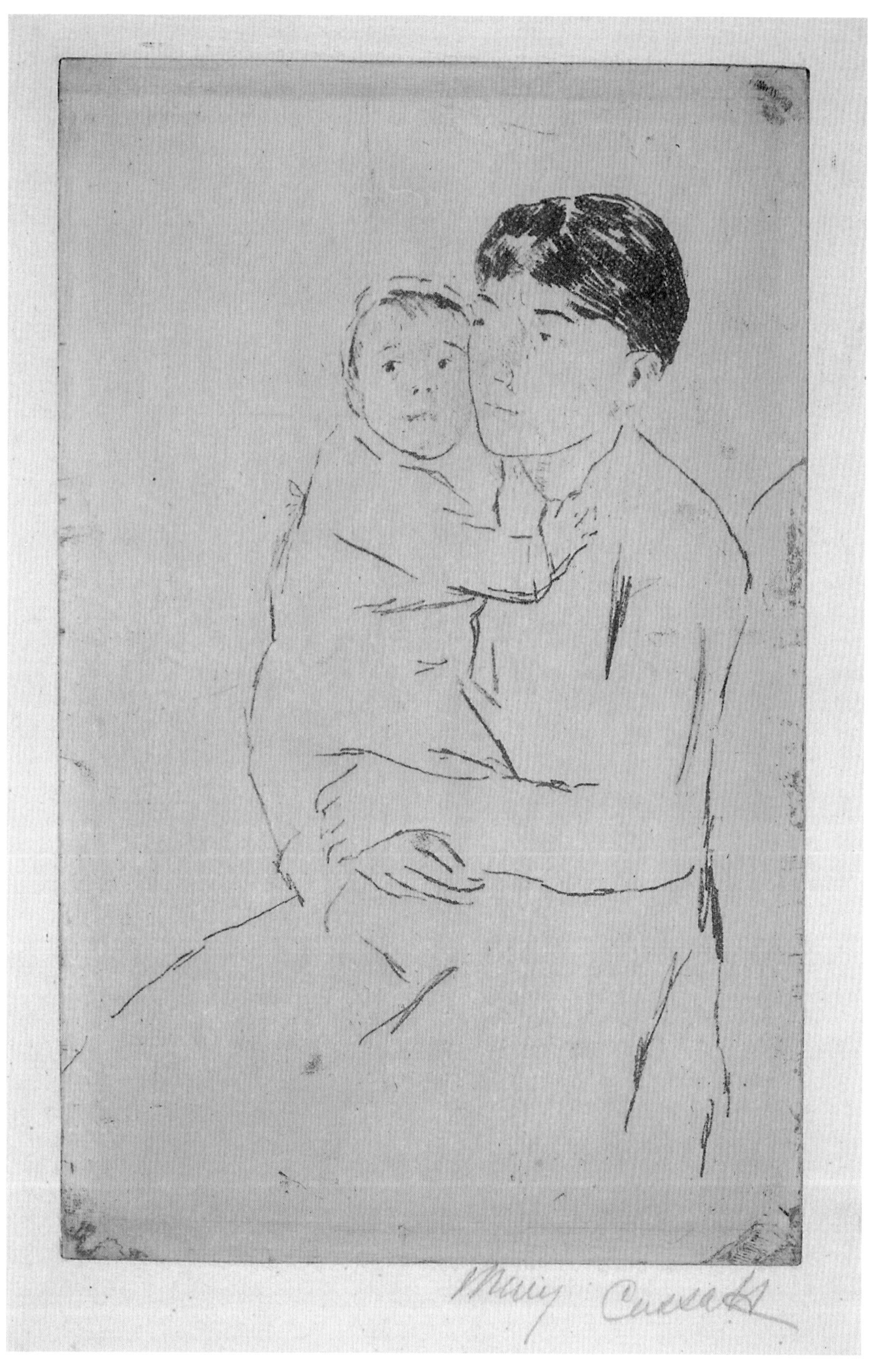

Nurse and Baby Bill (No. 2), c. 1889. Softground etching and aquatint on paper. First state (of two). 8⁹⁄₁₆ x 5⁷⁄₁₆ in. (21.8 x 13.8 cm). The Lunder Collection, 2012.312

Nurse and Baby Bill (No. 2), c. 1889. Softground etching in sepia on paper. Second (final) state. 8⁹⁄₁₆ x 5⁷⁄₁₆ in. (21.8 x 13.8 cm). The Lunder Collection, 2012.282

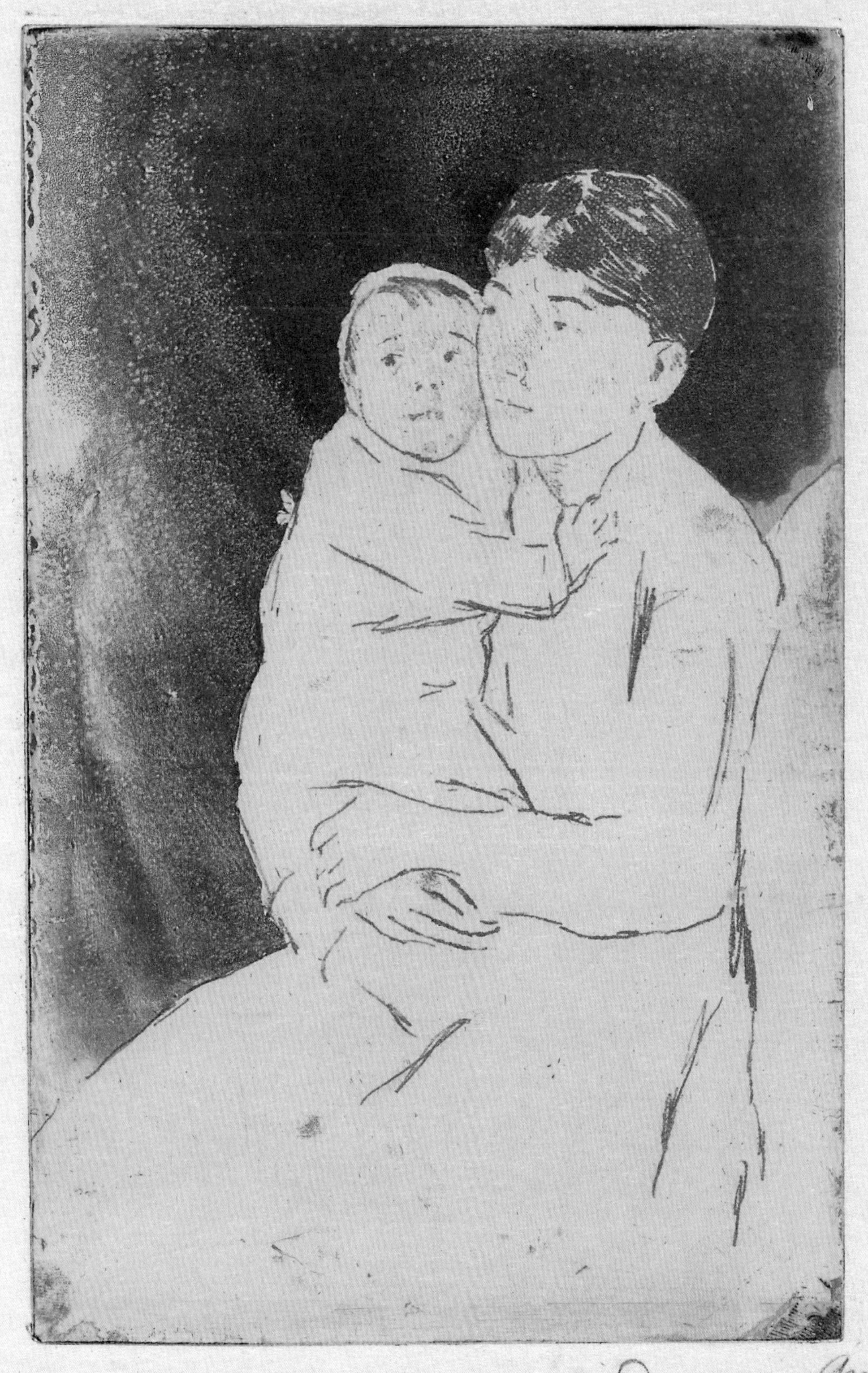
à Monsieur André Mellerio
Mary Cassatt

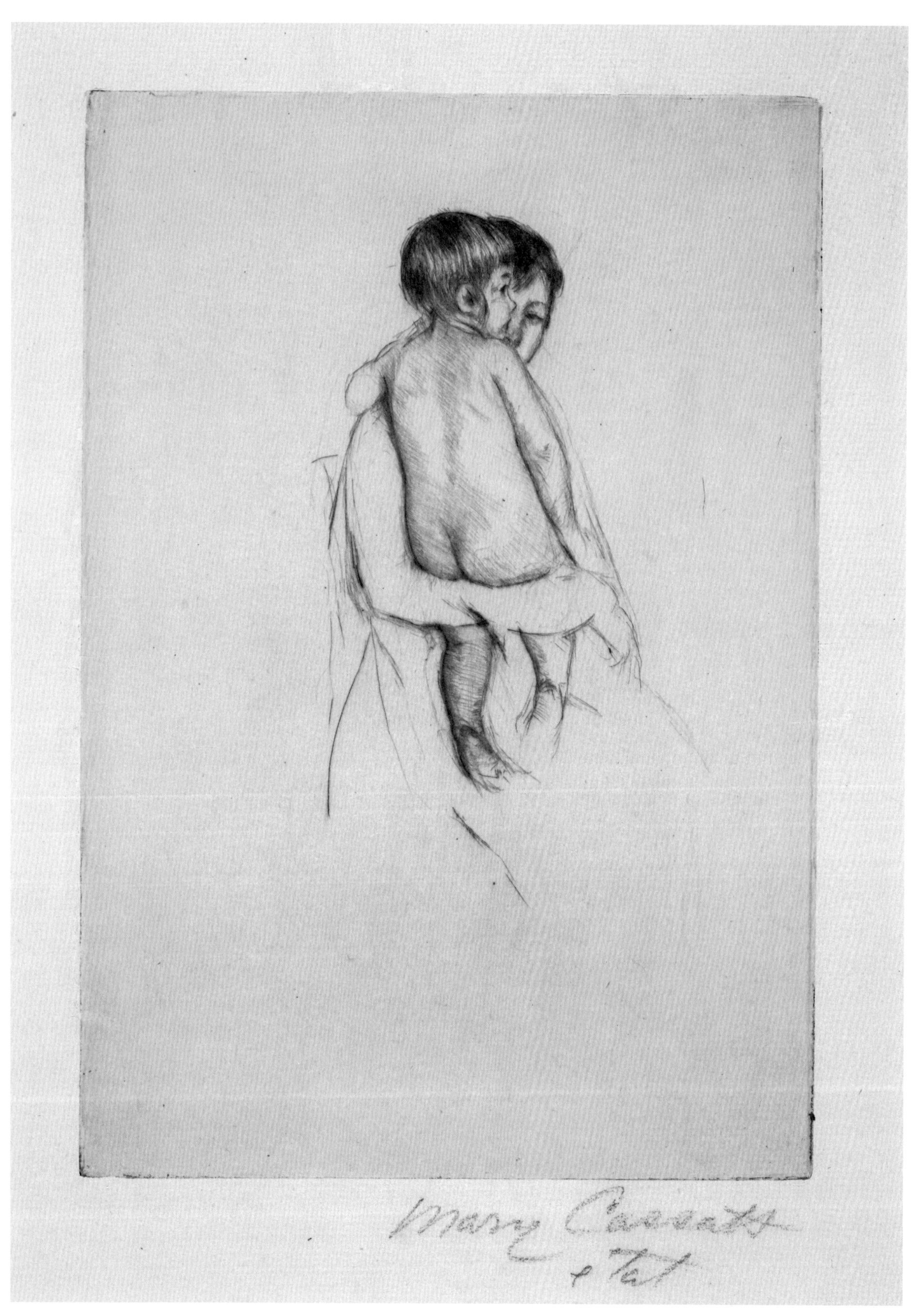

Baby's Back, 1890. Drypoint on paper. Second state (of three).
$9\frac{3}{16}$ x $6\frac{7}{16}$ in. (23.3 x 16.4 cm). The Lunder Collection, 2012.314

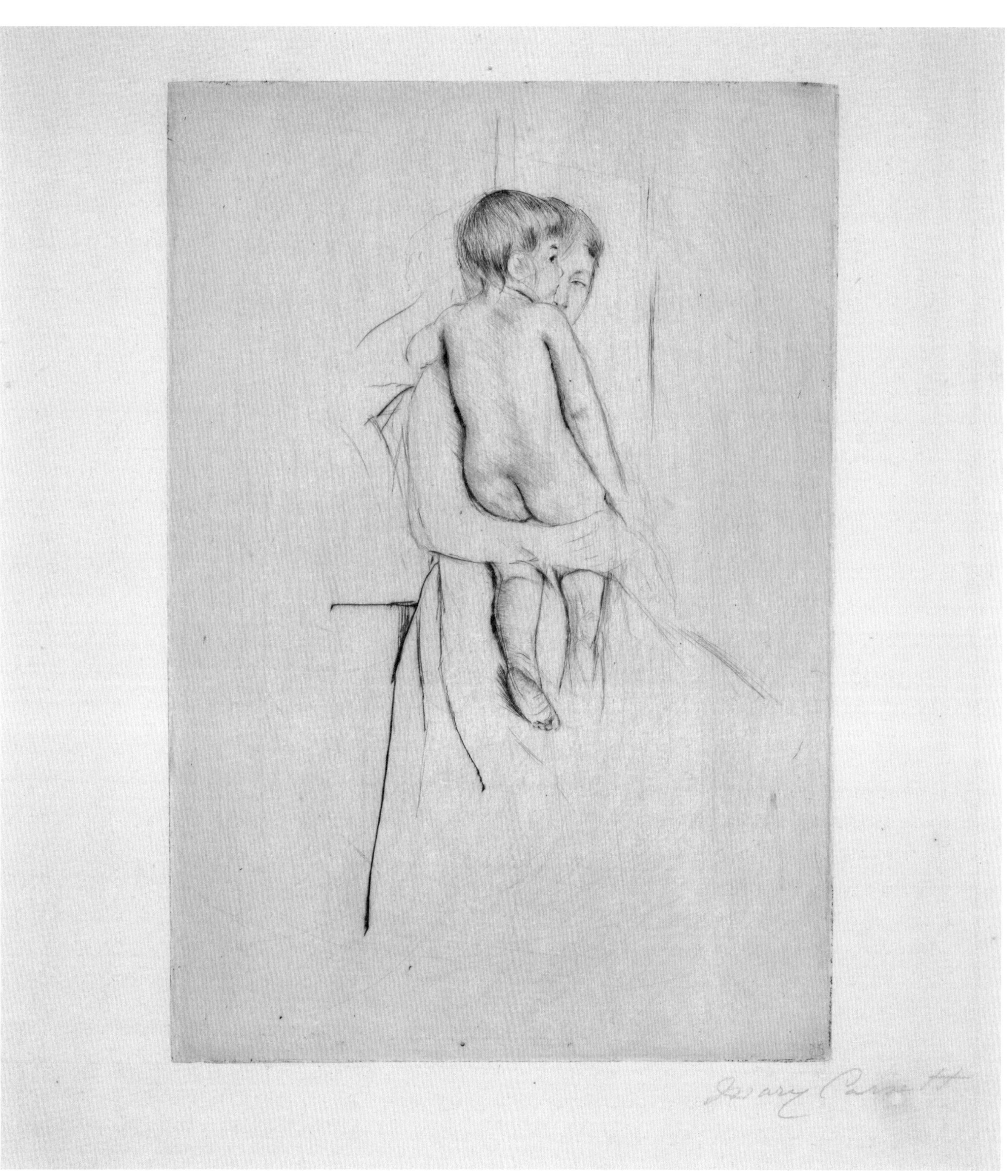

Baby's Back, 1890. Drypoint and softground etching on paper. Third (final) state.
9³⁄₁₆ x 6⁷⁄₁₆ in. (23.3 x 16.4 cm). The Lunder Collection, 2012.315

The Map, 1890. Drypoint on paper. Trial proof of third (final) state.
6⅛ x 9⅛ in. (15.6 x 23.2 cm). The Lunder Collection, 2012.313

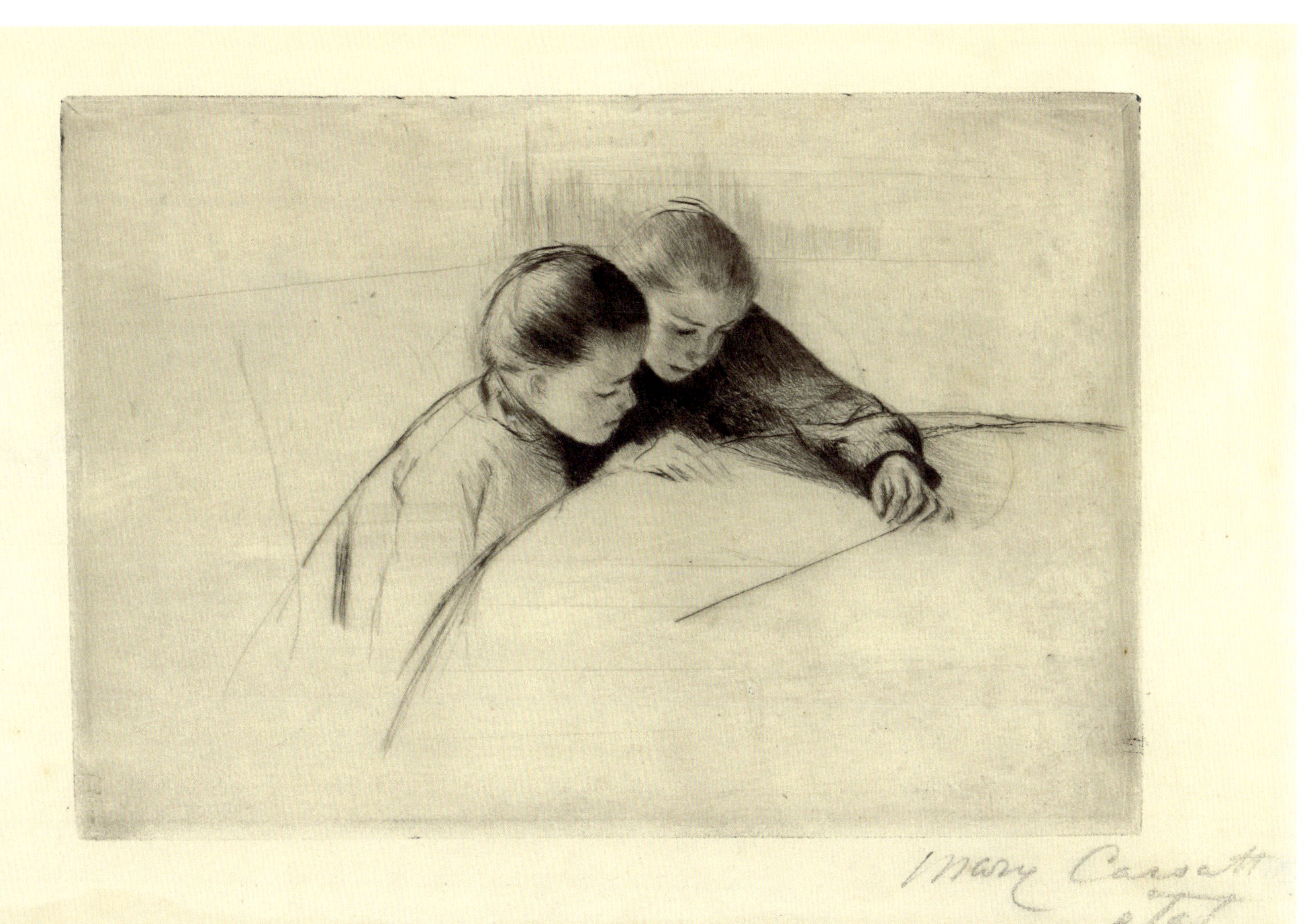
Mary Cassatt

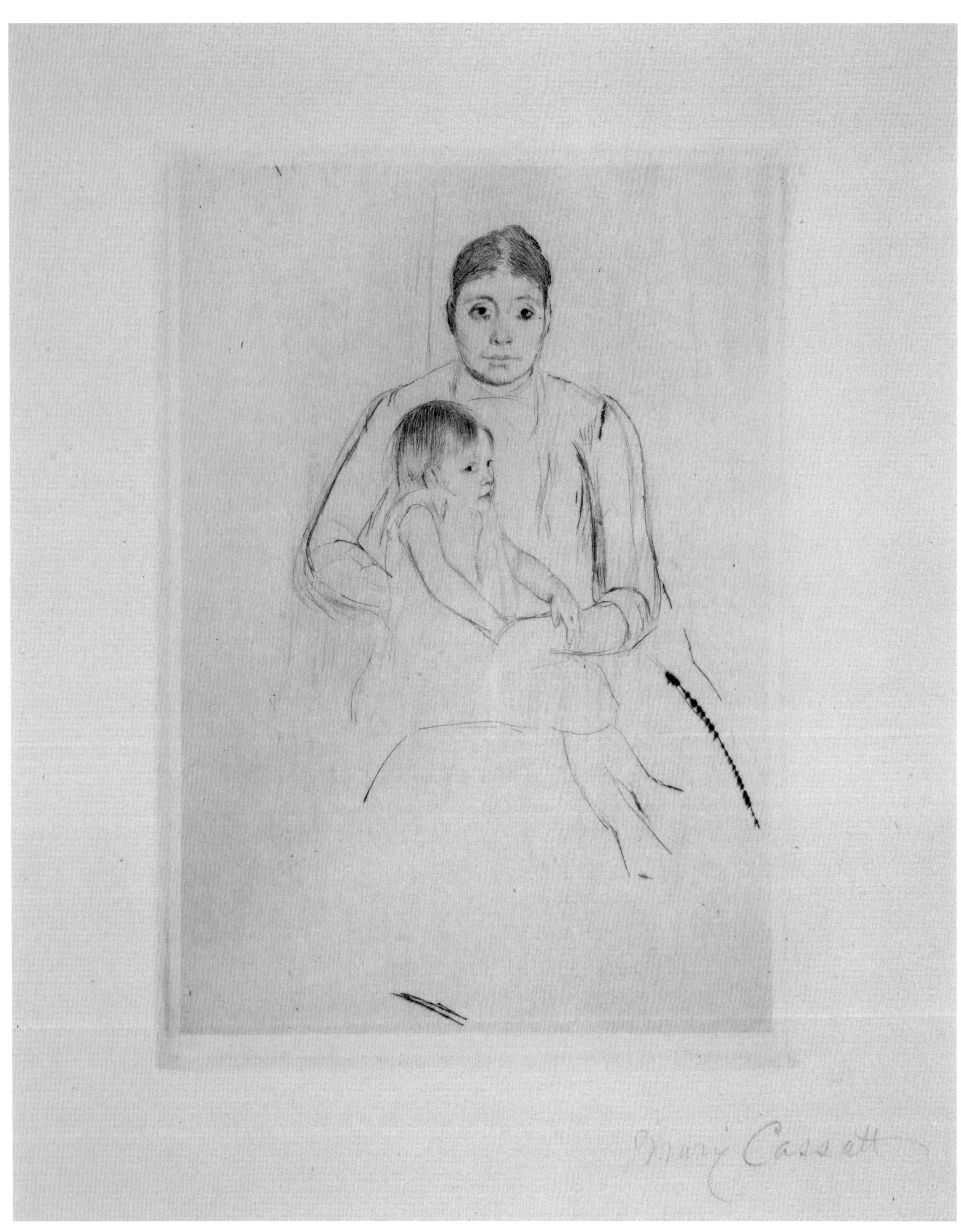

Repose, c. 1890. Drypoint on paper. Second state (of five). 9¼ x 6⁹⁄₁₆ in. (23.5 x 16.7 cm). The Lunder Collection, 2012.318

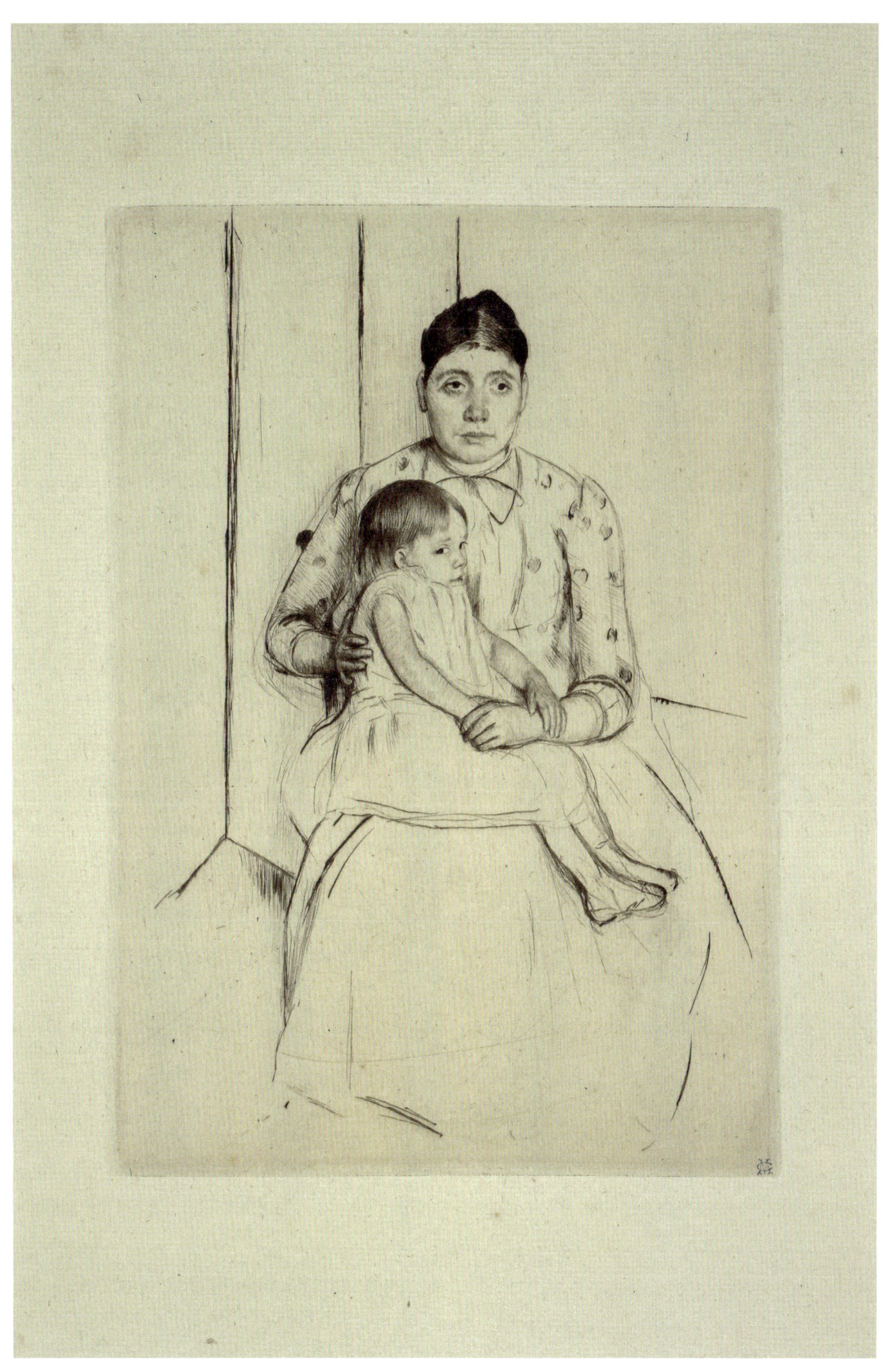

Repose, c. 1890. Drypoint on paper. Fifth (final) state. 9¼ x 6⁹⁄₁₆ in. (23.5 x 16.7 cm). The Lunder Collection, 2012.319

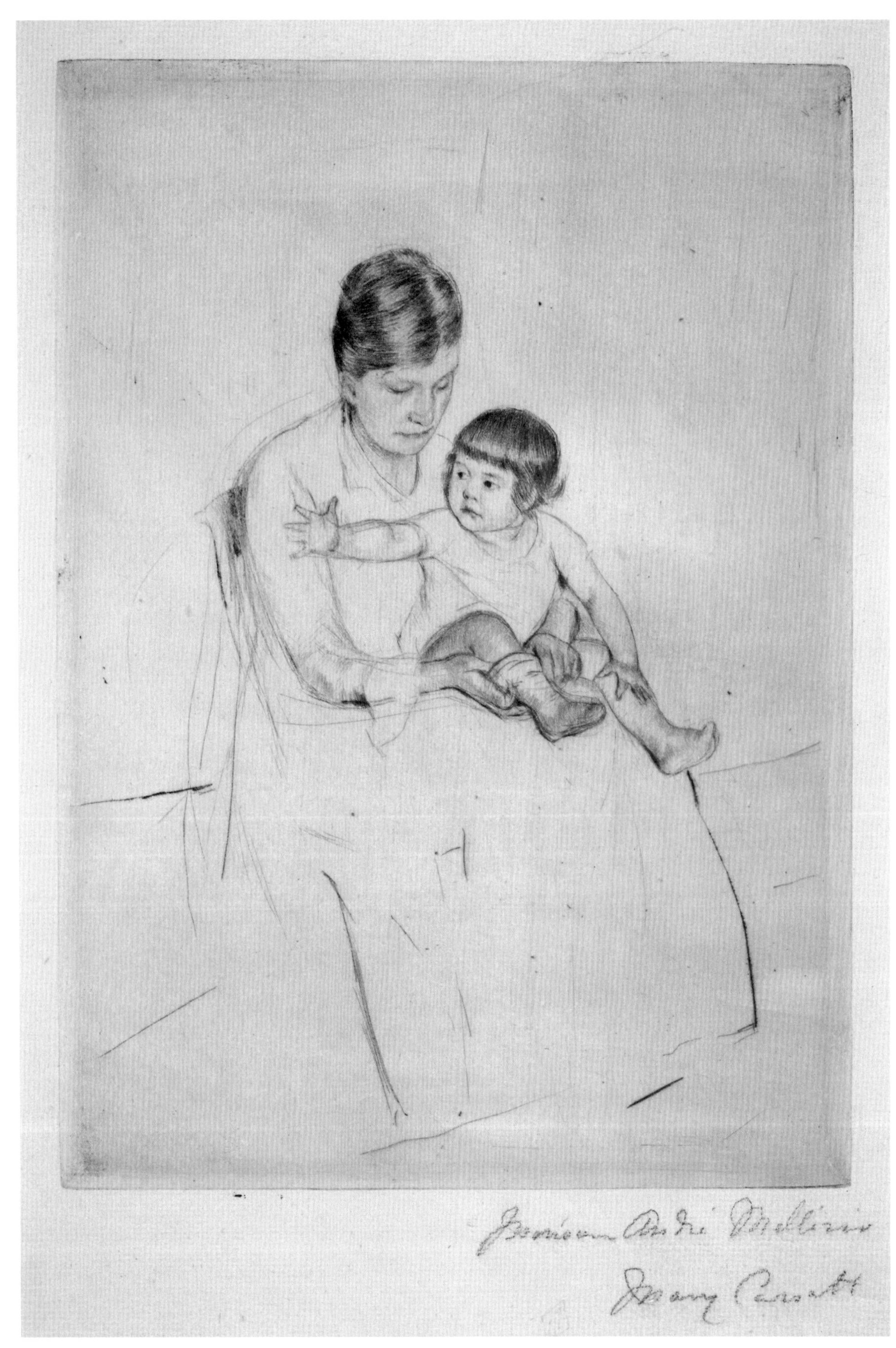

The Stocking, 1890. Drypoint on paper. Fifth state (of six). 10 3/16 x 7 5/16 in. (25.9 cm x 18.6 cm). The Lunder Collection, 2012.316

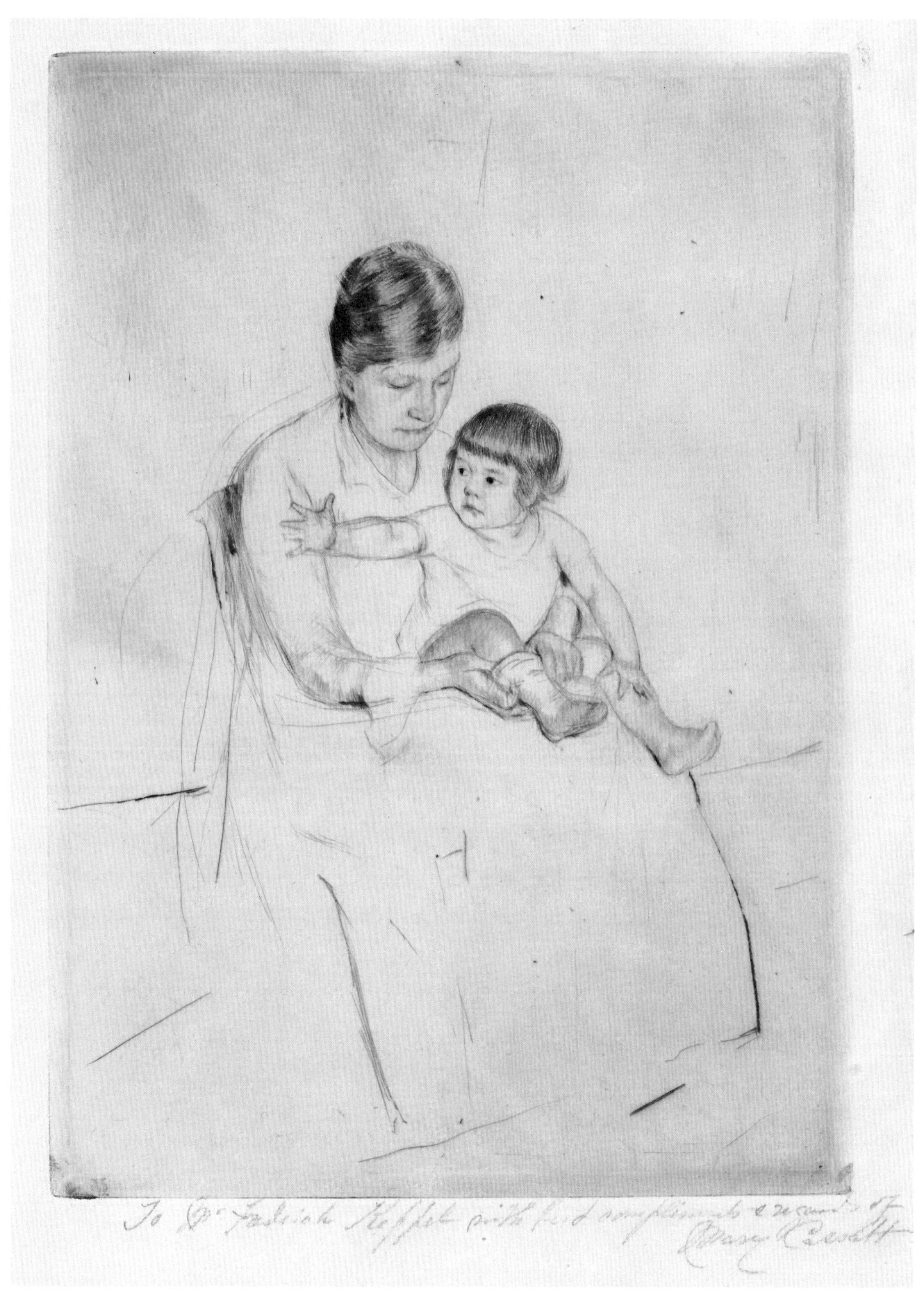

The Stocking, 1890. Drypoint on paper. Fifth state (of six). 10 3/16 x 7 3/8 in. (25.9 x 18.7 cm). The Lunder Collection, 2013.037

Tea, c. 1890. Drypoint on paper. Fifth (final) state. 7⅛ x 6⅛ in. (18.1 x 15.6 cm). The Lunder Collection, 2012.320

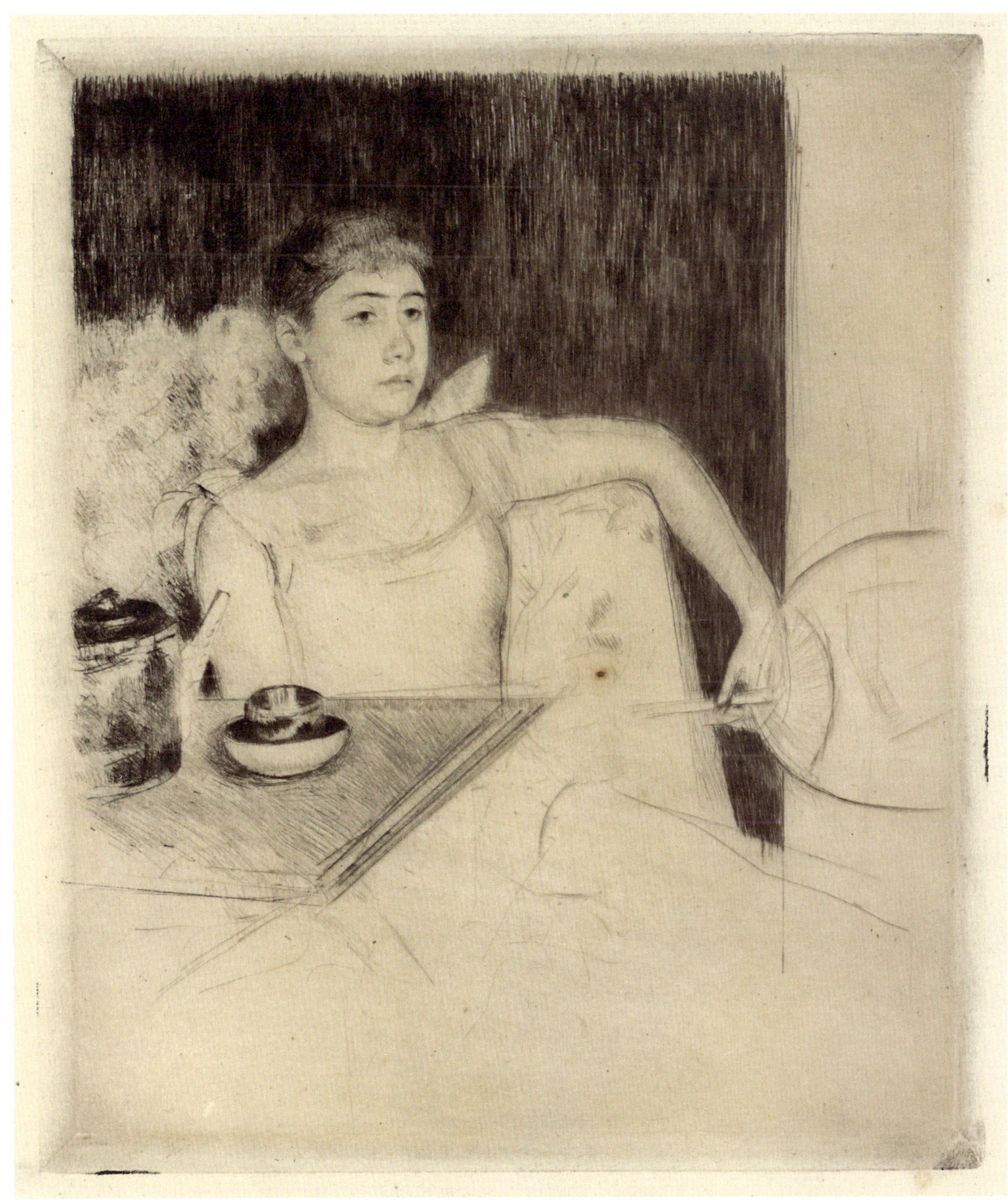

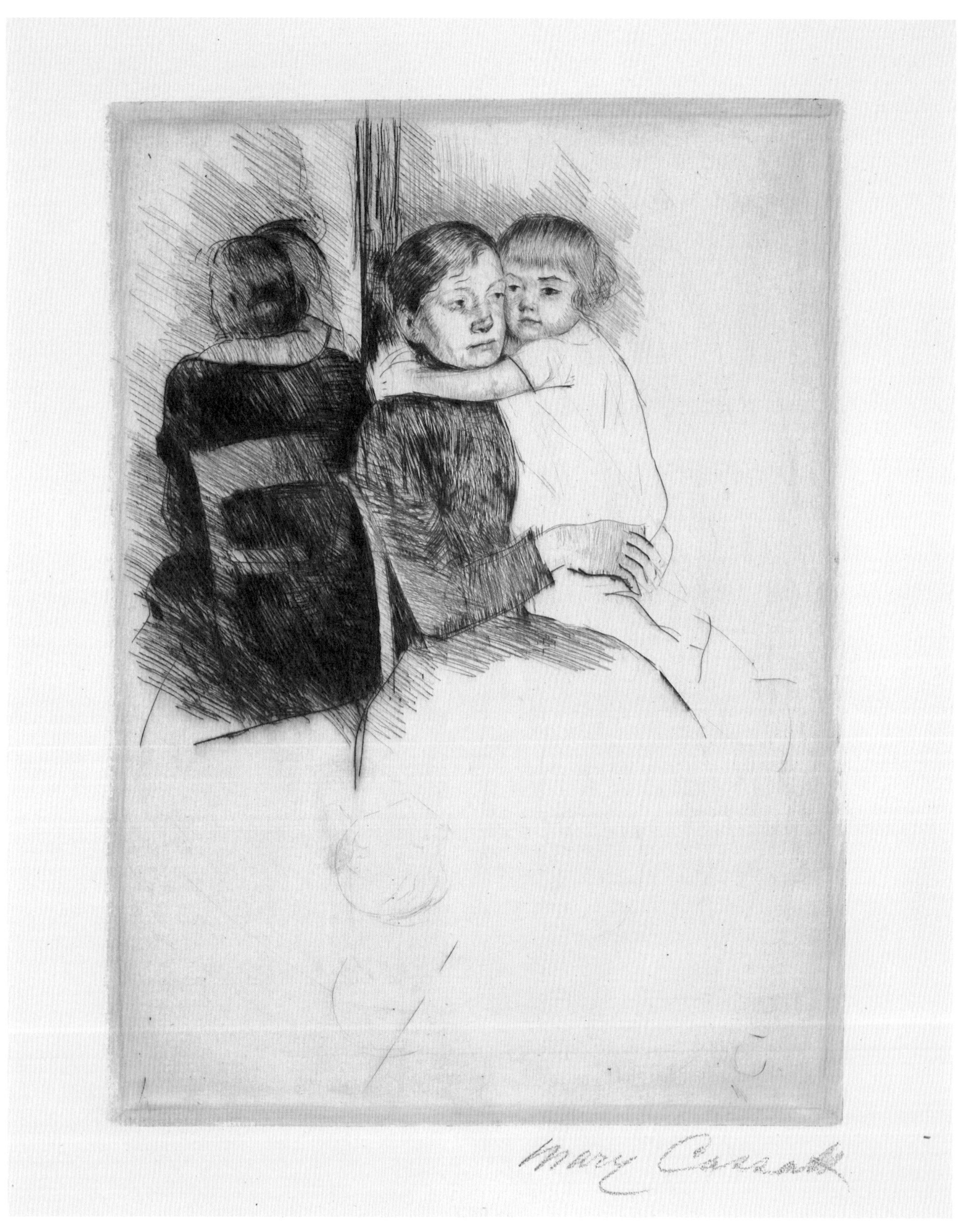

The Mirror, c. 1891. Drypoint on paper. Third state (of seven). $8^{15}/_{16}$ x $6^{11}/_{16}$ in. (22.7 x 17 cm). The Lunder Collection, 2012.321

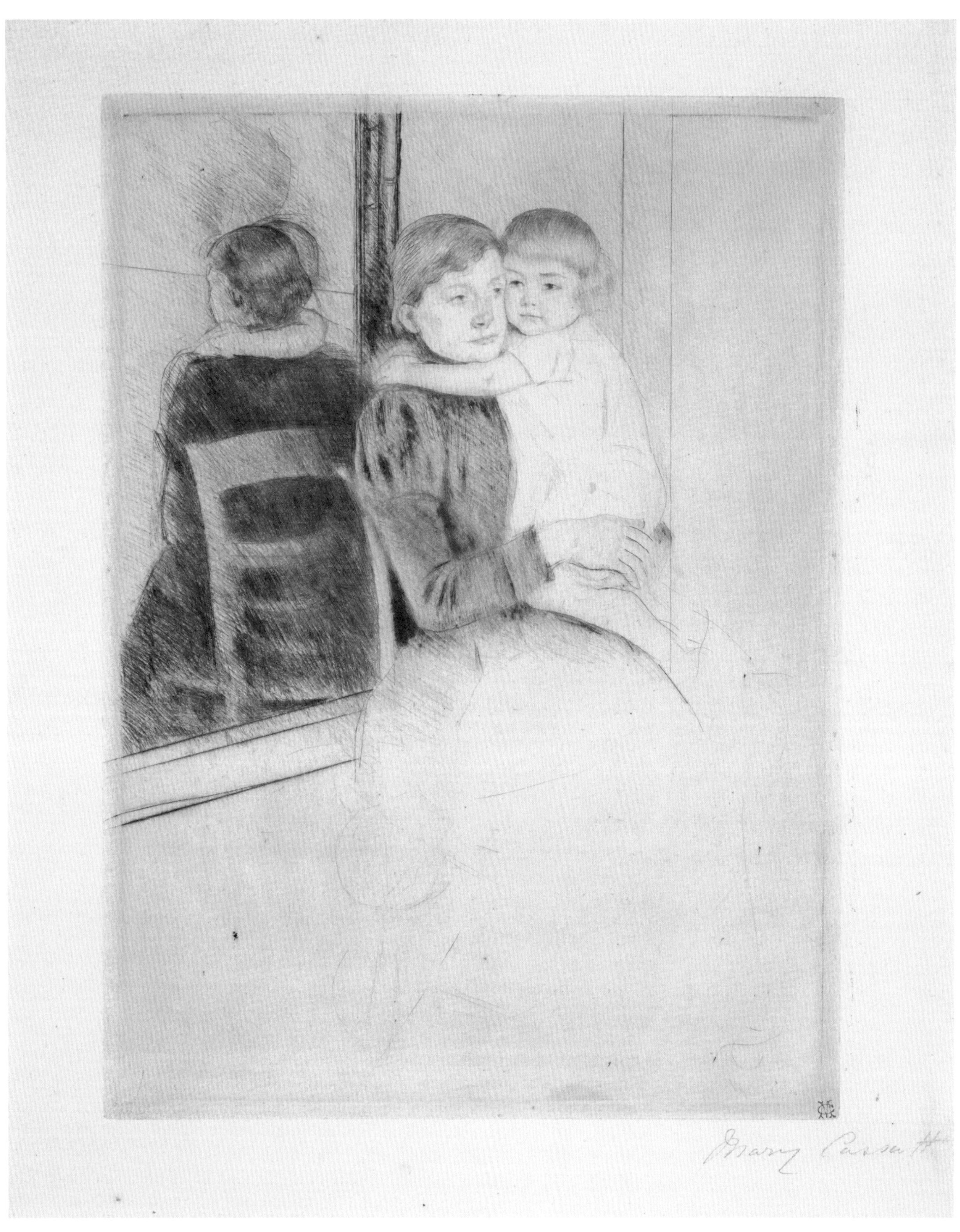

The Mirror, c. 1891. Drypoint on paper. Sixth state (of seven). $8\frac{7}{8}$ x $6\frac{11}{16}$ in. (22.5 x 17 cm). The Lunder Collection, 2012.322

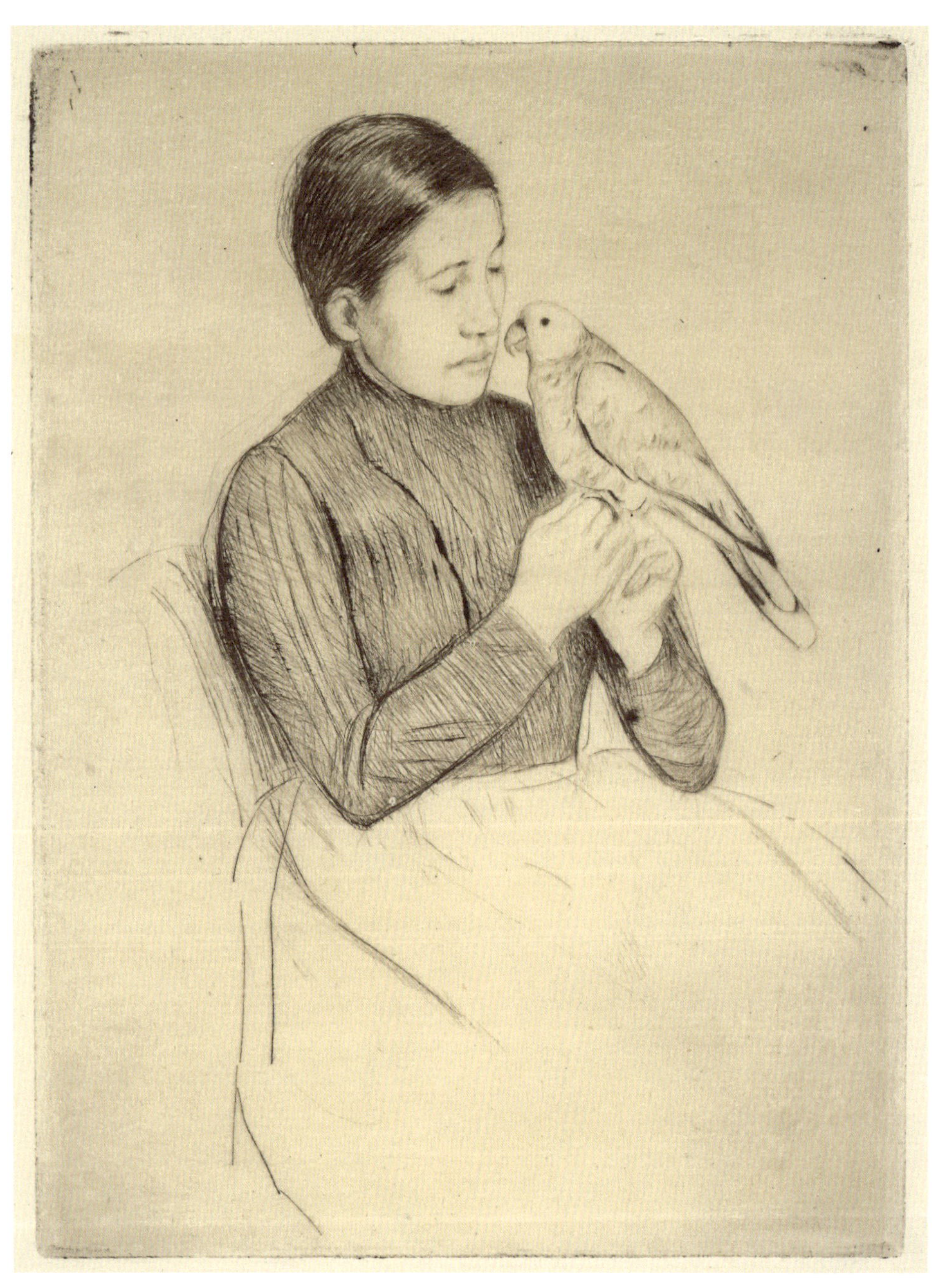

The Parrot, c. 1891. Drypoint on paper. Fifth state (of seven). 6⅜ x 4¾ in. (16.2 x 12.1 cm). The Lunder Collection, 2012.323

The Banjo Lesson, c. 1891–93. Drypoint on paper. Second state (of four). 15⅜ x 10⅛ in. (39.1 x 25.7 cm). The Lunder Collection, 2012.326

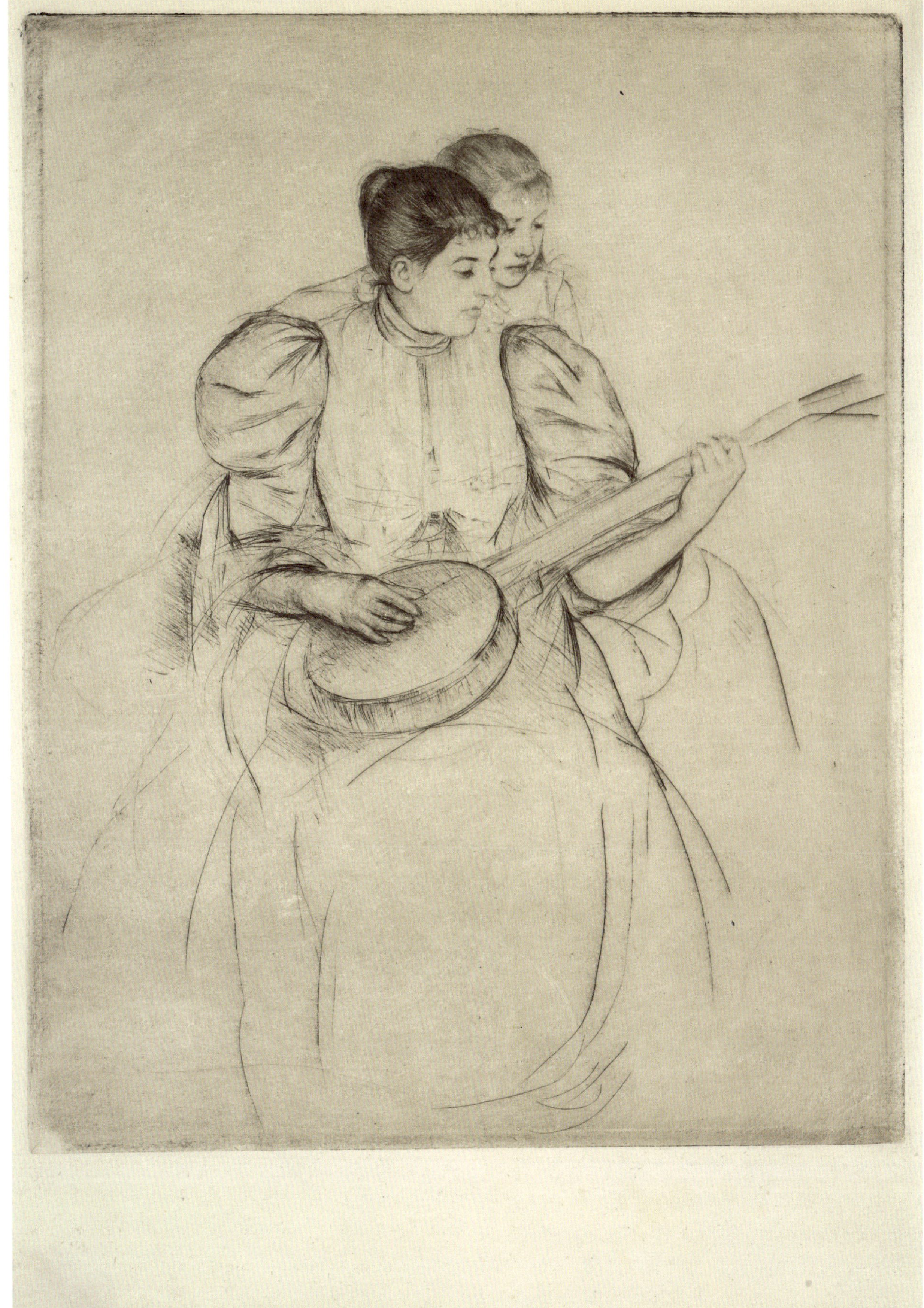
Mary Cassatt

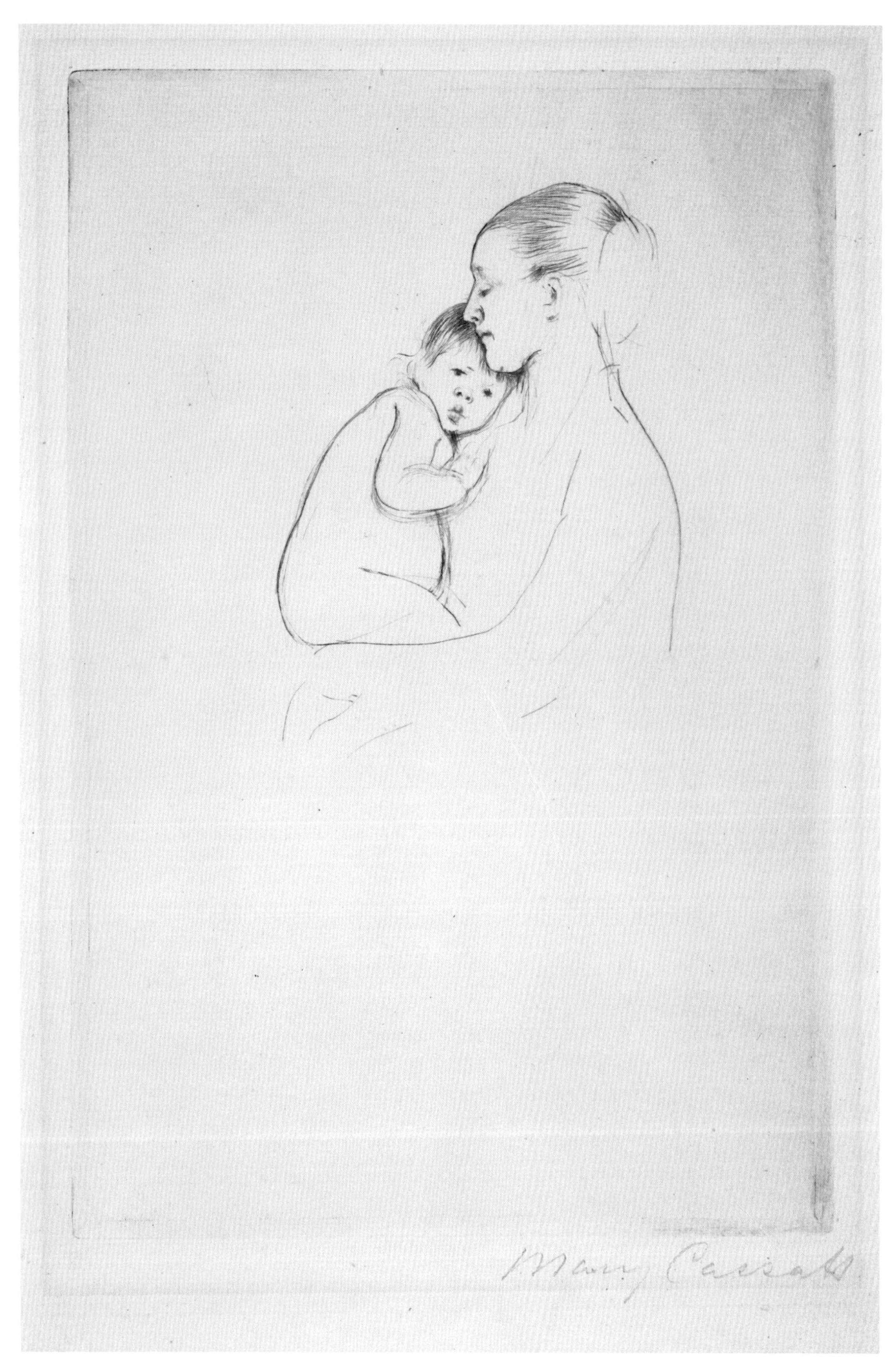

Quietude, 1891. Drypoint on paper. Second state (of five). 10¼ x 6⅞ in. (26 x 17.5 cm). The Lunder Collection, 2012.324

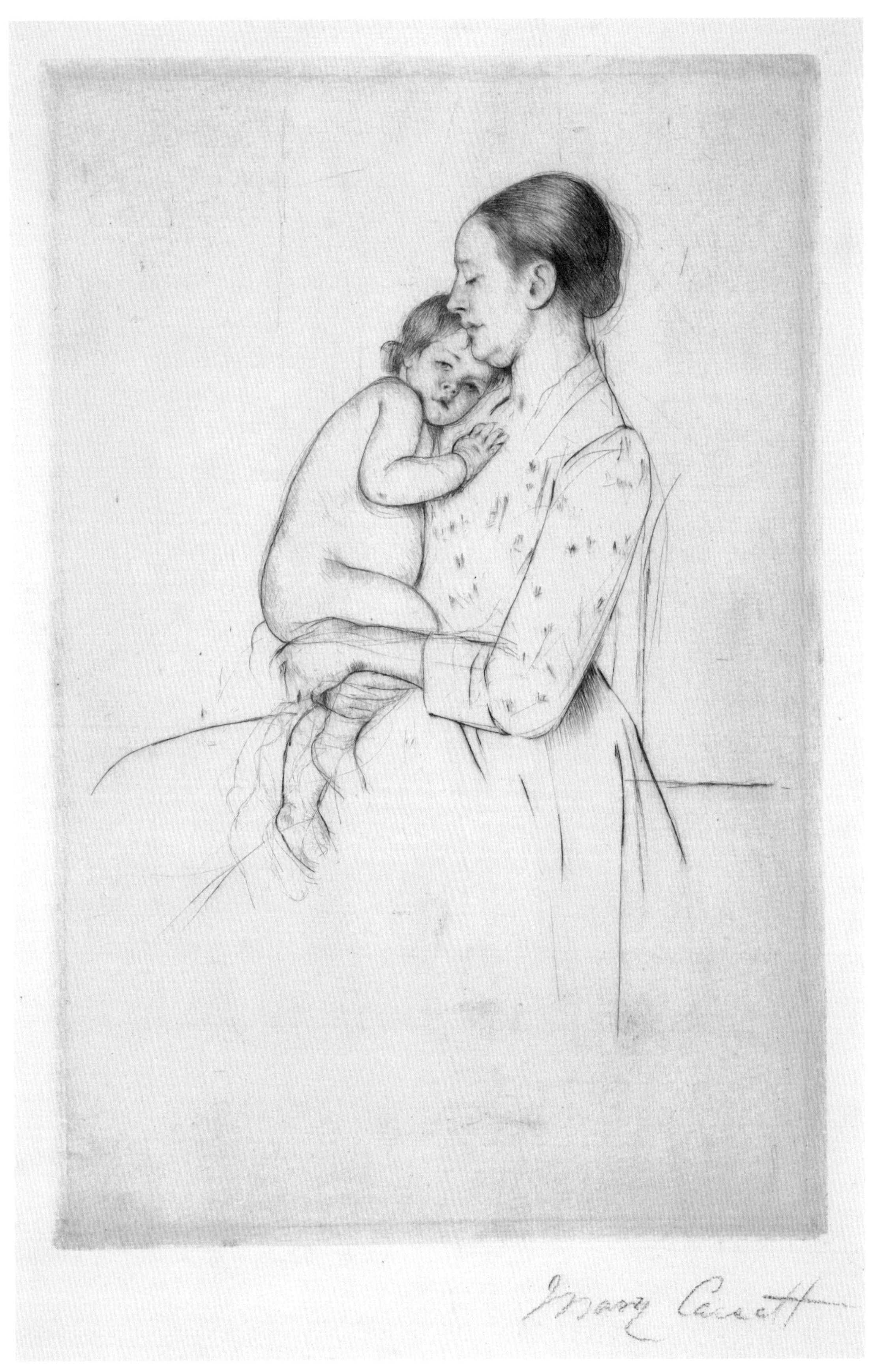

Quietude, 1891. Drypoint on paper. Fifth (final) state. 10¼ x 6⅞ in. (26 x 17.5 cm). The Lunder Collection, 2012.325

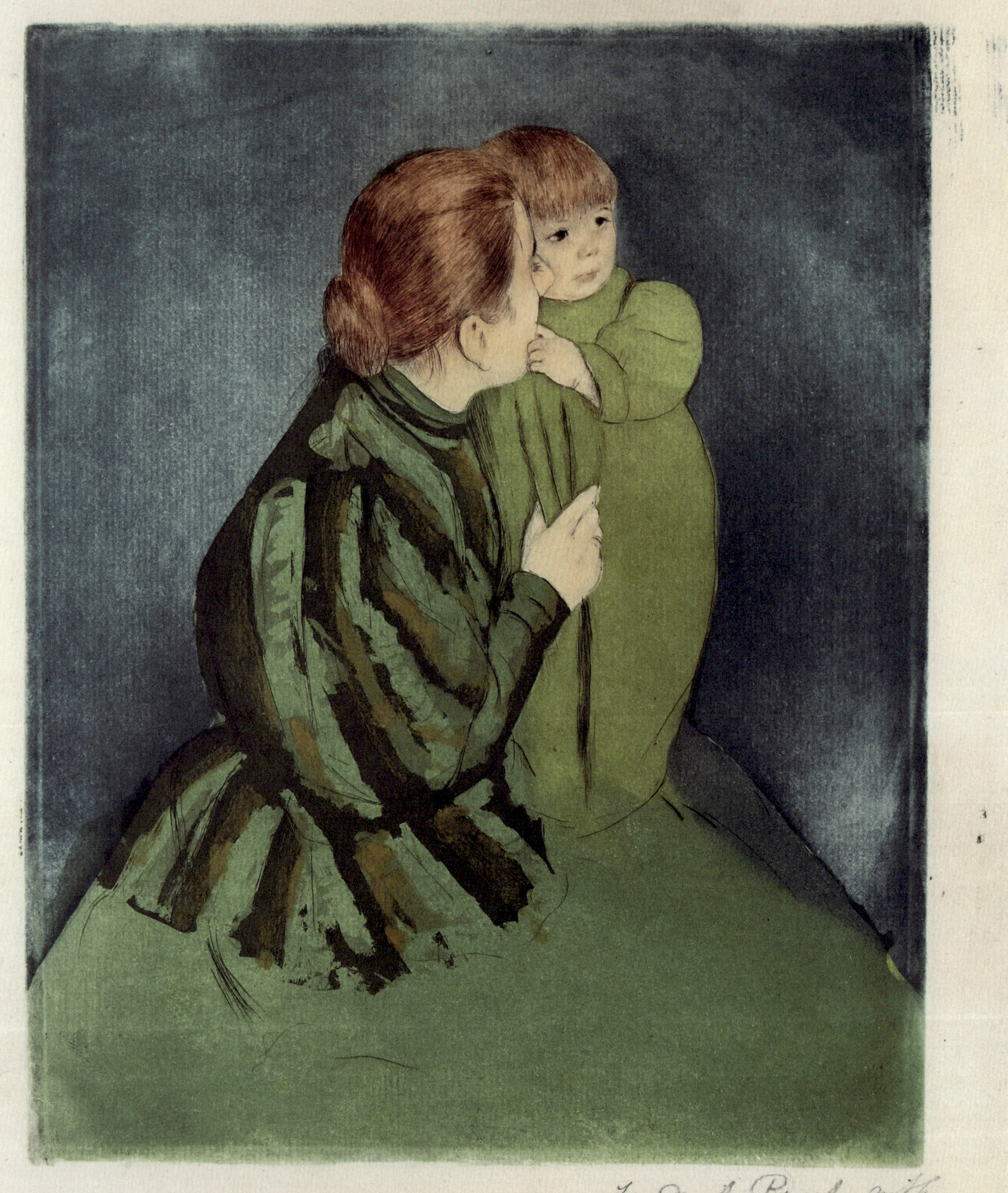
To Miss Paget with
sincerest regards
Mary Cassatt

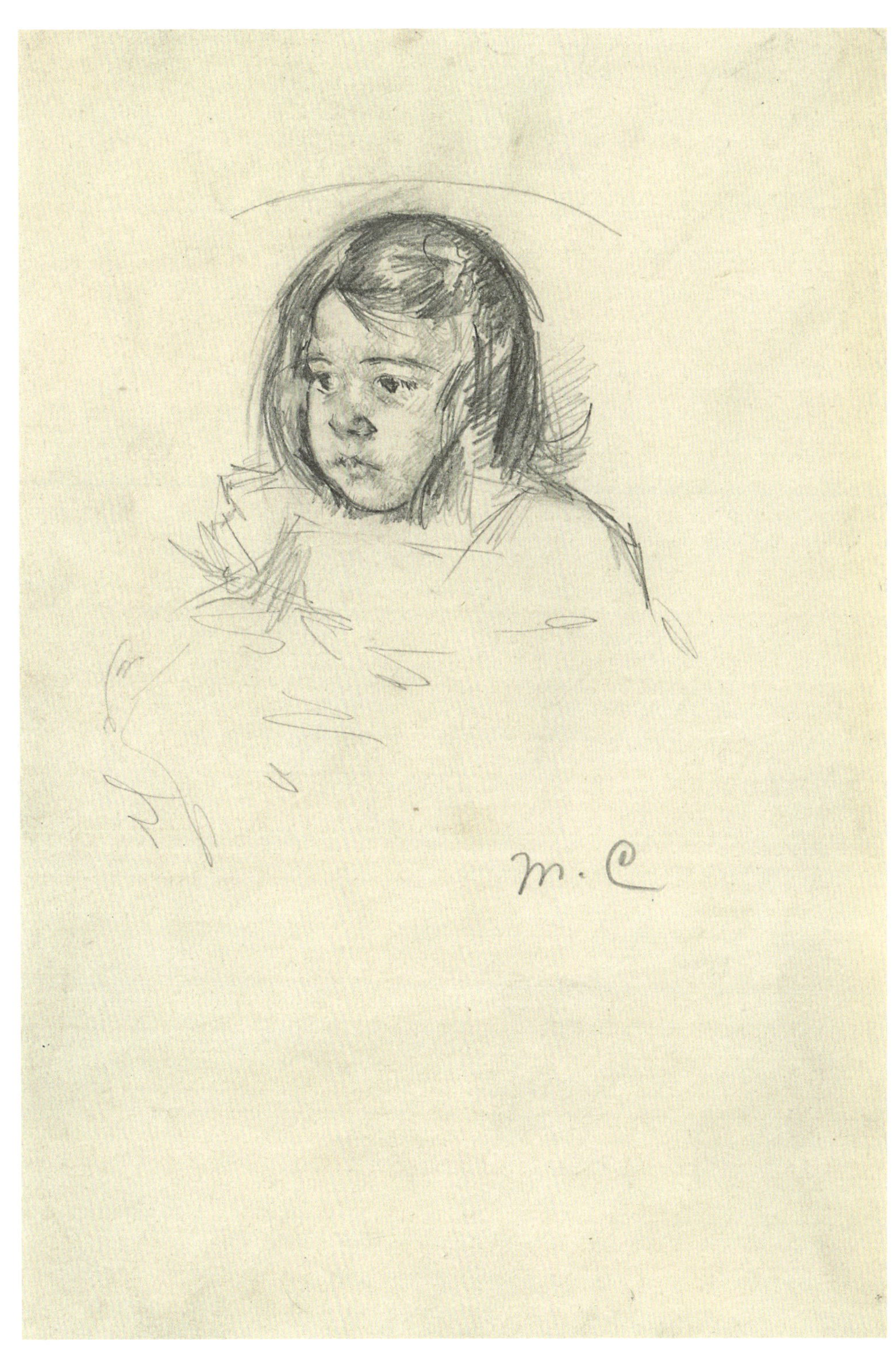

Peasant Mother and Child, c. 1894. Drypoint and aquatint on paper. Tenth (final) state. 17¼ x 11¼ in. (43.8 x 28.6 cm). The Lunder Collection, 2017.468

Sketch for Sara Smiling (No. 2), 1903–4. Pencil on paper. 11⅞ x 9⅜ in. (30.2 x 23.8 cm). The Lunder Collection, 2013.036

Mother Berthe Holding Her Nude Baby, 1898–99. Pastel on paper. 22½ x 17¼ in. (57.2 x 43.8 cm). Gift of Alan B. Mirken '51 and Family in honor of Peter and Paula Lunder, 2013.549

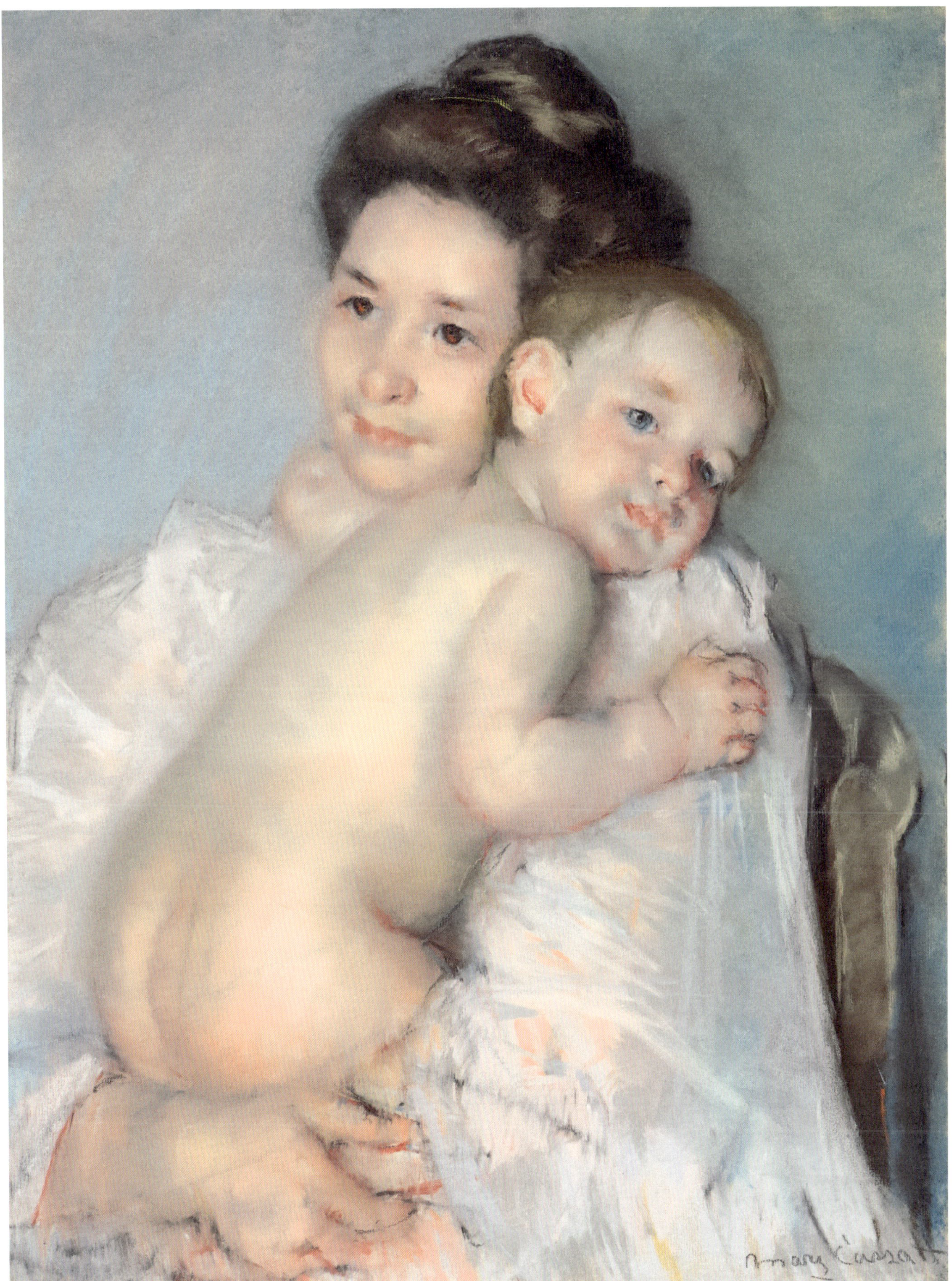
Mary Cassatt

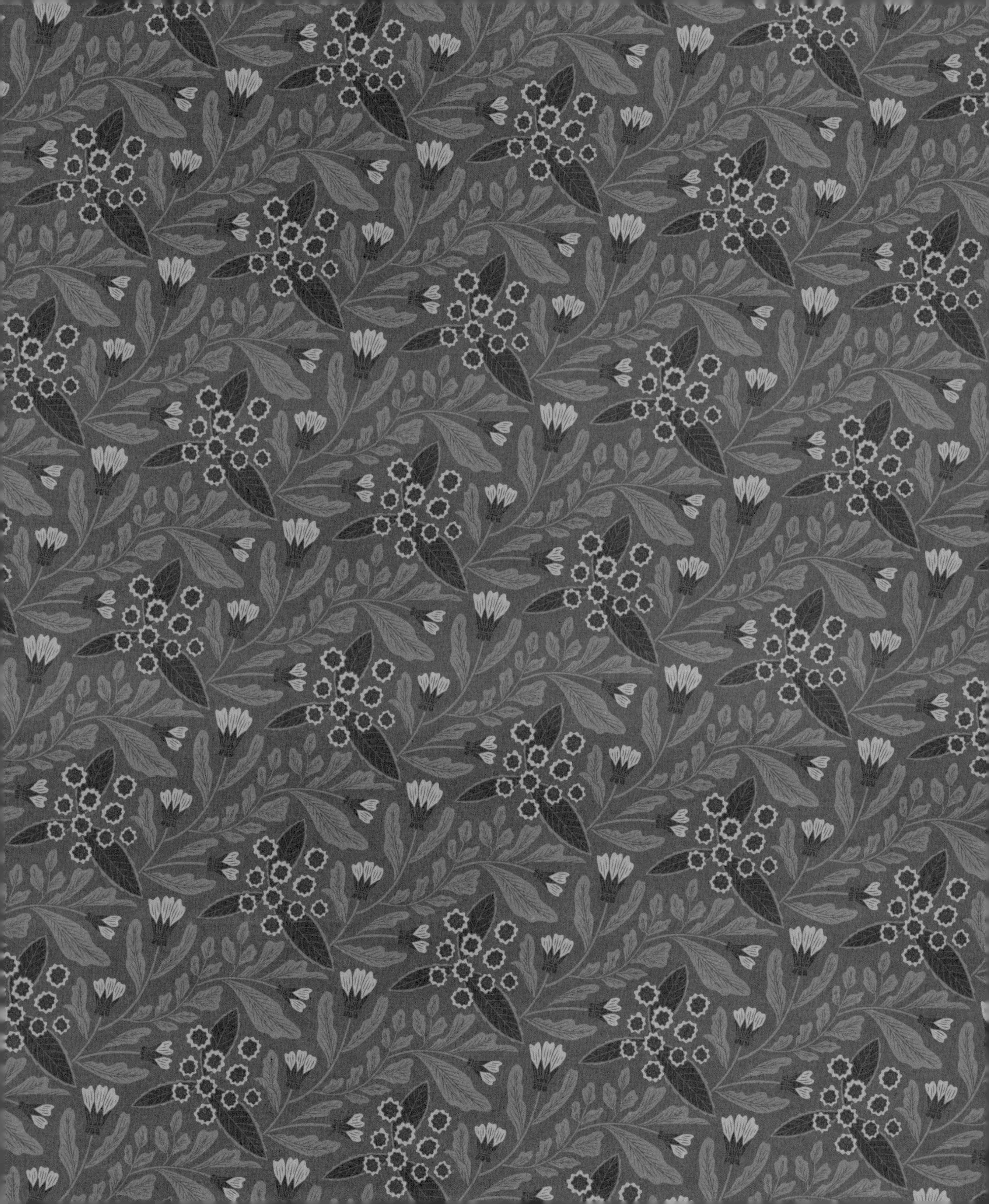

Works in the Exhibition

All works by Mary Cassatt are in the collection of the Colby College Museum of Art unless otherwise noted.

Pensive Roman Girl, c. 1872. Oil on canvas. 18¼ x 15 in. (46.4 x 38.1 cm). The Lunder Collection, 2013.038

At the Dressing Table, c. 1879. Softground etching, aquatint, and etching on paper. Trial proof of third state (of four). 6¼ x 8¼ in. (15.9 x 21 cm). The Lunder Collection, 2012.285

The Corner of the Sofa (No. 2), c. 1879. Softground etching on paper. Second state (of three). 8⅛ x 6⁷⁄₁₆ in. (20.6 x 16.4 cm). The Lunder Collection, 2012.290

Waiting, c. 1879. Softground etching and aquatint on paper. Third state (of four). 8⅝ x 5¹³⁄₁₆ in. (21.9 x 14.8 cm). The Lunder Collection, 2012.286

Woman Driving in a Victoria, c. 1879. Softground etching on paper. Third (final) state. 5¼ x 6½ in. (13.3 x 16.5 cm). The Lunder Collection, 2012.289

In the Opera Box (No. 2), 1879–80. Softground etching on paper. First state (of three). 12³⁄₁₆ x 9³⁄₁₆ in. (31 x 23.3 cm). The Lunder Collection, 2012.292

In the Opera Box (No. 2), 1879–80. Softground etching and aquatint on paper. Second state (of three). 12³⁄₁₆ x 9⁵⁄₁₆ in. (31 x 23.7 cm). The Lunder Collection, 003.2010

In the Opera Box (No. 3), 1879–80. Softground etching, aquatint, and etching on paper. Fourth (final) state. 14¹⁄₁₆ x 10⅝ in. (35.7 x 27 cm). The Lunder Collection, 2012.294

In the Opera Box (No. 3), 1879–80. Softground etching and aquatint on paper. Trial proof of fourth (final) state. 3⅜ x 7⅜ in. (8.6 x 18.7 cm). The Lunder Collection, 2012.293

The Bouquet, c. 1880. Softground etching and aquatint on paper. First state (of three). 9⁹⁄₁₆ x 6½ in. (24.3 x 16.5 cm). The Lunder Collection, 2012.291

Mrs. Cassatt Reading to Her Grandchildren (No. 1), c. 1880. Softground etching on paper. First state (of three). 6⅛ x 11¾ in. (15.6 x 29.9 cm). The Lunder Collection, 2012.302

The Visitor, c. 1880. Softground etching, aquatint, etching, drypoint, burnishing, and fabric texture on paper. Second state (of six). 15½ x 12³⁄₁₆ in. (39.4 x 31 cm). The Lunder Collection, 2012.297

Warming His Hands, c. 1880. Softground etching on paper. Only known state. 6⁵⁄₁₆ x 4⁹⁄₁₆ in. (16 x 11.6 cm). The Lunder Collection, 2012.295

Lydia at Afternoon Tea, 1880–82. Softground etching and aquatint on paper. Trial proof of third state (of five). 5½ x 8¹³⁄₁₆ in. (14 x 22.4 cm). The Lunder Collection, 2012.306

Knitting in the Library, c. 1881. Softground etching and aquatint on paper. Second state (of three). 10⅞ x 8⁹⁄₁₆ in. (27.6 x 21.8 cm). The Lunder Collection, 2012.296

Lydia Reading, Turned Toward Right, c. 1881. Softground etching and aquatint on paper. Second (final) state. 7¹⁄₁₆ x 4⅜ in. (17.9 x 11.1 cm). The Lunder Collection, 2012.304

Profile of Mrs. Cassatt Reading, with Glasses, c. 1881. Pencil on paper. 8¼ x 5¼ in. (21 x 13.3 cm). The Lunder Collection, 2013.035

Before the Fireplace (No. 2), c. 1882. Softground etching and aquatint on paper. Only known state. 6⁵⁄₁₆ x 8⅝ in. (16 x 21.9 cm). The Lunder Collection, 2012.305

Reading the Newspaper (No. 1), c. 1882. Softground etching with fabric texture on paper. First state (of two). 5½ x 8¾ in. (14 x 22.2 cm). The Lunder Collection, 002.2010

Mr. Gardner Cassatt Reading the Paper, c. 1883. Etching and drypoint on paper. Only known state. 10⅞ x 6⅞ in. (27.6 x 17.5 cm). The Lunder Collection, 2012.307

Sketch of the Black and Green Bonnet, c. 1883. Drypoint on paper. Trial proof of only known state. 3¹³⁄₁₆ x 2⁵⁄₁₆ in. (9.7 x 5.9 cm). The Lunder Collection, 2012.299

Pattern design by Frances MacLeod, 2020

Susan Looking Down at Her Hands, c. 1883. Drypoint on paper. Only known state. 8¾ x 5½ in. (22.2 x 14 cm). The Lunder Collection, 2012.301

Emmie and Her Child, c. 1889. Softground etching, aquatint, and drypoint on paper. Only known state. 8⅜ x 6⅛ in. (21.3 x 15.6 cm). The Lunder Collection, 2012.309

Nurse and Baby Bill (No. 1), c. 1889. Softground etching, aquatint, and netting texture on paper. Intermediate state between first and second state (of four). 7⅜ x 5⁵⁄₁₆ in. (18.7 x 13.5 cm). The Lunder Collection, 2012.311

Nurse and Baby Bill (No. 2), c. 1889. Softground etching in sepia on paper. Second (final) state. 8⁹⁄₁₆ x 5⁷⁄₁₆ in. (21.8 x 13.8 cm). The Lunder Collection, 2012.282

Solicitude, c. 1889. Drypoint on paper. Fourth (final) state. 7⅜ x 5¹³⁄₁₆ in. (18.7 x 14.8 cm). The Lunder Collection, 2012.308

Baby's Back, 1890. Drypoint on paper. Second state (of three). 9³⁄₁₆ x 6⁷⁄₁₆ in. (23.3 x 16.4 cm). The Lunder Collection, 2012.314

Baby's Back, 1890. Drypoint and softground etching on paper. Third (final) state. 9³⁄₁₆ x 6⁷⁄₁₆ in. (23.3 x 16.4 cm). The Lunder Collection, 2012.315

The Map, 1890. Drypoint on paper. Trial proof of third (final) state. 6⅛ x 9⅛ in. (15.6 x 23.2 cm). The Lunder Collection, 2012.313

The Stocking, 1890. Drypoint on paper. Fifth state (of six). 10³⁄₁₆ x 7⁵⁄₁₆ in. (25.9 cm x 18.6 cm). The Lunder Collection, 2012.316

Repose, c. 1890. Drypoint on paper. Fifth (final) state. 9¼ x 6⁹⁄₁₆ in. (23.5 x 16.7 cm). The Lunder Collection, 2012.319

Tea, c. 1890. Drypoint on paper. Fifth (final) state. 7⅛ x 6⅛ in. (18.1 x 15.6 cm). The Lunder Collection, 2012.320

Quietude, 1891. Drypoint on paper. Fifth (final) state. 10¼ x 6⅞ in. (26 x 17.5 cm). The Lunder Collection, 2012.325

The Mirror, c. 1891. Drypoint on paper. Sixth state (of seven). 8⅞ x 6¹¹⁄₁₆ in. (22.5 x 17 cm). The Lunder Collection, 2012.322

The Banjo Lesson, c. 1891–93. Drypoint on paper. Proof of second state (of four). 15⅜ x 10⅛ in. (39.1 x 25.7 cm). The Lunder Collection, 2012.326

Peasant Mother and Child, c. 1894. Drypoint and aquatint on paper. Tenth (final) state. 17¼ x 11¼ in. (43.8 x 28.6 cm). The Lunder Collection, 2017.468

Anne and Her Nurse, c. 1897. Oil on canvas. 27½ x 23½ in. (69.9 x 59.7 cm). Portland Museum of Art, Maine, gift of Elizabeth B. Noyce in honor of Roger and Katherine Woodman, 1966.12

Mother Berthe Holding Her Nude Baby, 1898–99. Pastel on paper. 22½ x 17¼ in. (57.2 x 43.8 cm). Gift of Alan B. Mirken '51 and Family in honor of Peter and Paula Lunder, 2013.549

Meditation, 1906. Oil on canvas. 26½ x 22½ in. (67.3 x 57.2 cm). Gift of Thomas J. Watson, Jr., 1972.002

Cecilia Beaux, *Ethel Page as Undine*, 1885. Oil on canvas. 39 x 31 in. (99 x 79 cm). The Lunder Collection, 2019.433

Julia Margaret Cameron, *Heaven (Mary Hillier with Freddy Gould and Elizabeth Keown)*, 1864. Albumen print from wet collodion negative. 9½ x 7½ in. (24.1 x 19.1 cm). Museum purchase from the A. A. D'Amico Art Collection Fund, 2014.060

James McNeill Whistler, *The Duet*, 1894. Lithograph on paper. 10⅛ x 9 in. (25.7 x 22.9 cm). The Lunder Collection, 2013.448

James McNeill Whistler, *The Sisters*, 1894–95. Lithograph on paper. 8¾ x 11¼ in. (22.2 x 28.6 cm). The Lunder Collection, 2013.479

James McNeill Whistler, *Afternoon Tea*, 1897. Lithograph on paper. 15⅞ x 9¾ in. (40.32 x 24.8 cm). The Lunder Collection, 2013.311

After Kitagawa Utamaro I, *Mother Nursing Child Before Mirror*, 1797. Color woodblock print. 15 x 9¾ in. (38.1 x 24.8 cm). Gift of Charles Hovey Pepper, 1959.211

Contributors

Justine De Young is chairperson of and assistant professor in the history of art department at the Fashion Institute of Technology (SUNY), where she specializes in the intersection of art and fashion. She is the editor of *Fashion in European Art: Dress and Identity, Politics and the Body, 1775–1925* (Bloomsbury, 2019). Her work has been generously supported by grants and fellowships from the Metropolitan Museum of Art, Getty, and The Kress and Mellon Foundations. De Young previously taught art and fashion history at Harvard, Wellesley, and Lesley University. She has published many essays, notably contributing to the exhibition catalogues for *Impressionism, Fashion & Modernity* (2012–13) and *Tissot: Fashion & Faith* (2019–20). She is currently completing a book on fashion and feminine types in art of the second half of the nineteenth century.

Daniel Harkett is an associate professor of art at Colby College. His research focuses on nineteenth-century French visual culture, addressing topics such as the afterlife of art from the French Revolution, the role of art in elite salons, and the politics of popular exhibitions. With Katie Hornstein, he coedited *Horace Vernet and the Thresholds of Nineteenth-Century Visual Culture* (Dartmouth College Press, 2017).

Shalini Le Gall is the chief curator, Susan Donnell and Harry W. Konkel Curator of European Art, and director of academic engagement at the Portland Museum of Art in Maine. Le Gall recently co-curated the exhibition *River Works: Whistler and the Industrial Thames* (2019) at the Colby College Museum of Art, and has also published articles on the British Pre-Raphaelite painter William Holman Hunt and the French photographer Charles Marville. She has also contributed to various exhibition catalogues and forums on best practices in museum education. Her research and curatorial interests include French modernist painting, American and British art of the Victorian era, nineteenth-century photography, and postcolonial and ecocritical approaches to art history. Prior to coming to Portland, Le Gall was the Linde Family Foundation Curator of Academic Programs at the Colby College Museum of Art. She received her BA from Georgetown University, and her MA and PhD in art history from Northwestern University.

Justin McCann is the Lunder Curator for Whistler Studies at the Colby College Museum of Art. In that capacity, he oversees and programs the museum's collection of over 350 works by James McNeill Whistler and assists in managing the Lunder Consortium for Whistler Studies, a collaboration between Colby, the Art Institute of Chicago, the Freer-Sackler, and the University of Glasgow. He curated the exhibition *Whistler and the World: The Lunder Collection of James McNeill Whistler* and edited the accompanying catalogue. He has delivered papers on Whistler at the Frick Collection and the Clark Art Institute, and was a member of the editorial board for the paintings catalogue raisonné for Whistler. He is currently finishing his PhD dissertation on Whistler and masculinity at Rutgers University. In addition to his work on Whistler, McCann has also curated shows on Old Master prints, John James Audubon, George Bellows, John Marin, and Pablo Picasso.

Museum Staff

Jessamine Batario, Mellon Postdoctoral Fellow for Artistic and Scholarly Engagement and Programs, Lunder Institute
Jordia Benjamin-Sands, Mirken Senior Coordinator of Programs and Audience Engagement
Kristin Bergquist, Mirken Curator of Education and Engagement
Megan Carey, Barbara Alfond Manager of Exhibitions and Publications
Elizabeth Carpenter, Manager of Registration and Collections
Lorraine DeLaney, Registrar for Exhibitions and Loans
Daisy Desrosiers, Director of Artist Programs, Lunder Institute
Paige Martha Doore, Registrar for the Permanent Collection
Anna Fan, Coordinator of Board and External Affairs
Elizabeth Finch, Lunder Curator of American Art; Interim Director, Lunder Institute
Olivia Fountain, Anne Lunder Leland Curatorial Fellow
Theaster Gates Jr., Distinguished Visiting Artist and Director of Artist Initiatives, Lunder Institute
Julianne Gilland, Deputy Director
Khristina Kurasz, Manager of Operations and Special Projects, Lunder Institute
Sheri LaVerdiere, Assistant for Museum Visits
Justin McCann, Lunder Curator for Whistler Studies
Jaime McLeod, Communications Manager
Liz Herring Menard, Director of Museum Development
Abigail Newkirk, Linde Family Foundation Senior Coordinator of School and Teacher Programs
Jamie O'Brien, Museum Development Officer
Chris Patch, Senior Preparator
Tanya Sheehan, Distinguished Scholar and Director of Research, Lunder Institute
Jacqueline Terrassa, Carolyn Muzzy Director
Diana Tuite, Katz Curator of Modern and Contemporary Art
Miriam Valle-Mancilla, Linde Family Foundation Coordinator of Academic Access
Jason Weller, Manager of Installations and Operations
Karen Wickman, Executive Assistant to the Director
Qianni Zhu, Mirken Family Postbaccalaureate Fellow in Museum Practice

Museum Security

Michael Benecke, Associate Director of Security and Museum Security Manager
Lori Cutter
Randy Gerry
Ryan Ridky
Thomas Savinelli

Installation Crew

Nancy Bixler
Nishant Chandrasekar
Bethany Engstrom
Stew Henderson
David Holbrook
Michael Hudak
Scott Mosher

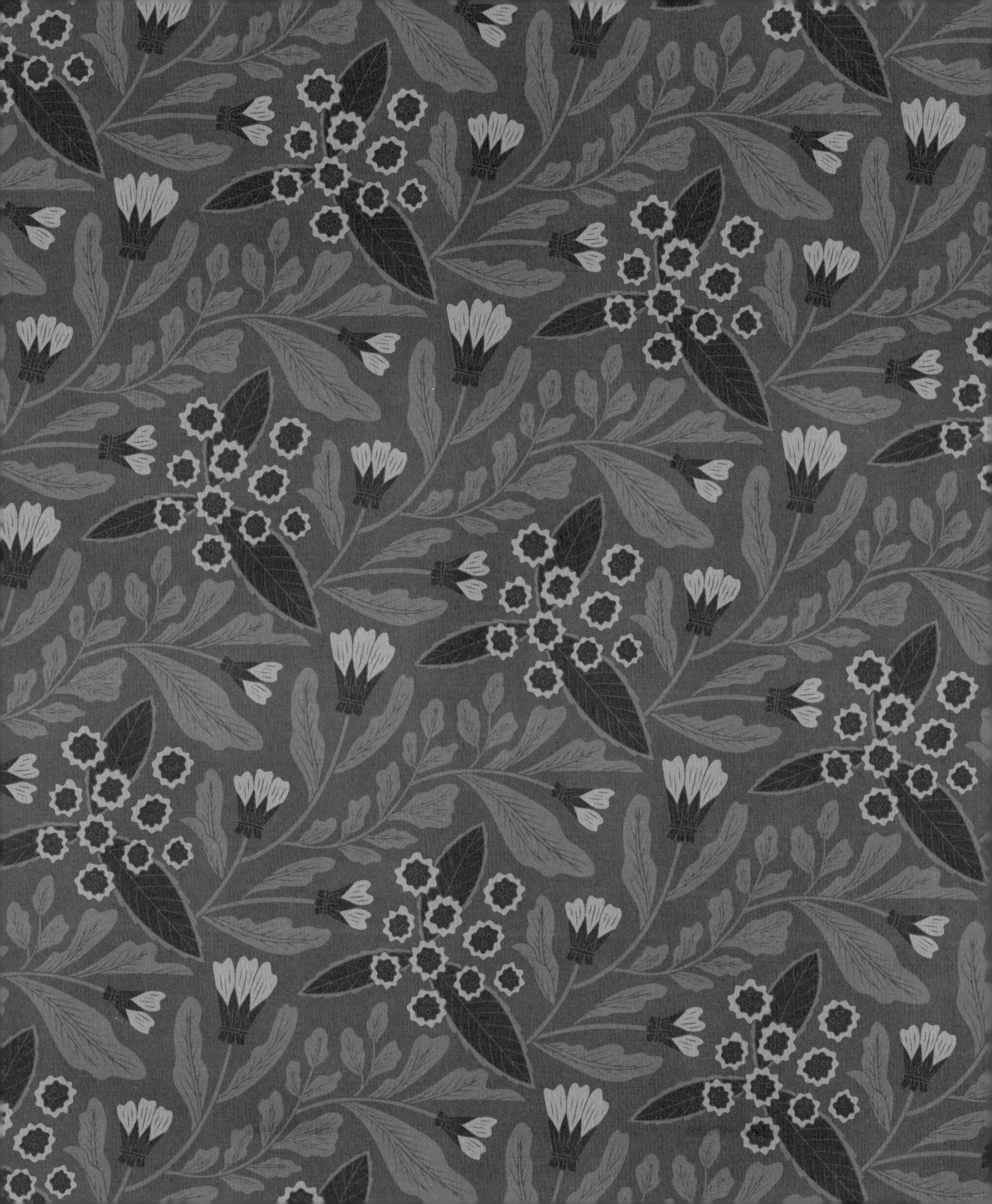